Ordinary Gifted Children

*The Power and Promise
of Individual Attention*

Ordinary Gifted Children

Children

The Power and Promise
of Individual Attention

JESSICA HOFFMANN DAVIS

TEACHERS
COLLEGE
PRESS

Teachers College, Columbia University
New York and London

Published by Teachers College Press, 1234 Amsterdam Avenue, New York, NY 10027

Library of Congress Cataloging-in-Publication Data

Davis, Jessica Hoffmann, 1943–
Ordinary gifted children: the power and promise of individual attention / Jessica Hoffmann Davis.
    p. cm.
  Includes bibliographical references.
  ISBN 978-0-8077-5096-4 (pbk. : alk. paper)—ISBN 978-0-8077-5097-1 (hard-cover : alk. paper)
  1. Hoffmann School for Individual Attention (New York, N.Y.)—History. 2. Alternative education—New York (State)—New York—History—20th century. 3. Individualized instruction—New York (State)—New York—History—20th century. 4. Hoffmann, Ann, d. 1980. 5. School principals—New York (State)—New York—Biography. I. Title.
  LD7501.N5144D38 2010
  372'.97471—dc22   2010001301

ISBN 978-0-8077-5096-4 (paperback)
ISBN 978-0-8077-5097-1 (hardcover)

Printed on acid-free paper
Manufactured in the United States of America

17 16 15 14 13 12 11 10   8 7 6 5 4 3 2 1

For All Ann Hoffmann's Children

Contents

Acknowledgments

L IKE THE HOFFMANN SCHOOL, Teachers College Press has embraced this work's individuality over expected norms. I am grateful for this—and more—to my extraordinary editor, Carole Saltz, and to Emily Ballengee, whose thoughtful direction has been invaluable. For skillfully shepherding this work to the light, I thank Adee Braun, Michael McGann, Nancy Power, Beverly Rivero, Leyli Shayegan, and Lori Tate. I thank my sister Trudy Bolter for the sweet recollecting that only we could do. For his loving input, I thank Ann Hoffmann's only living sibling, my spectacular uncle Nino Luciano. For their insightful commentary on early drafts, I am indebted to William Corbett, Joshua Davis, Ronne Hartfield, Andy Hrycna, and Sara Lawrence-Lightfoot. For reading and encouragement, I thank Mary Ann Albert, Benjamin Davis, Carol Davis, Frances Davis, Monique Devine, beloved Eleanor Hackett, Faye Hill, Miriam Miller, Margaret Ramsdell, Carly Simon, Barbara Seagle, and Barry and Pam Zuckerman. I will always treasure the generosity of the Aaron family (especially Lisa), Robert Barone, Rosalie Capone, Robert Choderker, Michael Eschelbacher, Judi Falk, Austin Hill, Franklin Ilfelder, Richard Levine, Rebekah Marler, Phyllis Robinson, the late Richard Robinson, and Erica Sloane. For tireless interest, editorial genius, and unyielding applause, I thank my true love Will. For purpose and inspiration, I am forever grateful to our children and theirs: Joshua, Jennifer, Emerson, Malcolm, Katy, and Andrew; Alexander, Frances, and William; and Benjamin, whose careful reading promises a movie or play. May they all know better from what is here that they too are Ann Hoffmann's children: ordinary, gifted, and loved.

Introduction

NINE-YEAR-OLD Chester[1] had already been asked to leave three schools. His size betrayed his young age. He had the height of a small adult, a stocky build, freckled face, and large brown eyes that seemed in wounded warmth more defensive than defiant. A fully zipped, seriously outgrown jacket hugged his round body tightly. When Chester arrived for his first day at Hoffmann School, the principal, my mother, was waiting to greet him. Ann Hoffmann[2] had admitted Chester into her school because she believed in him. As he encountered this figure of authority and welcome, Chester must have sensed that.

"Would you like to see your classroom?" Ann Hoffmann asked politely.

The youngster shook his head. "No."

Her interest increased. "What would you like to do?"

After casing the small eclectic lobby outside the principal's office, Chester pointed to a tall mahogany antique chair, rococo in detail, no doubt throne-like to a young child. This well-placed hand-me-down from decorators in the Hoffmann family provided a perch from which its inhabitant had full view of the scene. The office traffic (parents and teachers dropping by, children delivering messages or collecting Band-Aids), orderly disorderly walking ("No running") up and down the stairs, and straight-backed, dark brown Emma in her white uniform, carrying trays of juice and crackers to the various classrooms for morning snack.

"Okay," my mother said. "Make yourself comfortable. You can let me know when you're ready to join your class."

My family lived in an apartment on top of the converted mansion that was the Hoffmann School for Individual Attention in the Riverdale section of the Bronx. At that time, in the late 1950s, I had graduated from Hoffmann School and every morning came down the steps from our attic apartment to set out on the 20-minute walk to my secondary

1

school. I think Chester's mother must have driven him to school because sometimes he was there quite early, well before the 8:45 a.m. arrival of the hired cars that delivered the rest of the 90 children from their houses or apartments scattered throughout Manhattan and the Bronx. "Good morning, Chester," I'd mumble as I raced past the place where he sat resolutely in the hall. Sometimes his eyes would move to acknowledge me; other times he appeared lost in thought. Almost busy, he seemed, sitting in that chair.

I don't know when I first noticed something that resembled a smile in response to my greeting, but Chester sat there for more than 2 months until one morning he went into my mother's office and told her, "Ann Hoffmann, I'm ready to go to class." Chester went on from Hoffmann to schools of his choosing and to a career practicing medicine somewhere in New York. As with so many of her alumni, Chester stayed in touch with my mother. He would visit from time to time or drop a line at junctures in his life about which he thought she should know. But it's been almost 3 decades since his last contact, a note of tribute and gratitude written in 1980 on the occasion of Ann Hoffmann's death.

Chester's turnaround is emblematic of the stories associated with that little school—that place where children whom others had given up on felt safe to explore their individual possibilities. In a manuscript about the school that my father was writing in the 1940s, he described the plight of a prekindergarten child who would not nap. His frustrated teacher had labeled the child's resistance "bad," and that intolerable word had found its way to the then-fledgling school director. Ann Hoffmann took immediate action. With the teacher's permission, Ann hid behind a screen at the next rest period and intervened when the teacher's patience began to wear thin.

"What would you like to do?" my mother asked the restless four-year old.

"I'd like to be on that swing," he replied, pointing to the small playground adjacent to the nursery classroom. According to my father's admiring account, the child was on the swing for a very short while, pumping vigorously and then coming to a stop and slumping over to one side. "I'm tired now," he explained, as he returned to his little cot and fell asleep.

"What would you like to do?" she would ask the children, believing in her heart and mind that children knew exactly what they needed and that the adult's job was to listen carefully enough to follow their lead.

"Every child has special gifts," my mother told me. "It's the teacher's responsibility to discover the individual gifts in each of her children." Every child, all children, ordinary children—they came to school bearing gifts. I thought of presents differently wrapped: patterned paper, silken ribbons, or plain white tissue and string. Sometimes the outer layers took quite long to undo; other times a treasure was gifted without fuss. All of us with different bounty and the teacher at full attention—watching, listening, ready to recognize and receive.

Half a century later Ann's closest colleague, child psychologist Richard Robinson, who worked as mental health advisor to the school for more than 20 years, tells me, "Her educational philosophy was quite simple. She believed, first, that every child could learn, and, second, that every child could learn to love learning." I wondered if Dick knew this philosophy from years of working with and observing my mother or because she expounded it out loud. The latter possibility seemed unlikely. My mother did not talk about education. She did it.

Helen Parkhurst, founder of the Dalton School and an advisor to my mother in her earliest years as director, awakened me to this phenomenon. I was no more than 10 years old and "Parky," as we called her, was in her sixties, retired from Dalton, and on the road spreading her progressive educational ideas through consultation, lectures, and writing. Her greatest wish, her dream, she told me, was to have Ann Hoffmann stand at a podium and tell student teachers what it was she did. Did Parky say that if Ann would do this, a generation of great teachers would emerge? Or the future of early childhood education would be transformed? Whatever her exact words, they were of great importance and a dramatic version of something I would often hear again: "If only we could bottle what Ann Hoffmann does" or "Schools of education cannot teach what Mrs. Hoffmann knows."

It was my first encounter with the notion that good teachers are born, not trained; that talent in teaching, like talent in art, is given and not acquired. Certainly, it was the first time in my life that I realized that, like so many dedicated and overextended educators, my mother was all action, without the time or inclination on top of the rest to explain to others what she did. Perhaps she was like those artists who fear that if they think too hard or talk too much about what they do, their magic will disappear. Or perhaps she realized, as I suspect I did even at that time, that speaking in public was not her strongest suit. Although she ran both a school and a summer day camp, everywhere projecting an image of competence and confidence, it was my father, a lawyer and writer, who wielded the words in our family. Imposing at 6'6", Malcolm Hoffmann would frequently and eloquently address audiences at school functions on behalf of his 5'2" wife (standing right beside him) or on behalf of the school (past and present) itself.

"Why don't you write it down?" I asked my mother, understanding that it might be hard for her to speak in front of a lot of people and knowing firsthand what a pleasure it was to put words on paper. Parky had raised my preadolescent concern that the work of great educators should not be confined to the limits of their own practice, and I was proud that my mother's work counted in that dilemma. Ann Hoffmann responded to my question with earnest attention. She looked at me fully, taking me in as more than someone she loved, but as someone she respected and in whom she believed: "I'm counting on you to do that, Jessie." She spoke quickly, simply, clearly—as if it were something she'd considered or known for a very long time.

I don't know what I said—whether I nodded, openly agreed, or stared solemnly as was my wont. But at that moment, a promise was made. Engraved with the earnest commitment of a child, it is a promise that has stayed with me throughout my adult life, serving alternatively as a beacon, a burden, and a bond. On its account, I would deliberately study the field of education to gain context and skills with which to make sense of whatever it was my mother did and would or could not get up in front of teachers to explain. On its account, I would unexpectedly discover more fully a life I thought I knew and perpetuate a conversation with my mother long after her passing.

In the pages that follow, more than half a century later, I finally write it down. I tell the story in hopes that it will reach individuals like those Helen Parkhurst thought should hear it. Beyond that, I hope it will be of interest to anyone who is curious, as I am, about the substance and reach of early education and the extent to which professional portraits are framed in personal narratives. But most of all, I write it down in hopes that the Hoffmann School, a tiny dot in the vast landscape of educational reform, may touch more parents than those who were able to find it and more children than those who were able to attend. This may seem the story of an unusual place and an unusual educator, but surely it is in consideration of the unusual that the usual becomes clear. Moreover, I have come to see that just as my mother was moved by the gifts she recognized in ordinary children, she was herself an ordinary educator. And like so many ordinary educators, her particular gifts changed very many lives.

My preparations for writing ranged from grand scale to small detail. On the life-changing level, in order to dedicate myself fully to the project, I retired from my teaching position at the Harvard Graduate School of Education. The move from overwrought to self-directed schedule was not without challenge, but the prospect of finally digging in has kept me almost diligently on course. I assembled in one place the many scattered boxes of information about my mother and the school that I had been saving for years. I sought out individuals who remembered, attended, or had worked at the school, especially those whose time there coincided or overlapped with my own. I spoke to them on the phone, and in person, asking each of them the same set of questions. Their recollections and insights expanded my understanding; their voices resound throughout this work.

As if I were assembling pieces of a physical puzzle, I studied and sorted the photographs, letters, and documents that predated the school's founding in 1921 by my great-aunt Rebecca Hoffmann and extended through my mother's direction from 1944 to 1980. Deciding what was relevant was torturous. I found all of it fascinating and hard to set anything aside. I bought archival acid-free envelopes and white cotton gloves and still felt the thrill across generations of my hands touching the same pieces of paper as relatives I had never met. The addresses on their letters were minimal and effective: "Abraham Hoffmann, Trudeau, New York." In beautiful handwriting on aging papers that fell apart at my touch, everyone started a letter with some version of "You must hate me or will you ever forgive me for taking so long to reply to your last letter." Were I beginning this book with a letter to my mother, it might take a similar turn.

It was among the copious piles, oddly labeled files, and partially bound collections of yellowing papers that I uncovered pieces of the draft manuscript that my late father was writing about the school in the 1940s. Thanks to that discovery, I have also enjoyed a reunion with him, learning and quoting from his words, joining our voices through my text, and tackling the same challenge he chose in that and other writing. My father frequently recited that cheerful Edgar Guest poem[3] about some task that folks assumed couldn't be done and one man who "wouldn't say so till he tried." Whatever the exact words, what is most vivid is the raised arch of my father's eyebrows as he would light up and say, "And the job that couldn't be done? He did it!" In part, I feel just that: That impossible child's promise that I planned to keep? I did it! But accounts like this one are never definitive and the job therefore is never really done.

Readers who remember the school may be moved to add or rewrite chapters; others who are meeting the school for the first time may have experiences that resonate with those I describe or shed new or other light on the portrait I have created. Throughout, I have tried to tell the story in a way that is faithful to the shared recollections of individuals who attended the school and to the memories of my immediate and extended family. But as I recognized when a close colleague posed to me the same set of questions that I asked of others, the story I have to tell is my own and in the end can only be truly faithful to my experience of it all.

Mine is the story of a child for whom life was school, school was life, and home was situated somewhere therein. It is the story of a child who was primed to be an educator and who fulfilled that expectation, recreating the Hoffmann School throughout her personal and professional life. But it is most importantly the story of a visionary educator, Ann Hoffmann, and her school—a remarkable place where a diverse, challenging, and challenged group of ordinary students was believed in authentically and with extraordinary results. It is at last the story I promised my mother I'd tell.

Chapter 1

Ordinary Gifted Children

The first Hoffmann School building.

CONSCIOUSNESS

FORMER STUDENTS WHO expected to remember little if anything about their early education were astonished at the accuracy with which they could recreate the stage set on which it had transpired. They entered the gates of the Hoffmann School and followed the driveway past the fieldstone schoolhouse on the right, the small duck pond on the left, out to the playground across the road from the swimming pool and the art barn, beyond that to the athletic field and the tree-covered knoll that many of us called "Sherwood Forest." "To me, it was like totally the

Top: Libby Castle.
Bottom: 215th Street, where Malcolm and Ann met.

country," my classmate Stephen told me 50 years after his last visit to the school, " but it was close to home in a number of ways." From the short time it took to get there from downtown, to the scale and warmth of the building, to the freedom and safety of the grounds, Hoffmann School was close to home in a number of ways for most of its students.

Wide stone steps led to the schoolhouse's columned front porch and its heavy glass and mahogany double front doors. A turn-of-the-century country estate, the original residence had approximately 20 rooms. That count included the string of attic rooms that ultimately comprised our apartment, but not the warren of chambers in the partially above-ground basement or the apartments in the attic of the barn or in its adjoining garden sheds. These tucked-away spaces spoke to us of the help who had once lived in the margins of these structures. Architectural touches throughout the schoolhouse resonated with gracious family life in another era: home for sure, with a capital *H*.

French doors opened from the kindergarten and nursery rooms that flanked the center entrance hall onto opposite sides of the expansive front porch. In both those rooms elegant fireplaces—one beneath a carved stone crest monogrammed with the original family's hallmark—were closed off and refitted with shelves for holding read-aloud books in one room and wooden building blocks in the other. No doubt igniting my enduring passion for sifting and sorting data (and sporadic attachment to organizing drawers), I enjoyed putting the blocks away in those shelves at the end of kindergarten building time. The half blocks could be doubled and aligned with the long ones; the arches fit perfectly atop one another; all of them entered with small ends out gave the look of a uniform mosaic. The high ceiling of the nursery classroom allowed for a playhouse loft in which 3- to 5-year-old children could easily stand. This magical space, accessed by steep stairs, sheltered cubbies underneath and was outfitted with costumes, plastic dishes, a wooden stove, table, and bed. Its vaulted location marked both the separation between pretense and reality and the honoring attention afforded to dramatic play.

On the second floor, the first-grade classroom must once have been all or half of the master bedroom. Its large adjacent bathroom was tiled in green-edged pink marble squares that set an elegant backdrop for the child-sized sinks and toilets subsequently installed. The bay window off the art room in the front of the building opened up to a spectacular view of the Hudson River and a glimpse of the beautiful neighboring estate that extended, with small houses for help and guests, down the steep hill toward the Riverdale station's train tracks at the edge of the Hudson River. Villa Pauline was a precise replica of an Italian villa built and inhabited, until his death in 1957, by the world-famous classical conductor Arturo Toscanini.

We enjoyed sightings of the reclusive white-haired Toscanini standing on his balcony or coming and going in his chauffeured limousine. On occasional spring and summer nights, my family would have dinner on the school's open front porch (in later years both sides were closed to add additional classrooms) and music would waft through the trees. The maestro, practicing or reveling with small groups of musicians, was "serenading" us, my father would say. "Some day this will seem important to you." A few decades later, Toscanini's home would be leveled to accommodate the sprawl of the religious school that bought his property. Scouting the scene, I drove down his driveway and found a group of young mothers collecting their children from that school. I was excited to tell them that the great Toscanini once lived where they now stood and was surprised by the message behind their blank expressions: "Toscanini who?"

Hoffmann School alumni speak longingly of the foliage: the sweet gum trees and the spreading horse chestnut in the back near the little wooden outdoor stage we used for spring festival. Within the prickly shell of the horse chestnuts that fell to the ground, we found lustrous brown seeds to polish and collect. Beneath the garnet-leaved maples, among the beetle-laden magenta peony bushes, and on a very good day, children from St. Nicholas Avenue, Central Park West, or Gun Hill Road could easily find a bright pink salamander or a small garter snake. From uptown, downtown, the Village, and the Bronx, we were New York City kids at Hoffmann—New York City kids who went to school in a wooded dell 15 minutes from Times Square.

My father wrote of it sentimentally: "Three and a half acres of grounds means trees, means shrubbery, means flowers, means space to be used by children in their many playful representations of life. . . . Three and a half acres also means an abundance of living creatures: the transcendental caterpillar, the laughing squirrel, and the proud pheasant." Three and a half acres of grounds also allowed for the planting of children's gardens and the gathering of fruit from trees. Large purple grapes peeked through the jagged leaves that crowded the row of arbors separating the older children's playground from the athletic field. Wisteria fell heavy from the trellis over the steps to the youngest children's playground, offering shade to the shirt-staining black mulberries that we tasted each spring.

The grounds afforded a hill steep enough for sledding and skiing, playgrounds with swing sets, climbing structures, slides, and sand boxes equipped with spoons discarded from the kitchen, small shovels, and buckets for packing and turning out towers or cakes. The large barn out back was originally used to keep horses and perhaps a carriage, but now was opened and outfitted for spring and summer arts and crafts. Adjacent to the arts barn, a series of sheds seemed home to Tony, who took care of the gardens and grass on which we played, the sheep and chickens that we got to pet and feed, the white ducks that lived on the island at the center of the small pond on which we rowed flat bottom boats, and a few cats who had their kittens in secret recesses of the barn. The big ones that Tony did not give away grew to be strictly outside cats, in charge of containing the rodent population: tiny brown field mice and huge slick black water rats that found their way up the hill from the river.

This groundsman-gardener seemed to us to be quite ancient (he was almost 70) and he spoke English infrequently and with a thick Italian accent. My father wrote of Tony that "he worked on and about the soil with a love that proclaimed that trees, and flowers, and vegetables were mistresses to be touched and enjoyed by him alone. His energy was inexhaustible; his ego and independence unsurpassed; his proclivity toward petty larceny a thing of beauty and a wonder to behold. Small tools and farm implements purchased for the children disappeared with a rapidity that must have brought joy to their manufacturers."

There were few apartment buildings in the Riverdale of that era and adventuresome men called "hobos" rode the trains and fished sturgeon out of the then-clear waters of the Hudson. We would often sneak through the woods across from Toscanini's and peer through branches to watch these journeymen cook their catch on open fires in makeshift camps. In similar but more permanent residence, on the other side of the wall abutting the school's baseball field, there lived a squatter who was always or had become a friend of Tony's. Like Tony, Mr. Raduli spoke Italian with more passion and range than English and tended his garden with tireless attention. Mr. Raduli wore a fedora hat and would daily come over the wall with a large glass jug to take his drinking water from the pipe out of which fresh spring water flowed into our pond.

Raduli had built as his home a tin-roofed hut with a mud floor, sunk like a bunker underground in the undeveloped open space on that side of the wall. The mud floors were beautifully covered with oriental rugs taken to my parents' obvious and oft-cited distress by "someone" out of the school's basement. My father would write of Raduli that he was "a simple man given to solitary virtues. He loved the soil and he loved red wine. He was impervious to weather and the blandishment of work [and] . . . he began to resemble in his habits the mole which finds its refuge in the ground . . . his skin and face caked with a brownish earthlike tinge, suggesting his terrestrial habits."

Toscanini's opulent village-like spread on one side of the school was rivaled by the charm of Mr. Raduli's playhouse-like abode on the other. In both directions we were bordered by adult experts in the real subjects that we studied at Hoffmann School. Toscanini's life was filled with music as was ours; Mr. Raduli planted a bountiful garden, as did we; and their respective abodes for different reasons were as fantasy-like as our imagined futures. Perhaps ironically, or on account of some great equalizer, when Mr. Raduli died many years later, his children, left behind in Sicily, inherited his squatter's land and sold it off to urban developers for a formidable fortune. My father had foreseen this windfall when he noted in his writing, "It is possible lawfully to steal land and become the owner of it, if one does so openly and notoriously under claim that the land is his and succeeds in occupying it for 20 years."

From the fresh spring water that fed the small pond to the rambling dry wall between Tony's back gardens and Raduli's homestead, the grounds at Hoffmann School were, as Stephen had noted, "like totally the country." Indeed, they were only by virtue of geographic location the slightest bit urban. I should have known all along that the selection of a quasi-rural atmosphere was entirely, and for all 60 years of the life of the school, by deliberate educational design. Each of the six buildings that housed the Hoffmann School from 1921 to its final move to Riverdale in 1942 was surrounded by open land, ranging from 3 to 10 acres, and almost always providing a view of the Hudson River. Founder Rebecca Hoffmann, known affectionately to family as Buddy, believed firmly that "grass and woods, and water . . . should be among children's neighbors," and from the inception of the school in 1921 to its close in 1985 they were.

The various settings for the school were all easily accessed by the West Side Highway beginning with its original location in a clapboard arts-and-crafts homestead on Riverside Drive at 177th street and including its next move to Fort Washington Avenue at 193rd Street to the vine-covered Libby (sometimes called Woodcliff) Castle, built in 1855 and apparently lent to Rebecca for the school's use by John D. Rockefeller. School materials describe its setting as, "at the highest point of Manhattan Island so that from its ample porches and grounds the eye can sweep in the whole of Manhattan and the Bronx and can follow for miles in either direction the graceful flow of the river, winding two hundred feet below." After Hoffmann School had moved on and in spite of its historical value (it was home to politicians including Tammany Hall's infamous Boss Tweed), Libby Castle, like Toscanini's Villa Pauline, was leveled to the ground for new construction—in its case in 1939 to make way for a housing project.

The next move would be to the red-brick building on West 215th Street where in 1935, my mother, a young teacher in Rebecca's school, would meet my father, a Harvard Law School student. There would be two more moves, a year at Gouveneur Avenue near Van Cortland Park and another at 227th Street, before Rebecca would find the school's final location at 254th Street and Independence Avenue in Riverdale, a neighborhood of 3 square miles that pressed the boundaries of the Bronx, sitting just 10 blocks south of the city of Yonkers. Relatives attributed the school's many moves to Rebecca's complete disregard for monetary constraints: "Buddy was always getting kicked out because she couldn't pay the rent." More interested (and vocally so) in serving orphans and the children of workingwomen, Rebecca tended to eschew rather than to attract the wealthy parent population that might benefit the school. My father's brother described Rebecca's financial management: "She is always two steps away from success; two steps ahead of the sheriff!"

In 1942 Rebecca Hoffmann took a 5-year lease on the fieldstone mansion and bucolic grounds that my classmates and I knew as the Hoffmann School. Like the locations that preceded it, the Riverdale site provided a regal setting for children's construction of their understanding of that noble concept "school," and for their understanding of the sorts of fine settings that their education deserved. School brochures from the 1920s and 1930s specified the importance of physical setting: "The aim of the school is to teach the children in the open air amid beautiful natural surroundings in order to insure the fullest development of their health and of aesthetic and spiritual consciousness." This was a time when educators felt free to discuss precious intangibles: the development of awareness and attention to beauty, and even the cultivation of something called the human spirit. Daunting objectives that put into drab perspective twenty-first-century emphases on standardized testing—quantifiable measures that can be neatly counted and tracked. The Hoffmann School was never about them.

A friend wrote to my father in 1942 that "Rebecca's new school is a thing of beauty—a handsome stone building, three acres of grounds, a pond, a garden; in brief, the accoutrements of a country estate. With advantages of this kind, plus an active market of prospects for private schools, she has every opportunity and I should not be at all surprised to see her reverse the trend of many years and run her business profitably." Buddy ran the school in that country estate, though not profitably, until March of 1944 when she became gravely ill and turned to her family for help.

Making short a story whose real length I may never know, my parents came directly (perhaps even in a matter of days) to Rebecca's rescue—helping out first and temporarily through her difficult illness, and then taking over for the long run when she died. The move from Washington, D.C., either precipitated or was well-timed with my father's invitation to become a special assistant to the Attorney General at the United States Courthouse at Foley Square in New York. My parents, married in April of 1939, had moved that summer to Washington so that my father could work as a lawyer for the National Labor Relations Board.

For my mother, the change would be more drastic. Her 5 years as an at-home wife and mother, giving birth to my sister in April 1940, and me in December 1943, were to come to an abrupt end. Within months she would return to work overseeing not a classroom, but an entire school. She would abandon the Arlington Village duplex apartment where she and my father and sister had lived for almost 4 years and move with her husband and two children to a second-floor classroom at Rebecca's Hoffmann School. Photographs from their time in Arlington Village show my mother radiant in her late twenties, looking younger than I ever remember seeing her in person, wearing an apron with ruffles on the shoulders, hanging out behind the apartment complex with women friends who have children about the age of my sister. They are pictures of the sort of regular home life for which I longed. A mother free to play with her child in their backyard; a home that was home only to the family that lived there.

Ann Hoffmann looks in these joyful photos as if she has transitioned perfectly to her new life and community. But a curious journal entry, written in her familiar graceful penmanship, reveals the tension she experienced adjusting to her new role. She entitles her comments "A Teacher Becomes a Parent":

> Never in your classroom did you ever use "do" or "don't." Now what about your 2-year-old? She never pays attention to any indirect suggestions and completely ignores your direct suggestions. And what about the backyard situation? What is all the fighting and tearing of hair and scratching of skin about amongst the youngsters? You know your 2-year-old is eager to play with the older children and is absorbing all that is going on in order to parrot and be accepted by the children. Why don't these mothers do something? But they have ideas about child training also. Poor misguided and badly executed

to your way of thinking and from your experience, but the soundest principles as far as they are concerned.

I have heard that motherhood—that is, a teacher becoming a mother herself—will soften the animosity that can persist between teacher and parent, enabling a teacher to better understand, for example, what seems like unnecessary anxiety on the part of the parent or the roots of well-meant parental intrusion on a teacher's careful plan of action. But even as a young mother, Ann Hoffmann identifies herself as a teacher first, a teacher impatient with parental wrongheadedness. She is outraged by the other mothers' allowance of the sort of rough housing ("the fighting and tearing of hair and scratching of skin") that she would not have her child learn and that she would go on to disallow in her nonviolent school.

Surely at the time she released her frustration in these written words, Ann Hoffmann believed that her years of teaching were substantively behind her. She was the wife of a government lawyer and entrenched at home. She might even have expected that our family would someday move to a typical suburban house with a front garden and a backyard. Perhaps she imagined herself, as I always did, spending more time in ruffle-edged aprons. Whatever her immediate or long-term expectations for family and home, Rebecca's illness would change all that. The teacher-turned-parent would turn educator again, and this time, as school administrator. Those 4 years in Arlington Village would be all Ann Hoffmann would know of the at-home housewife's life that I used to believe she romanticized as much as I.

DIVERSITY

Nineteen fifty-five was the year that Hurricane Diane tore fiercely through the Hoffmann School playgrounds, breaking down treasured bushes and well-established trees. It was also the year that Walt Disney's first Cinemascope cartoon, *Lady and the Tramp,* opened at our local movie theater, the now defunct RKO Marble Hill on Broadway and 231st Street. Hurricane Diane was frightening, thrilling, humbling; *Lady and the Tramp,* long awaited and enchanting. But for me the standout event of 1955 was the graduation from Hoffmann School of my sixth-grade class. In our graduation photo, you see the four of us, as we never were, all dressed up. On regular school days, we wore some variation of play clothes: blue jeans and tee shirts, anything that could get dirty without causing distress. Un-surprisingly, there were neither uniforms nor a dress code in a school that was dedicated to individual identity and expression.

Our daily explorations in style relied on accessories: big-buckled cow-boy belts, genuine sailor caps, cowboy neck bandanas, a fringed frontier jacket, or raccoon-tailed Davy Crockett hat. These were costume-like de-tails that, beyond fashion, placed us at the ready for pretend play. But for graduation I wore a calf-length, white organdy dress, handmade for the occasion by my grandmother, and the boys wore grown-up navy blue three-button suits. I felt regal with the traditional graduation daisy crown secured to my head and a bouquet of white baby's breath in my hand. Flowers were reliable markers of special occasions at Hoffmann School. I am surprised that my mother chose carnations for the boys' lapels. She hated those flowers because they reminded her of death.

I stand in the photo at an awkward angle, my shoulder length brown hair set off by unreasonably short bangs, my tentative smile taking in the camera with cautious pleasure. Stephen stands with shoulders back, head up, triumphantly grasping in one hand, as we all do, a ribbon-bound di-ploma. Some overseeing adult has arranged the rest of us elbow to elbow with arms entwined. Wiry and a head shorter, Arthur smiles cheerfully, his posture straight as a soldier, his feet close together, heels touching. Jacob stands out for several reasons: the color of his tie, his blond hair and blue eyes. But most conspicuously, Jacob is unsmiling while the rest of us beam with pride.

Beneath the luster of dress-up clothes and flowers we are a motley crew—surely not the Three Musketeers and Maid Marion, conflating sto-ries and characters that entered our 1950s pretend play—not a merry band at all. We are distinct individuals; we four children aged 11 to 13, who in our tiny class size, imbalanced gender distribution, and range of projected dispositions, herald rather than reflect the much broader wave of diversity that permeated Hoffmann School. Actually, we had a lot in common. Arthur, Jacob, and I lived in Riverdale, Stephen in Manhattan. With varying iterations thereof, we all lived in apartments: Arthur's was a separate entrance first and garden; Jacob's and Stephen's were upper floor flats in multilevel buildings; and mine was a small collection of rooms on the top of our school. Our fathers were all well-educated professionals: a businessman (Stephen's), a doctor (Jacob's), an engineer (Arthur's), and an attorney who longed to be a full-time writer (mine). Half of us lived with both our parents and had mothers visibly connected to the school. Half of us lived with mothers who had weathered a divorce. My mother was the school's principal; Arthur's mother for some time worked as her secretary. Stephen and Jacob had mothers who, at a time when it was less common, were raising children on their own. Jacob characterizes the challenge: "I went to overnight camp when I was 3½!" While Arthur was an only child on whom both parents doted, Jacob's life as an only child took a turn when his mother remarried and had two more children. I lived with a precocious sister 4 years older; Stephen's brother, 4 years younger, had what Stephen describes as "mild retardation." Within the shadow of the Second World War in a "wannabe suburban" Bronx community in which anti-Semitism was ripe, half of us (Jacob and me) were Jewish, half (Arthur and Stephen) were not. We four were together at Hoffmann for all of elementary school, although several other variously remembered children joined us for sojourns of 1 to 5 years.

Through fourth grade there was my best friend Gracie. Now a social worker, she was then a "tomboy" like me. Her father was a well-known actor who was blacklisted in the McCarthy era. When the listing took a toll on his career and fortune, the family moved out of the city to a more affordable suburb. There was a history at Hoffmann School of parents in theater, dating back to Rebecca Hoffmann's friends from the Moscow Art Theater and including in Ann Hoffmann's time the children of Dustin Hoffman and the venerable Captain Kangaroo (Bob Keeshan). A card to Rebecca from the National Bureau of Private Schools referring a child in 1936, notes that the parents, active in Yiddish theater on the Lower East Side, were looking for a "progressive" boarding school. It makes sense that artists would have a penchant for progressive schools; progressive schools have always had a penchant for the arts. In the 1950s our schoolmates included the daughters of television comedian Milton Berle and the radio announcer known as "the Voice," Ken Roberts. The urban backdrop of New York City was filled for all of us with glitterati, and a number of Hoffmann School children went at night with their parents to grown-up restaurants, theater, or nightclubs a stone's throw from home.

In second and third grade I was also close to Betsy, a stalwart little girl with curly black hair and an unforgettably contagious giggle. When Betsy turned 9, her family invited us all to a black-tie birthday party at Bill Miller's Rivera nightclub in Fort Lee, New Jersey. It was a dazzling adult evening—bright lights and lots of noise—and as Betsy's friends, we felt at its center. My mother saved the professional photo of me beaming in yellow dotted Swiss, another party dress made by my grandmother. The photo's paper frame is autographed by comedian Jack E. Leonard, who performed that night. I was thrilled to get that autograph, perhaps the only one I have ever collected. Under the category of art and music, my third-grade Hoffmann School report reflects my enchantment with my friends: "Jessica has not been paying as much attention as she might. She gets involved with Gracie and Betsy and forgets about music."

One of the first names remembered by the men who had been boys in my class was Fred, a tiny but relentless bully—almost a parody of a bully, the way he pushed and poked the other boys. What had my mother seen in him? Stephen—like me, bigger and more afraid—recollects as a moment of triumph his just once (in the art room) pushing Fred back and insisting successfully that he leave him alone. At 62, Stephen's boyhood moment of self-protection is fresh in his mind, perhaps serving still as a touchstone of self-reliance. I have to wonder where the art teacher was when the pushing occurred. Had he purposefully looked away for a moment? Or did the exchange happen too fast for the standard intervention—the talking through disagreements mandated at Ann Hoffmann's peaceable school.

Other boys at Hoffmann included sweet Nathanial, small for his age with an oversized heart that too soon proved fatal, and independent Jonathan who made his way through the school on little wooden crutches. Norman was an unthinkably skinny boy with a tremendous stutter. He loved to tell jokes and the playfulness of his demeanor and dress—short pants, plaid bow ties, elastic suspenders, cockeyed wire-rimmed round glasses—added to his humor and warmth. He was patient with his stammer, holding you in his sparkling gaze until the balance of his sentence or the punch line of his joke found its way home. A few years behind us was Donald, a markedly quiet boy who ate inappropriate things. Heavyset and slow moving, Donald would make and pop into his mouth paste balls coated with seeds and sawdust from the collage table in art class. More stealthily, he would chew off bits of the knee of the giant papier-mâché policeman that was proudly mounted on the front hall newel post. His friend Bruno, uncomfortably 6'3" at age 11, remembers Donald as "morbidly obese." Alternatively, Louisa was delicate if not fragile and always seemed a bit "out of it," I think because of medication she took to avoid the grand mal seizures with which we all grew familiar. Other children came and left the school, sometimes like Gracie because of family moves and sometimes for reasons unknown to us.

Arthur described his experience of community at the Hoffmann School: "You were there and you were part of everything and you knew everything. It was a completely unique experience." And it was true of our class that we four knew everyone in a school that at its peak would have 120 students but in the 1940s and early 1950s had no more than 85 students in nursery through sixth grade. In 1955, in a sixth grade combined with fifth, bringing us to a total of eleven (with me still the only girl) we were close to the younger students in our extended class. Gregarious Kurt was unmistakably proud to be the son of the school's well-loved music teacher, who also sent Kurt's older and younger sisters to our school. All three children sang beautifully and regularly had solos in concerts and leads in school musical productions. Kurt and I were aligned in our attachment to "in charge" grown-ups. But where he was apparently proud, I wanted to be invisible or undistinguishable from the other children who, like Kurt, had other homes they went to at the end of the day—homes that were not the Hoffmann School.

The son of a firefighter, Marcus was a mild-mannered boy with cocoa-colored skin and soft-brown curly hair who dressed for school as if it were someplace to go. A photo taken on a class trip to the Metropolitan Museum of Art shows Marcus wearing a dress shirt open at the collar, a collegiate looking v-neck cardigan with two stripes on one arm, neat khaki pants, loafers, and a cowboy hat—a few sizes too small—tied under his chin with a wooden clasp. Marcus's face seemed always fixed in a gentle quizzical look but his demeanor could turn in a heartbeat from cautious respect to raucous laughter. He seemed to do his schoolwork easily, and his penmanship pleased our teacher as much as mine. Marcus had a great pitching arm, and when he was baseball captain for the week and stuck with me on his team (I was always the last one chosen), he came early every day to teach me how to hit the ball. By himself, he rode the Hudson Line train for the six stops from 125th Street in Harlem to the Riverdale station at the bottom of our hill. In his early thirties, he paid a surprise visit on a weekend that I was staying with my parents. Tastefully dressed and with a graceful manner that seemed inevitable, Marcus spent a while talking to Ann Hoffmann in her office and then walked the grounds with me. I was eager to tell him how his teaching me to hit a baseball had served me throughout time. But his update was more sobering. He told me he had recently been in jail—something about working in the post office and abusing his station. Marcus begged me never to tell my mother. Tears edged his eyes as he shared, "She would be so disappointed." I wonder still why he had told me and what his homecoming to Hoffmann School had really been about.

Razor-smart Aaron was handsome, neat, small for his age, and born with only one arm. He used the stump of his absent arm to do so many things that it seemed as if he had no real use for the rest of it. I pondered the mysteries of circumstance that allowed me to have all my parts and Aaron not his. But I never felt sorry for him. He was resourceful and fair, and everyone liked him. Above all, I can hear still the shivering sound of the bat cracking against Aaron's head when I first took a real hard swing following Marcus's directives. I did everything as Marcus had explained but did not understand that the eye must check surrounds even as it stays on the ball. The cracking sound echoed through the air, but Aaron just staggered a bit, and then looked at me holding up his one hand, "I'm okay."

Earnest was bigger than the rest of us and struggled mightily in school. He was as tall as our teacher with a babyish face, and he was relentlessly clumsy. He laughed too hard at offhanded jokes and stayed by your side all day if you were the least bit nice. I know I liked him even though I was impatient with the time he took to get things done. We'd be assembling our nature journals, carefully holding a leaf to blueprint paper or dipping it into water, and Earnest would take forever, studying our movements and trying to coordinate his own. Earnest met frequently with one of the floating teachers who, with varying objectives, regularly took children out of their classes at Hoffmann. No matter what amount of help he was getting, however, it was clear that when Earnest was asked to read aloud, it was much harder for him. While the rest of us were urged to "read with expression," Earnest would be congratulated for just getting through. And when he finished, he would smile and sigh as if he'd done a really great job. It was hard listening to him sound out even the easiest words (I'd want to speak them out for him), but it made me feel good too when he was so proud to finish. Stephen, who since his mother's death has taken care of his challenged younger brother, remembered painfully Earnest's struggle to keep up with our high-testing, quick-talking, softball-hitting little class. I feel ashamed for all of us to hear Stephen say, "The other students were often cruel and I felt very sad for him."

The personal and physical characteristics of the children I've described are typical of the diversity of the Hoffmann School student body at a time and in a section of the Bronx in which more cookie cutter schools prevailed. From a range of socioeconomic backgrounds, children at Hoffmann came in all colors and sizes. All fitting Ann Hoffmann's porous designation of "bright," they had learning profiles that ranged from precocious to delayed and confronted physical challenges that included cerebral palsy, pica, brain injury, blindness, heart disease, epilepsy, childhood cancers, and accident-related paralysis. And they came from two-parent, single-parent, biracial, foster, and adoptive homes and saw psychologists and psychiatrists as frequently as pediatricians and dentists. Before there were terms like *special education* and *mainstreaming*, Ann Hoffmann installed throughout the school handrails and other mobility and safety features to accommodate individual children's needs.

These features served as well a faculty in which diversity also reigned. With male and female teachers of various ages, several were people of color, and some had disabilities like the withered hand that Stephen remembered oddly increasing the dexterity of an inspiring young art teacher. With a background in the arts and music and a strong sense of the aesthetic, Stephen explained his noting of such details and his compassion for others: "From a very early age I had this empathetic sympathetic gene . . . that I could really feel other people's anguish to some extent and that may have informed even my politics. I mean, how can you possibly live such a happy life when the world is in such trouble?" Given the distress and courage of so many of the individuals around us at Hoffmann School, how could any of us not have asked the same question?

The performance categories on a 1952 Hoffmann School report card feature empathy/sympathy as educational objectives that were no doubt among my mother's incentives for diversifying the school community. Looking under "Emotional Habits," I note with pleasure the check boxes for "Cheerful" and "Sense of humor" even as I consider how the diversity that Ann Hoffmann cultivated gave particular meaning to "Works and plays well with others"; "Contributes to the good work of others"; and "Assumes responsibilities for acts." In such a small community, where did we draw lines to separate self from other? Was the assumption of responsibility for our own actions connected to our contributions to others? What did we learn of ourselves, our capabilities, and the individual challenges we faced from experiencing so closely the range of limitations and the many shapes of promise that surrounded us?

Hoffmann School Graduation 1955.

EMPATHY

"Want to learn something about yourself?" my mother would ask. "Do something for someone else." Throughout the lifetime of the Hoffmann School, students were made aware of and encouraged to attend to the needs of less fortunate children. We collected canned foods when disasters struck far away, wrapped and donated presents for children we would never meet, and each year raised money to contribute to the *New York Times* Neediest Cases Fund. On Christmas Day 1948 the *Times* excerpted Ann Hoffmann's written explanation of how her pupils earned $110 selling handmade goods in a school bazaar. I can see in my mother's description that no child's effort went unmentioned: "stuffed dolls, wastebaskets made from empty gallon ice cream containers, vases made from glass jars, cookies, candy, gumdrop animals, sandwiches, original music manuscripts, plastic aprons, Christmas cards, and Christmas trees made from painted pine cones, . . . gift items modeled from clay as well as hand-painted scrapbooks." She added that two wooden bookcases, "were supposed to be given to the parents for holiday presents, but the two young carpenters decided to auction them off and give the proceeds to your fund. . . . We hope that this contribution will help to make some other children as happy as ours are."

The Hoffmann School letter that the *Times* would publish 2 years later was written by burgeoning business woman Patrice Zayner, Grade 5, who demonstrates that the attendant mathematics in selling and covering costs had become a formal part of the learning encounter. Patrice specifies proudly that from the bazaar "we netted a profit of $135." Still clear on the purpose of their financial efforts, Patrice adds: "All the children at our school are happy. We would like to share some of our happiness with others in this way. . . . May this bit help other children who need it." Happy. Happy within ourselves and happier still to be doing for others: children in need, children who face greater challenges than we.

In my father's mid-1940s novel, he describes the new principal's difficult decision to admit a little girl who, on account of her reaction to the smallpox vaccine at age one, had "lost control over her central nervous system." In his florid prose, he explains that the young director, seeking out promise, found that the child's "reaction to the vaccine had not affected her mental powers, that her memory was extraordinarily good, and that she had an irrepressible spirit which demanded release from the restraints that her tortured body imposed upon her." A plan was set in place. The young director "would play upon the child's strength to give her acceptance, and that lay in her memory which was remarkable."

Accordingly, this child (he called her Roberta) was assigned the responsibility of keeping track of the changing tasks of the kindergarten's Cleanup Committee. Roberta was able to remember all the children's names and to recite their various duties as needed. Instead of teasing the child for her limitations, the other children were impressed by and praised her "mnemonic" skills. His almost too-good-to-be true summary nonetheless illuminates Ann Hoffmann's point of view:

> The child was important and began to feel it was true. Her physical
> frailties began to become a part of the obligation of the group. The
> children themselves delighted in helping Roberta with her cloth-
> ing and pushing her [wheel]chair to the table. The time came when
> Roberta could climb the stairs independently. She became a little
> surer in the use of her hands and the doctor said that it would not
> be long before she would acquire a normal control of her faculties.

[The young director] was proud in the knowledge that there were few schools which would have accepted Roberta for admission and that not only had Roberta been helped by the school, but also the children had learned a valuable lesson in living together.

Jade, a grade behind me at Hoffmann School, was older but much smaller because, we were told, she was born prematurely. She had cerebral palsy, and it was very hard for her to climb the stairs, or speak a sentence, or move in rhythm with the music, even though she was with us at school doing it all. At age 11, Jade was strikingly thin with pale skin, fuzzy beige hair, and eyes in search of direction. She moved jerkily but with determination, as if she were made of unhinged joints. I was troubled by Jade's mouth, always half open and fixed in some kind of smile, and I was alarmed (though flattered) that she became cheerfully agitated when I would stop to say hello. I recall my curiosity and discomfort more clearly than compassion, but Gracie, my best friend in fourth grade, believes today that her empathetic reaction to Jade may have been an early sign of—or perhaps even a stimulus for—her destiny as a social worker.

The school car that took Gracie to and from her family's elegant Park Avenue apartment also transported Jade from her modest Johnson Avenue abode. Jade's family lived on the Bronx side of the Spuyten Duyvil Creek that joins the Hudson and Harlem rivers. Unaware of the more accepted translation "in spite of the devil," I always thought it was the place where the devil spat and separated Manhattan from the Bronx. On account of their locations, Jade was picked up after Gracie and dropped home before, allowing Gracie to witness Jade's daily departure from and reunion with her mother. Gracie told me, "I was so tied into her . . . her mother would be letting her go every day with this disability and she was doing her best to let her daughter be separate from her and meet the challenges that she would have to face." And as Gracie watched this selfless action, she remembers, "the tears would roll down from my eyes." Similarly, she watched "the mother's joy and relief when Jade came home and they would run into each other's arms," a parent-child relation so different from her own. Gracie explained:

> I was the opposite. I was like the poor little rich girl. I saw my parents hit or miss and there was some sort of a caretaker/nanny type person to meet the car when I came home, and here in contrast was this poor and disabled child and she and her mom had this incredible bond. She had cerebral palsy—one side was partly paralyzed and all I remember was that scene and that she had a mother who adored her

and was there for her. I had this interpretation even as a child that it was an act of great love that the mother could let her go like that . . . that she clearly didn't want her to go but that she should go to school like a regular kid.

Whatever notions of sameness are evoked by the term *regular kid*, at this small progressive school—across physical, personal, and cognitive variables—irregularity reigned. Indeed, it may be said that difference at Hoffmann School was the only norm. The art historian Ernst Gombrich has likened the artist composing a visual image to a woman arranging flowers in a vase, knowing for example, just where red was needed on one side to balance the green on the other.[4] If Ann Hoffmann was an artist composing a balanced whole out of the children she selected for the school, we would have likened her process more to the assembly of a wild outdoor garden than to a careful arrangement in a vase.

Ann included flowers and shrubs that she enjoyed watching grow, took a chance on unpromising seedlings, and was always prepared to defend as flower that weed on the edge of removal. She was unlike those school directors who reached for symmetry, admitting this many boys and this many girls in each class, enough children to fill a chorus or an advanced math class. Indeed, she may have been drawn to asymmetry, attending to each child as an individual, disinterested in where or whether he or she would fit, perhaps thinking disruption had more to offer than balance. I consider Ann's eclectic garden more human than Gombrich's balanced vase and her preoccupation with imbalance a most effective way to view any student body. Hoffmann School taught students to be wary of homogeneity and other falsehoods that obscure or devalue the precious differences that distinguish and connect us all. My classmate Stephen said that he was greatly influenced by the mix of people at Hoffmann School. He felt it made him "appreciative" rather than "afraid" of difference.

But the school's emphasis on difference and diversity raised the curiosity if not downright suspicion of outsiders looking in. What sort of school was it anyway? For what sort of child was it designed? While Ann Hoffmann's wild flower garden pleased her sensibilities, myopic outsiders were mistrustful. My father portrayed some of the upper-middle-class Riverdale neighbors in the 1940s peering through binoculars from their abutting properties to take in the school's population. He said that they protested alternately that the name Hoffmann was German, that the children were Jewish, or not American, or black. Among the threats and attempts to close the school that he described, he noted one neighbor complaining contemptuously, "Fine people have built this neighborhood and we do not want it spoiled."

Our young director did not shrink from the community's sharp-toothed challenge. Her thinking was typically pragmatic: "If we only had more children drawn from the neighborhood," she offered, "community acceptance would come about overnight." According to my father's manuscript, Ann arranged a display of children's artwork and served refreshments "from 4 to 6 on Thursday, December 19, 1945." The announcement was distributed throughout the two blocks surrounding the school. Apparently, neighbors even without children dropped by out of "sheer curiosity" and most of them were positively impressed. While overnight acceptance may not have been achieved in fiction or history, as the years went by more and more local children did attend the school and Ann Hoffmann's outreach to the neighboring community—often around displays of the art of children and adult artists—continued throughout her real-life directorship. Perhaps ironically, after the school was closed in 1985, even ambivalent abutters suffered the loss of its well-kept grounds and the musical sound of children's voices. In the end, they were obliged to watch the ravishing of it all by vandalism, fire, and neglect.

Again crossing fictive and real lines, the Hoffmann School for Individual Attention was one of the many New York private schools that the eccentric Auntie Mame was considering for her nephew in the popular mid-1950s novel by Patrick Dennis.[5] In spite of local legend, however, it was not the wacky place that she selected: a Second Avenue loft where neither teachers nor students wore clothes. I do not believe that perceptions of the school ever reached such extremes. Nonetheless, while it was listed alongside them in the *Registry of Independent Schools*, the Hoffmann School was a certain and persistent outlier to the more conventional independent schools that Mame was urged to consider.

At the secondary level in 1955 a desirable cluster of independent schools known as the "Hilltop Schools" (all located in Riverdale) included Horace Mann, then a boys school for the intellectually elite; the more accessible Barnard School (which has since merged with Horace Mann); Fieldston, a progressive coeducational Ethical Culture School; and the Riverdale Country Schools (separate then for boys and girls), which were solid, traditional, and solely directed toward sending each student to the "college of his or her choice." Leaving the soft womb of Hoffmann School for seventh grade, all four of us in the graduating class of 1955, with varying levels of scholarship support, went to Hilltop Schools. I went to the then inappropriately (at least for me) straight-laced Riverdale Country School for Girls; Arthur, a sprightly athlete, to the daunting Riverdale Country School for Boys; and gentle Stephen and erratic Jacob to heady Horace Mann. Regardless of the learning and social challenges that we all remember facing, as it was with Chester, "out of Hoffmann," with its/our eccentricities, we were pretty much in demand by—and apparently well prepared for—the competitive private school sector.

We all went on to college and various versions of graduate study. I am mindful of Hoffmann School's emphasis on empathy and on the arts as I note that I grew up to be a developmental psychologist focusing on artistic cognition; Arthur, a clinical psychologist specializing in drug and alcohol abuse; Stephen, a textile conservationist with a passionate interest in well-being; and Jacob, a lawyer dedicated to charitable organizations. Two of us stayed in New York; the other two ended up in Massachusetts. But in spite of the overlap in our Hilltop secondary school experience and our subsequent geographical propinquity, the four of us have had little or no interaction since graduation from sixth grade.

Reflecting on the lifelong friends his children made in their local elementary school, Jacob wonders whether Hoffmann School, with its focus on individuality, did not set the stage for enduring childhood friendships: "None of us seemed to have maintained a relationship even though we were in this small closely knit group thrown together for so long," he observed. "We were classmates not friends." Considering that possibility, I am reminded that Hoffmann School kids were not like children in suburban communities who every afternoon walk home from school together, participate in after-school activities, and share a sense of neighborhood. Hoffmann School students didn't get home until nearly 5 o'clock and were taken in cars on different routes to dwellings and communities that were often quite far from one another. Well, the other children were.

At the end of the school day, I would go to the school kitchen where Estelle, who cooked for our family and the school, would have prepared a snack for me: usually two tuna fish salad sandwiches on soft white bread taken from an industrial size loaf and a tall glass of milk. An extremely large and most loving woman, Estelle always wore a white dress, full apron, and one of those high chef's hats. Her bright white uniform contrasted greatly with her dark brown skin and belied in its formality the fact that Estelle was prone to peals of uproarious laughter. Both Gracie and Stephen remembered across decades Estelle's warm presence and the particular comfort of her embrace: her upper arms, soft as pillows, the

wide and ready smile that twinkled with a gold front tooth, and the im-
possibility of passing her by without an adoring hello.

After conversation and sandwiches with Estelle, I would usually play
outside until dark. Absorbed in one or another dramatic sequence, talking openly to myself, I roamed the quiet school grounds accompanied
only by my trusty bike as horse. Sometimes my grandmother, Nanny—
my mother's mother who lived with us and could sew anything from
dresses to drapes—would walk slowly with me along the flat stone path
that led from the schoolhouse to the back of the property. I knew my
grandmother had been born in Italy, but it surprised me that after 50
years in this country, she spoke English hesitantly, if at all. Nanny would
cheer reliably for tricks that I had mastered like going backward down a
slide (hard to brave when others were waiting their turn) or jumping off
a swing (not allowed at school). Indoors, I would sometimes play teacher
alone in an empty classroom—making marks on a clean green blackboard
and addressing the empty desks. But my pretense seemed more authentic
in a room away from school. Unfettered by the trappings of real school
elements, I would spread guest towels on the floor of our apartment's
little bathroom and read aloud to the imaginary and often misbehaving
children resting on those mats.

The Hoffmann School was my neighborhood; its staff and my family
members were my friends, and my after-school activities were all contained
therein. In discussions with my three classmates after so much time, one
thing was certain. For each of these individuals, and I think quite rightly,
I was not just another member of our class. Where as a child I'd carried
the social burden of being the principal's daughter, half a century later
it seemed I had become to my former classmates the school itself. Jacob
said simply, "I cannot disassociate the two." I don't know whether that
perception intruded upon or enriched our exchanges, and I was pleased
when I heard it was a "delight" or "eye-opening" to realize how much,
how poignantly, and what in particular mature individuals remembered
from long-ago elementary school days. For me, home, school, and self
were literally intertwined. With their shared recollection of the "homeyness" of Hoffmann School, others seemed similarly attached.

After a few phone conversations, Stephen e-mailed the following:
"Jessie (hope you don't mind 'Jessie' from school days), I can't tell you
how exciting this revisiting the days at Hoffmann School has been. It's
not even a heavy dose of nostalgia, but it seems to be somehow woven
into a psychological fabric of the moment, creating something new rather

than just a sentimental rehash. Hope you can make sense of that last statement." Soon after that message, a carefully wrapped package arrived from Riverside Drive. Ripping it open, I found within the most beautiful object—a sea green ceramic bowl that Stephen had cast for me and sent along with a note of appreciation and reunion.

I was struck that Stephen expressed his sentiment by making something. I am similarly inclined to thank a friend with a small painting or a pen-and-ink caricature, or to celebrate an event with endless deadly doggerel. Friends will ask where I learned so easily to express myself in multiple ways. I have always thought it came from Hoffmann School where students were encouraged to speak in languages that went beyond words and included the making, movement, and sound of visual and performing arts. In this light, Stephen's gifting seemed to me such a Hoffmann School thing to do. Seeing it as more artistic than utilitarian, I placed the bowl in full view on a living room table. It stands for me as the "something new" that Stephen has created out of the past—open, circular, embracing, filled with possibility. I do hope he can make sense of that last statement.

PAIN

Although she was only 5'2", Ann Hoffmann was seen by her students as of "ample size," "large," "an authority figure," "in charge," a "head of state." While other children seemed to me to have young stylish mothers, my own mother, whose long black hair went gray early on, never seemed young at all. Full-figured, she stood with perfect dignified posture and always dressed as a school principal in sensible shoes and conservative clothes. She wore double-breasted coatdresses, woolen skirts and tailored blouses, and unexpectedly bright-colored sweaters draped like shawls on her round shoulders (purple and red was her favorite combination). Her light blue eyes peered over green reading glasses that hung from a cord round her neck in the way I thought grandmothers' glasses were meant to be worn. If, as school psychologist Dick Robinson had said, "she was always playing the role of a school principal," Ann Hoffmann had the costume down to a T.

I longed for a mother like the others had: someone glamorous like Jacob's very young mother; someone with free time to play as I imagined would Stephen's at-home mother; someone who might wear an apron and a dress with a waistline as slim as Arthur's diminutive mom's or as the mother played by Jane Wyatt on my favorite television show, *Father Knows Best*. Someone who would be waiting for me when I came home from school, unaware and eager to hear of the many things that happened—or that I could say happened—in my place away from home. Instead, my mother knew the workings of my and everyone else's every day. I never had the privacy to keep from her my indiscretions in school for certainly, and perhaps even as a conscious equalizing gesture, I was sent to her office at least as much as, but I think more than, other children (though it was infrequent for all of us). "Just sit there," she'd say to me understanding my discomfort, "and think about whatever it is that's brought you here."

I'd think about the injustices of the world and especially my sorry lot as the principal's daughter. How that miserable identity kept me from ever having a triumph of my own. How the other kids thought everything was easy for me and would say, "Oh, that's because you're the principal's daughter," if ever a teacher praised me for anything. And I could see through the teachers' thinly veiled plots, sending me to the office when it was never my fault just to make it seem to the others that they didn't treat me specially. That's the sort of self-pitying reflection in which I would indulge as I sat in my mother's office. Watching her buzz around efficiently, calling for this and that, I would be wishing that it was after-school time and she could be her real self and give me the warm hug that I needed and deserved.

This was not a time when the mothers I saw on TV or in magazines worked full-time as mine did, overseeing the school during the day, planning at night the class schedules or car assignments or meals for the week. How many times did my mother run up and down the three flights of stairs between her office and our apartment, remembering at the end of the day as she left the space that was school for the space that was home that now she should be fully available to my sister and to me and especially to my father? My father would frequently bring home surprise guests for dinner and was accustomed to the beautiful meals she planned, the gorgeous tables she set and taught us to set, and the fresh red lipstick she managed to apply minutes before he trekked up the steep stairs, bellowing his nickname for her, "Hoffie," as if she had been waiting there for him all day.

How many times did she scale those three flights of stairs before her death at 66? One might think the endless exercise—out on the grounds, up and down stairs responding to whatever crisis and/or child called her—would have kept her in shape and promised her a much longer life. I have often thought that all the demands, both physical and administrative; the responsibilities to children and parents and teachers and family and staff; the expectations for miracle working with children in need; were taken together too much for one person to bear. But she bore them all right to the end. School psychologist Dick Robinson was able to tell us at her funeral that a week before she died, Ann Hoffmann had called him about a child, with the same urgency with which she had always asked for his services. "This child is in pain, Professor," she told him. "Let's get on with it."

Jacob was surely a child in pain. While I align our sixth-grade graduation with the most exciting events of 1955, Jacob remembers standing in front of the school, dress shoes firmly planted on the stone steps, tears streaming down his face, waiting for his stepfather who finally and not atypically showed up more than an hour after the ceremony. Had I not seen Jacob there as the rest of us enjoyed cookies and punch on the front porch? Was I too absorbed in my own feelings of personal injustice to attend to the miseries of my classmates? I do retain images of Jacob crying and acting out, but I question the veracity of our vivid recollections of him eating crayons and grass and hiding under his desk from loud noises. On the one hand, he was this handsome well-spoken student who read big books and knew how to spell; and on the other, he was an emotional explosion waiting to happen. Was this the sort of behavior that was unacceptable at other schools and just another reason to call Dick Robinson at ours? I know that we were advised to be patient and told that Jacob's life was difficult. But I'm not sure that I ever understood why.

Perhaps I had heard the word *divorce,* not infrequently spoken at Hoffmann School, but regarded as a challenge to child rearing. Something about the Holocaust (though we didn't call it that)—that event in history that was too terrible to talk about, that could never happen here, only in a safely faraway country called Germany. Although it unravels now as childhood myth, I thought that Jacob and his mother had survived in a concentration camp because they both had white blonde hair and blue eyes that made them look anything but Jewish. Alternately or additionally, I believed that Jacob had chilling numbers inscribed somewhere on his arm (he didn't), and that—whatever the facts or details—his unsettled countenance was the result of the most horrific wrongdoings of the adult world. With slight variations in plot ("survivor guilt," "traumatized by the war"), my classmates shared these misapprehensions. I am surprised to learn that he was actually born in the states and impressed by the facileness with which children weave enduring tales out of bits of truth and falsehood.

In his well-appointed office half a century later, Jacob welcomed my interest in his recollections of Hoffmann School, although he let me know up front that this was not a happy time in his life. Like everyone I spoke to, Jacob apologized at the start, certain that he would not remember very much and not be able to be of much help: "How am I going to sustain this conversation for more than 5 minutes in terms of my memories?" I told him that Arthur and Gracie said the same thing but they remembered a lot and in great detail. "Well," he said, "let's face it. They're both shrinks. They've been talking about their childhoods for years. I've carefully not thought much about mine."

Much to his surprise, Jacob recounted details of the double room in which we had a combined fifth and sixth grade and the placement of our teacher's desk where the doors between used to be. Clear to him still was the mahogany balcony overlooking the first floor where, he said, "I had a massive tantrum with the banging of hands and kicking of legs because I refused to hand in my math homework, which I refused to hand in because I hadn't done it!" He pressed further and pictured the fields and the slides, the expanse of green grass, and the fact that the famous conductor, Arturo Toscanini, was an immediate neighbor. I ask about his beautiful mother, who was born in Germany and whose sister died in a concentration camp. He tells me she is now in her eighties and incapacitated, attended lovingly still by the stepfather ("in many ways a wonderful man") who missed graduation.

I heard for the first time of the plight of Jacob's mother, first married at 17, divorced and single in Jacob's earliest years. It had been just the two of them through her sadness and loss, and that was hard. But most devastating to Jacob was her remarrying and going on to have one and then another child—siblings he now cherishes, but then rude intruders on his 6-year-old life. At Jacob's suggestion, I review a book his mother had written in which she describes her lush childhood in Germany and the unthinkably long time it took for her comfortable Jewish community to understand the magnitude of Hitler's evil. I try to imagine her confusion and despair, arriving with friends at her favorite places for swimming and skating and finding mounted over the door: "Jews and dogs *verboten!*" Her writer's voice is part diary, girlfriend, keen observer, and outraged citizen. Across time and space, it seems familiar, embedded as were our childhoods, in the global anguish of the 1940s.

Although it wasn't directly discussed, the horrors of that era—whispered words like *dictator* and *concentration camp*— permeated our nightmares and our play. It was chilling or hilarious (I could never decide) to sing along to the melody of the Disney tune, "Whistle While You Work": "Mussolini is a meany. Hitler is a jerk." Just as the Second World War had provided a shadowy backdrop to the early development of the eclectic Hoffmann School, Nazi Germany contextualized our misunderstanding of this complicated little boy. Jacob was quick to tell me what he thinks is obvious: His dramatic scenes in school were calls for the attention he felt slipping from him at home. As I look now at the photo of our class, after so many years as a teacher, I am most drawn to Jacob. His scowling demands my attention and piques my interest as students who wear their hearts on their sleeves always do. Do squeaky wheels annoy or intrigue? Are all teachers drawn to outliers, even as we are asked to cultivate and maintain a norm?

My mother must have admitted Jacob to her school because she saw through or in his behaviors both the pain he was enduring and his longing for success. But how did Ann Hoffmann pull it all off? With a school full of children with differing and well-identified physical, cognitive, and personal challenges, how did she and the other teachers keep up with each of them? I begin to see Ann Hoffmann as a timeless (exhausted) juggler keeping fast-moving balls in the air even as their shape and substance continuously change. Administration; teachers; the needs of the individual child; transportation; lunch; referrals; listening; challenging; athletics; the arts; social development, and more. Inevitably, mistakes would be made. A ball would have to drop from time to time.

As Jacob tells his story of how he learned that he would repeat first grade at Hoffmann School, I consider that it was half a century ago and that painful moments may stand out most in our early recollections of school. But I still cringe as he describes his recollection of coming to school on the first day of what he thought would be second grade and following someone from his last year's class ("a friend") to what turned out to be the wrong classroom. How could he not have been told before that moment that he would be repeating a year? Who and what had changed Ann Hoffmann's mind about his class placement and when had that decision been made? Jacob considers the possibility that there was more preparation for the event than he remembers, and he is certain the decision to hold him back was the right one, but what he remembers most clearly from his moment of discovery was what my mother so strongly fought against: disgrace.

Gracie tells me that after the formal interview, as she and her mother first toured the Hoffmann School, which they had selected because 4-year-old Gracie refused to go back for a second week of kindergarten at Ethical Culture, Ann Hoffmann asked her matter-of-factly if she still "wet her pants." While the scene seems somehow improbable, I understand when Gracie tells me she was "very offended" by that query. It was true that Ann Hoffmann supported open discussion and accurate language (no *tinkle* or *pee-pee*) regarding the natural activity of going to the bathroom. But how could she assume this formal little girl had similar cultural norms? Was it possible that she needed the information (perhaps she'd forgotten to ask Gracie's mother) and not thought it through? I envision Gracie's round freckled face, perfect posture, and well-brushed shiny hair parted in the middle. On special occasions, she wore freshly starched dresses to school. Perhaps she'd worn for that first visit her double-breasted tweed coat with the velvet collar—the kind you bought at Best & Company on Fifth Avenue, the kind that came with riding pants and a velvet brimmed hat.

Gracie was a fastidious child whose everyday school dungarees were carefully ironed with a crease down the leg. She was a lot of fun and she was good at everything. On those few occasions when I slept over at her apartment, she would win the in-house games. She could always stand longer in the very hot water with which we would fill the tub, and I would give up sooner when we took turns being bridges between the two beds in her room—lying with arms on one bed, feet on the other, while the other player walked across the bridge's back. Her deep bellowing voice, adult articulation of words, and easy confident manner hid well the fact that she was worried about such things as the height of the slide she saw in the school playground. Who knew she was distressed that her sled was sensibly kept in the dark basement of the school where it would be ready for her use rather than hidden away in an albeit nearby closet in her apartment building? She worried about it at night.

Perhaps my mother asked that impertinent question because at naptime the younger children rested or slept on canvas cross-legged cots separated by wooden folding screens that created room-like compartments. Did the lowering of lights in this setting present a challenge to young children still working to stay dry through the night? How many balls would the juggler have had to be balancing to casually confront this polite little girl with such a blunt question? Gracie remembers selectively that our third-grade teacher wore paper cuffs to keep her shirtsleeves clean. This is the same teacher who suggested on my report card that I take a "little more pride in neatness and correctness." Gracie sounds admiring of the cuffs even as she describes the action as "persnickety." Who would ask a persnickety little girl if she wet her pants?

Was it possible that a phone call from Jacob's mother the morning of the first day of school, perhaps reporting on a summer of limited maturing or excessive thumb-sucking, elicited the quick last-minute action that caused Jacob such distress? Is it possible that Ann Hoffmann knew Gracie didn't wet and thought she might be proud to respond in the negative? These encounters—misguided, accidental, or misremembered—are conspicuously at odds with Ann Hoffmann's emotional goals for her students: "respect for self and others, flexibility, empathy." These recollections position Ann Hoffmann as all-powerful, and Gracie and Jacob as small and vulnerable. This was not the rapport my mother desired. She set out to be to her children a good friend, and perhaps I should not be surprised that in spite of these painful encounters, Gracie and Jacob speak of Ann with affection and respect. Surely Ann Hoffmann reflected at the end of each day with strong measures of doubt and remorse even as she carried on with the steady proud countenance of what Hoffmann school lifer (K–7) Bruno called "the hard-nosed executive." His view was that, "she was every little child's friend, but she could really guide people and make the place run."

Bruno's promotion story, occurring 10 years after Jacob's, is very different. Describing himself as a "challenge" for his parents, Bruno explains that he was a child for whom "abstract thinking was very tough" so that subjects like arithmetic were difficult for him and he had a terrible time controlling his temper: "I'd break things and I was a handful." Substantially taller than the other children in his class, he was especially concerned when he "almost had to be left back in kindergarten." He made a passionate appeal to Ann Hoffmann, whom he found "very strict and very gentle at the same time." She agreed to make a deal with Bruno. "Look," she offered as a wise friend, "you can go into first grade if you agree that you will not be disruptive." And Bruno promised with a full heart, "Yes, Ann, I won't be disruptive." He tells me with assurance and sustained mutual pride that they "both kept the deal."

Diana attended Hoffmann School without interruption from kindergarten through sixth grade. A few years younger, Diana even at 8 or 9, had an exceptionally droll sense of humor. She was witty and clever—remarkable, I would say, for the warm glow of laughter and kindness that seemed to surround her. Heavy eyelids set off her enormous brown eyes and gave a sheepish edge to the friendly smile that invariably graced her lips. Diana seemed always in good spirits, was carefully groomed and dressed in well-matched outfits, and her thick dark hair was lovingly braided with ribbons each day. If she was heavier than the other children at school, I did not mark the difference or recognize it as of similar concern to the struggles that beset so many students at Hoffmann. But my peer perception was again out of touch with the reality of another child's pain.

When as an adult, Diana published a book on style and confidence for any sized women, it seemed another Hoffmann School success story. Diana had left Hoffmann for a demanding high school, gone on to study art and philosophy, and started a dance company for women of all sizes. In her writing in the early 1980s she was perhaps the first to break the boundaries of fashion and beauty for the neglected and rejected population of big women. And there it was, an outsider finding her safe haven at Hoffmann School and going off to re-create the Hoffmann experience, affecting social change as Ann Hoffmann strove to do—by championing outsiders.

Within the pages of her engaging book, I was moved to see that Diana wrote about the Hoffmann School and that in the photo she included of herself and her mother at the school when she was 11, the older girl of 13 whose back is to the camera is me. I have already moved on to the Riverdale Country School for seventh grade and I believe the photo is of a spring festival at Hoffmann School. My shoulders are rounded as they are now, my hands are folded behind my back as I still fold them, and my curly hair is mashed down into a lacquered straight bob that turns up tidily at the ends. The photo is black and white so I am uncertain as to whether the familiar plaid dress I am wearing is tan and white as I think, but it is for sure beset with crinolines and, as was the fashion in the late 1950s, the belt at my waist is pulled impossibly tight. Diana is seated and smiling as if she's heard or told a joke, with two of her friends whose faces are familiar and who are looking my way. I am the big sister returning to the family that was our school and the littler girls look happy to see me.

I wouldn't have missed the spring festivals for anything my first years out of Hoffmann. It was at these year-end events that the whole Hoffmann School community would gather under the flowering trees out back to celebrate the rite of passage that is graduation. I am sure that my return each spring was for me a kind of renewal. I would soak in the sound and spectacle of student voices filling the air in musical and dramatic production and the graduating sixth graders—the boys still dressed in suits with those white carnations in their lapels and the girls wearing the Hoffmann School trademark crown of daisies—receiving their diplomas. But as time went on and my social hemisphere expanded an inch or two, I was often too busy to come or unfamiliar with whichever children had moved up behind me at Hoffmann and were now celebrating their big day.

As Diana describes the school and its warmth, the familiarity of calling teachers by their first names, and the homelike atmosphere of the place, she writes in fullest detail about the dining room. She remembers the low tables and child-sized chairs, the Formica tabletops, and the two "enormous" dark-skinned ladies who cooked and served the food, Emma and Estelle. Still vivid are the overflowing platters of spaghetti and meatballs or macaroni and cheese and the good friends with whom Diana was surrounded. But what stands out most, apart from her own industry, success, and popularity, is the isolation she experienced in the dining room—the diet pills and separate dry lunches of turkey or tuna that made mealtime at Hoffmann for Diana a "hell on earth."

I see it again. Although she speaks of the school with love, it is the moments of humiliation that stand out for Diana. The time a medical clinic was set up in the dining room and all the children were weighed in front of each other. The exciting day when she was 7 (her second year in the school) and a huge concrete turtle was delivered—a climbing structure that seemed prehistoric in its proportions. Rather than face the embarrassment of climbing up the sides of it, awkward and plump and slipping around, Diana gathered spring flowers from the back of the grounds and wove together dandelion chains with feigned concentration, as if it were the thing she preferred to do, even as she kept a watchful eye on the new stone structure with its shell's shoe-sized indentations and the regular-sized children scaling up and down.

There is no doubt that my mother was aware of Diana's anguish. As a woman who struggled with her weight, Ann Hoffmann must have identified particularly with Diana's plight. My mother suffered many diets and occasionally went on retreats with one or another of her sisters to something they called a Milk Farm in order to lose a few pounds. She even went at one time to the famous New York City "Fat Doctor" (at least that's what she called him), who offered what I think were amphetamines as magic diet pills. I believe he was the same doctor that treated Diana. I am sure that my mother spoke to Diana about their common struggle as she always encouraged me to let younger children know when things weren't as easy as they looked for me. Perhaps she tried to prepare Diana for the public weighing in the dining room or comforted her after. Perhaps she recognized the potential pain of that situation and thought Diana's confidence would be enlarged by her endurance. Or perhaps there hadn't been time for the reflection that we know informs good practice. Another quick decision that could not be retrieved. How many such decisions face all of us who teach? A look, an offhanded remark or query—the smallest misstep can have consequence. Ann Hoffmann believed that the child was never wrong, that if school—a construction mediated by adults—was failing, it was up to adults to regroup and redesign. I believe she wrestled daily with the profound responsibility embedded in her belief. You could see it, along with the rest, in the darting, distracted, and vulnerable eyes of the hard-nosed executive.

Children in pain. Did Ann Hoffmann seek them out or did she consider anguish a part of everyone's childhood, ordinary childhoods? Each of us as surely as we were blessed with hidden or apparent gifts carried with us hidden or apparent pain. She did not isolate children in pain. They were her mainstream. They were the same children who realized that in the broad societal landscape they were the happy ones at Hoffmann School at the ready to share their joy and make better the lives of less fortunate children. I have to think the Hoffmann School helped Diana to see through her pain to the possibility of making of it all (and even using the arts) something from which others could learn. As I turn the pages of Diana's beautifully illustrated and well-written book, I feel myself fully as the Hoffmann School and I long to reach through the decades and wrap my approving arms around this brave, sad, funny, resourceful little girl.

Chapter 2

School as Home

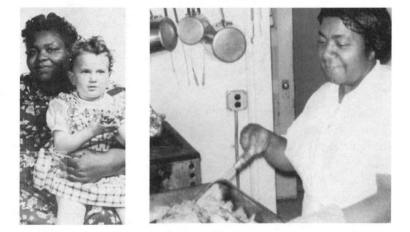

Lucy and Jessica (left). Emma in the school kitchen (right).

POROUS BOUNDARIES

S TEPHEN'S MOTHER SELECTED the Hoffmann School because she wanted Stephen to be in a warm homelike environment in a country
setting. She was trying to ease the pain of his father's abandon-
ment when Stephen was only four years old. Gracie's mother didn't want
Gracie to endure the same "uptight, strict, and demanding education"
that her immigrant parents had found for her in New York and that she
hated: "She wanted me to go to a school where you would love learning,
[a place] where you would want to be as a child, where you could express
yourself and discover your own strengths and talents and be nurtured
and not terrified." Jacob didn't know why or how his mother chose the
Hoffmann School, only that she miraculously always found the resources

Estelle and Ann at a birthday party.

to send him to private school. But I have to think that she was drawn to the school as a place where differences were honored, where children were not faulted for their origins, and where her little boy would never feel *verboten,* no matter what he did.

Jacob allows that even though he chose to stage tantrums rather than do his homework, he was never afraid to go to school. He loved to read and thinks the teachers at Hoffmann School must have done something to inspire that. "Please be candid," I say, urging him to elaborate his reservations, "no need to protect me." "Well, I'm protecting the Hoffmann School," Jacob admits, "but I guess you and it are one and the same." Of course he is right. I am the Hoffmann School. I realize this in the recurrent dream I have in which I am a house of many chambers—some tucked away and packed with interesting mementos from former owners' lives, others empty and flooded with light and possibility. But whatever the layout of new or familiar rooms, I invariably open a door that leads to a small gym, or a bathroom with child-sized seats, or an art room with many easels. And I am never surprised by these discoveries (somehow I knew they'd be there) even as I wonder how we will use these public spaces in whatever private house I am.

I think these dreams—these self imaginings—are the reason I was so moved by a particular moment in Doug Wright's magnificent play, *I Am My Own Wife.*[6] The subject of the play, the cross-dressing Charlotte von Mahlsdorf, stands alone on stage in front of her museum collection displayed as a pile of veiled chambers containing historical objects—timepieces collected over her tormented and courageous past. "I am my museum," she speaks quietly. "Yes," I think to myself and realize asleep or awake, "I am my school." Perhaps an obvious discovery for someone whose home was actually a school, but I wonder whether educators should be mindful that the spaces we create for learning (literally and metaphorically) are the people that our students will become. Like home, school imprints itself on every child, blurring the boundaries between context and self, helping to shape or to suppress individuality. Each of us stage center, making sense of internalized chambers replete with historical objects, personal challenge, and relative respect. Each of us reconciling home and school through indelible images grounded in literal space: cultivated or adequate, equipped or lacking, honoring or disregarding. I am the Hoffmann School and so is Jacob.

In the literal space that was our Hoffmann School, children were welcomed by warm wooden wainscoting in the main hall—where Chester would choose to sit—and invited up the curving stairway so well-worn by my mother's sturdy shoes. Above those stairs, daylight glowed through the pink, blue, and yellow panels of an arched stained glass skylight. Industrial gray linoleum covered the wooden steps that branched to left and right at the second level. The left access led to the double room that housed our fifth and sixth grades, two other classrooms, and the art room. The right stairwell led to the landing where each year we would sing holiday songs while parents looked up from below. We wore outside clothing to add a touch of winter to these occasions and held assorted unrelated books that we pretended to read as we sang the memorized words of ecumenical holiday songs. My mother was reportedly the first educator in New York City to introduce in 1947 a "Festival of Lights" in which Christmas and Hanukkah (in the late sixties Kwanzaa was added) were discussed in depth and celebrated with equal respect. Ann Hoffmann did not see difference between individuals or religions as a means or reason for separation. Looking within and across perspectives, she encouraged us to seek out and celebrate our shared humanity.

Beyond that Festival of Lights landing, and up a few steps was the music room where we sang daily, played psalteries and recorders, and all (boys and girls) took modern dance and ballet. At the end of the hall was the heavy door that separated downstairs school from upstairs home—that warren of six rooms where my family lived. As soon as you closed the weighted door with its heavy lock, you were surrounded by warmth and color: a space of smaller dimensions accented with the beautiful fabrics my mother selected for curtains, spreads, and the amazing slipcovers my grandmother would sew. Images on the walls included lawyers and workers: Spy caricatures of barristers and Irwin Hoffman (no relation) etchings of Mexican farmers and mine workers with lights on their foreheads. The small kitchen that doubled as stair-top entry hall held promise of Estelle's apple pie or Nanny's fried dough. Like the other school children, Jacob was aware of that space as a privileged arena, a secret enclave. He was also aware that I sometimes invited my schoolmates to visit with me there. Fifty years later, more bemused than accusatory, he raises new guilt: "I never went through that door."

Arthur would visit frequently during the years his mother worked as my mother's secretary and as a typist for my father, who was always in process on one book or another, trying to keep alive the writer's life for which he not so secretly pined. Malcolm had graduated from Harvard College (1934) and then Harvard Law School (1937), but only after a few disappointing attempts at becoming a radio announcer and some heartening success publishing short stories in magazines and collections. He would go on to write and publish two autobiographies—the first about his life as a government lawyer, the second about the larger journey—and to edit books and write articles on the law. He also published a collection of musings from the issues-based luncheons and talk clubs he organized throughout his later life.[7] In his very last years, he set out to write a mystery novel. But his stories from the 1930s, all featuring his heroic prose, tackle worthy themes like friendship, prejudice, and the possibility of forgiveness. At my father's funeral, a lifelong friend described Malcolm as Superman in deference not only to his bigger-than-life size, but also to his preoccupation with virtue, justice, and what he believed in as the American way. For me as a young child, that stick-thin, handsome man whose face looked like Gregory Peck's but whose fingers were yellow at the tip from the four and a half packs of cigarettes he smoked daily (and through the night) did not match the robust superhero models I saw in comic books and on TV. But I knew that my father was a hero to my mother and her school.

The Hoffmann School was Malcolm's opus as well as Ann's. My father worked all day in a downtown office and wrote all night at home, but the margins of his life were cluttered with the needs of the school. The survival of the school had redirected my parents' future; its struggle for success weighed heavily on their finances and personal dreams; and its very existence connected them viscerally to their origins and ideals, their industrious and creative families, and their rooted belief that education could make society better. The Hoffmann School made good use of my father's writing skills for promotional materials, correspondence over my mother's signature when a situation was sensitive, petitions for incorporation of the parents' organization, or the hard-won charter (finalized in 1968) for the school. Amidst a sea of contracts, ranging from registration obligations to snow removal, Malcolm's legal acumen was a boon. Similarly, his income as a lawyer (especially when he left the government and went into private practice) was helpful at those junctures when the school was just about running on empty.

I was never quite sure how it all fell out, the realities of budget and survival, in the school that was our home. My parents did not actually own the property for most of my childhood and they met monthly rent-like payments with the help of numerous giving, lending, familial, and otherwise friendly hands. My parents depended on the kindness of others, struggled to make ends meet, and rarely indulged in a vacation getaway or even dining out. Nonetheless, thanks to our unusual circumstance, our lives felt more opulent than modest. Our apartment, albeit garret-like, was perched on a castle top in a lush rural setting where we encountered beautiful grounds, wonderful architectural space, and easy city access. We also enjoyed the luxury of a staff whose services crossed the boundaries between school and home. Cook, porter, gardener, baby nurse, upstairs and downstairs housekeepers—these were not the usual employees of an unpaid schoolmarm. Even as they made life manageable for my mother, their relationship to us was, for me, as undefined and permeable as the home–school boundaries of physical and pedagogical space.

Not only did Estelle wait for me daily with a snack to quell my appetite until our family dinner at 7:30 p.m., she never let me stay alone at night in our apartment on those rare occasions after my sister had gone off to college when my parents were out. She would sit with me even though I was a teenager and, with momentary lapses of dozing, watch me do my homework—positioned in a chair in my room providing unasked-for protection from whatever lay beyond. When I was younger, she told me exciting and often scary stories that had been told to her and introduced me to a literary tradition that did not rely on the written word. And for all of my life at Hoffmann School, Estelle walked the steep hill up 254th Street every night at 9 o'clock after feeding our family dinner. As she and

I were older and I could drive, I would eagerly offer her the rides she'd refused from my weary mother, and she would praise my ability to drive all the way to her home. But I will not soon forget the more frequent image of that large lone unafraid figure moving slowly through the dark of night on the long walk to the bus that would take her to the train that took her to her apartment in the Bronx where she lived alone. Though she had a home away from us, I believe Estelle found her home in the school just as she helped make the school home for all of us.

Estelle's sister Emma, smaller and vivacious with a deep cleft chin, supervised the maintenance of the building, made sure lunch and snack came out on time, rode home as the strict supervising adult in a school car, and knew every child and where he or she was meant to be. Dignified and parental, with a truly playful edge, Emma felt more like a friend than a caretaker when she would take me on a Saturday afternoon to the movies. We would stop for a most delicious 10-cent hot dog at Woolworth's and sometimes shop together for a gift at the long-defunct Fuhrman's department store. With witty banter and reciprocated respect, Emma stayed close to my mother in all that she did. It was Emma who could make my mother laugh at the worst of times, who made sure my mother sat down occasionally during the day, and who never had a moment's fear of my mother's often-rigorous leadership. And when Ann Hoffmann died, it was Emma who helped me with the grueling task of packing up my mother's beautiful and carefully stored belongings. I was not surprised that Emma knew where and why my mother kept everything, from the already gift-wrapped small boxes of presents she stored on an upper shelf in her closet for staff or children on special occasions to the heavy cardboard box secured with rubber bands and carefully marked "Obsolete keys." "Maybe someone would want to play with them," Emma explained protectively, as I gasped at Ann Hoffmann's compulsive saving and labeling.

It seemed funny to me that Estelle and Emma were real family to each other even as they were some other kind of family to us. Lucy, my baby nurse, was Estelle and Emma's cousin or maybe another sister (it was never clear), and she was fired when I was 6 (an action I found unforgivable) because she restricted her duties to child care and would not take up while I was at school the ironing of sheets or dusting of floors required on the third floor. Or that was what I was told. I suspected that there had been words between Lucy and my mother—perhaps even that my mother was jealous of my attachment to Lucy who was the stay-at-home mother I needed and my working mother could not be. Throughout my childhood, my mother reminded me (and I her) that when Lucy left I would not speak to my mother for several weeks or perhaps it was or seemed like months. I was never sure why she spoke to me so frequently of my rage. Sometimes I thought it was because she was strangely proud of my stubbornness (a descriptor often launched in my direction), or perhaps not talking to one's mother was an action she recognized as a kind of developmental triumph. But I think now that it was her way of keeping me from forgetting that there had been Lucy and I had loved her.

More than a decade later when Lucy was very sick, my mother took me to visit her at Harlem Hospital. I was in my teens and surprised that without my knowing, Lucy had grown so old—that she wore a patch on one eye and that the lower portion of one leg had been removed, I believe on account of diabetes. Lucy's daughter Helen was there. Helen was about my age and remembered with me the times when we were little and she would come to the school and play outside with my sister and me. Emma was there with her daughter Lotte, a grown-up hospital nutritionist of whom Emma was most proud. There were a few other people in the hospital room whom I did not know. Lucy was happy to see Ann Hoffmann and said something to me that made me feel that she was also glad to see me: that I had been among the many children she'd cared for and of import, if it was really "Jessie" that she was seeing before her. Although her saying of my name struck a nostalgic chord, I realized in our awkward reunion how much more Lucy had meant to me than I to her—how foolish I was to have sent her notes throughout the years, letting her know that I was changing and growing and okay even without her. It was after the fact that I learned how ill she really was, and that I had been gathering with others at Lucy's deathbed.

Rebecca had hired Estelle and then Emma before we came to live at the school and for that reason they represented some continuity in our history. Among the disjointed episodes about the "young director fallen heir to an insolvent but democratic private school," my father tells the story of one of Estelle's birthdays at the school, how, with no expectations from others, Estelle had baked all day (with glorious sweet smells wafting through the school building) a large birthday cake. Not knowing that Ann Hoffmann had already had one made and decorated at a local bakery, that the children had all made cards and banners, that there was a party planned at the edge of the pond with marshmallow roasting and celebratory song, Estelle baked her own birthday cake. When she was called to the side of the pond where the children sang happy birthday and showered her with handmade tributes, Estelle began to weep. My father describes her breaking into song—singing a spiritual with such gusto that her deep full voice filled the loving scene, shook the trees, and made "everyone present feel very good for being alive and hearing Estelle's voice and eating the cake whose recipe was only known to Estelle and to St. Peter's first chef."

That joyful surprise could only have happened early on. For as long as any of us can remember, Estelle and Emma's birthdays were anticipated annual events. Emma and Estelle were always at the center serving—sometimes alongside Ann Hoffmann—whatever food accompanied celebrations, which at Hoffmann School food always did. At Thanksgiving there would be an enormous turkey dinner and we children would sing from our dining room chairs choruses of "Estelle put the turkey on," and "Emma take it off again," and "Let's have a feast!" We would clap our hands as Estelle and Emma, wearing their requisite corsages, would walk around the tables, Estelle laughing and accepting compliments for the dinner, Emma telling us to sit down and eat. These two women were heroines of our life at school and Ann Hoffmann taught us to honor and especially to thank those who made our happiness possible. Estelle's death in April 1964 would find me, at 20, away at college. She missed by 6 months meeting the man I would marry whose last name like hers was Davis and whose smile admitted light into the room just as hers did. I was bereft.

HOME SCHOOLING

I coveted my schoolmates' real apartment buildings with doormen and elevators or their suburban houses with friends on the block, but I knew the other children at Hoffmann were envious of my abode. While they were rushed in the morning, I could fall out of bed at my leisure and never be late to school. They saw as privilege my ability at day's end to play in the schoolrooms or on the grounds they had to leave for the separate places they called home. I knew they imagined wonders lying beyond the heavy door to our apartment and even beyond that in the tiny attic spaces in the peaked, red-roofed tower in the back of the building. What adventures might unfold beyond the crenellations that topped the wall outside my bedroom window? As a teen I would climb the fire escape and sit there, crouched tenuously in the well of a crenellation, self-consciously writing poems, featuring myself the heroine in Dodie Smith's wonderful book *I Capture the Castle*.[8]

Perhaps as compensation for my yearning for a regular home, I told many fictions (I knew they were lies but had a hard time with that) about the contents of those vaulted spaces. Arthur believed everything I told him. When we were 10, I taught him to ride a two-wheeled bike without training wheels before I knew how to myself. He assumed I was an expert even when I refused to demonstrate, explaining that, "every two-wheeled bike rider has his own style, and if I show you mine, you'll ride like me instead of developing your own style." I held the seat for him with authority as adults trying to teach me had held it for me, explained the balance thing, which was beyond my reach, and watched in amazement as he set off gracefully just as my teachers had expected I would. I learned from that encounter that it is more important that your students trust you than that you know firsthand the content of whatever you are teaching. Relationship was all. And with Arthur's trusting relationship, he was the recipient of many of my fictive accounts of the contents of the antique spaces above our apartment.

Arthur, like many of the other boys, was interested in guns (they were not allowed at Hoffmann School), and at home he cultivated a small collection of model rifles and toy pistols. Off the kitchen that was the walk-through hub of our small apartment, there was an eerie and exciting unfinished room that held, beyond an ironing board and various staples, intriguing vestiges of past Hoffmann history. There were small bottles and corks that may have been left over from a family perfume factory, glass eyes and other remnants from a family doll factory. Filled itself with plenty of inspiration for play, the room also promised access to the mystery-laden attic overhead.

As we mixed potions for our imaginary perfume company or plotted our next outside adventure, I would tell Arthur what was up in the attic. Alternately I described a complete collection of loaded guns or cannons that my father's brother David had brought home from the war, helmets taken off the heads of dead Nazis, and even a small plane—a full-scale version of whatever model was capturing Arthur's current attention. He believed it all: that I could ride a bike, or peek in on attic treasures (we were never allowed to go up there), or because my size exceeded that of the boys in my class, that I could actually beat them all up. He even believed that it was on account of such prowess, the responsibility of my might, that I avoided all aggressive physical conflict lest anyone get hurt.

All children at some time believe their teachers live at school, wave goodbye to them at the end of the day and then spend the night in their classroom homes preparing for their students' return the next morning. "Ann Hoffmann really does live at school!" an occasional child would declare, pointing to the anomaly that was our lives in a community that did not feel our own. We Hoffmanns were outside of the regular ring of family and neighborhood even as we comprised a recognized, if not always beloved, pillar in the local community. Mrs. Hoffmann pushing her overflowing grocery cart at the market bought gourmet treats that we would enjoy at home alongside gallon-sized bottles of pineapple juice and cartons of saltines for the school. She spoke in Italian to Mr. Pisacano at the fish market in Yonkers where she would alternately buy mountains of halibut for Estelle's preparation of school lunch or carefully selected shellfish for the bouillabaisse she prepared herself for her annual New Year's Eve party.

The lines between home and school larders were as thin as any of our home–school demarcations. I was the principal's daughter even when I went to the supermarket with my mother. There was no escaping the duplicity of my existence as a person whose home was a school and whose mother was a school head, no space that was home and not school, safe from the evening calls of anxious parents, the late-night scheduling of transportation routes and field trips, and the energy and exhaustion of a mother-in-charge. But Ann Hoffmann's role as mother-in-charge was at the core of the homelike quality of the school, that endearing feature that parents hoped would make school a less fearful place for their children than school had been for them, if not even a more secure home than home itself could provide.

Ann Hoffmann strove to balance in her practice the loving support of a caring parent and the pedagogical wisdom of an experienced educator. This was no small feat. Children's actions and dilemmas placed her constantly on call to turn on a dime, to act in the moment, to make decisions so quick that they sometimes seemed brusque. When, if at all, did she find time to reflect on and learn from the lightning-flash decisions she made as parent-educator with expediency and compassion, and no guarantee of success? There was an occasion when the class of 1955 put her resources to the test.

It happened on a warm spring day on which the fruit trees at Hoffmann School were bowing with blooms, providing shaded niches for hiding and cool spots of respite from the sunstruck, sweet-smelling, open green lawns. On such a day in what must have been fourth grade, Gracie, Stephen, Jacob, and I secluded ourselves on the rocky mound beyond the baseball field from which it was impossible to see out through dense trees. We were interested in investigating what each of us had hidden beneath our clothes. It was a "you show me yours, I'll show you mine" sort of exchange that took an awful turn when I finally dared to participate, looking up only long enough to see my mother barreling across the baseball field and moving in on us with obvious disapproval. We quickly collected ourselves and followed her back to the schoolhouse where she shared the worst.

Far from being out of sight, she told us, neighbors had observed us in our mutual investigation and called the school to report it. She spoke of how important it was to remember that we always represented the Hoffmann School in our behavior. I understood from a place deep within, where my mother had taught me came loyalty and family pride, that we had embarrassed the school, my family, my home. Out of that realization emerged a stinging shame that seemed so endless that I would have to tell myself alone at night, when it was most acute, that there was a chance it would be forgotten, perhaps someday when I was grown. Jacob had championed our initiative in the office conference, telling Ann Hoffmann that it was natural for kids our age to be interested in each other's private parts. I know my mother complimented him on his articulate defense; but more keenly I remember the agony of disgrace. Surely I, Ann Hoffmann's daughter, knew better than any of us to what extent the school was under surveillance by certain suspicious neighbors and how at peril it would be in the face of community disapproval.

Stephen thinks that Ann Hoffmann handled the situation very well. "She never said we were doing something wrong," and that had been important to him. I ask my co-conspirators if they think it was true that neighbors really had seen us or if that was Ann Hoffmann's strategy for avoiding overt disapproval of what had transpired. Stephen says quickly, "If it was, it was a good idea." A good idea? Did she have it, I wondered, as she swiftly traversed the long distance from the schoolhouse across the playgrounds through the baseball field to the tree-filled knoll on which we hid? Another on-the-spot from-the-hip quick decision, as might have been keeping Jacob back a year or questioning Gracie so bluntly? Had a teacher or another child reported us? Who could have been watching us? I think of all those scary outdoor moments when it looked like someone might get hurt because our game of war was getting too real—the running through the woods, the crunching of branches under our feet, the not-quite-faux-desperate "Look, a place to hide!" The grown-ups kept a very low profile during these realistic playful adventures. We thought we were on our own outside—independent, unwatched, autonomous. Did Ann Hoffmann always know exactly what was going on?

In my father's storytelling from the earliest days of the school, he shared the account of a pair of 4-year-olds who had engaged in similar show-and-tell in the narrow first-floor bathroom to the left of the back door entrance. It is the same room in which, as a 2-year-old nursery school child, I would seek refuge from rest period. Excused to go to the bathroom, I would run inside and close my eyes in order to become invisible. A tattered report card is dated December 1, 1946—4 days short of my third birthday. The teacher writes that I don't seem to be happy in school, that I am "very quiet" and "cry easily." Although I am reported to have good rhythm and a love for painting ("her favorite subject is ships"), my teacher says that I simply don't want "to come forth and be part of the group." In the far corner of that first-floor bathroom, my back to the door, my eyes pressed tight shut, I could leave the demands of school and disappear into the vastness beyond vision, floating away from the cots and the dark room at rest time onto the lap of my nurse, Lucy, who was waiting for me upstairs. Sometimes I was triumphant, and they would call Lucy to come down and get me. I was only 2 and too young for a full day of school. My place of refuge was the scene of the 4-year-olds' investigative incident.

In the aftermath, as my father tells it, the young heroine-director gets a phone call from the mother of the boy involved. The mother speaks proudly of her son's precocity both in wondering about gender differences and in convincing a little girl to help educate him. "Is your son in the room as you are speaking to me?" the young director asks. "Yes, but why?" and Ann Hoffmann responded with a small lecture on balancing acceptance of what had happened with expectations for mutual respect, and not heralding (and especially not to him) her small son's exploration as a coming-of-age male triumph. The mother of the little girl, on the other hand, had been outraged and embarrassed for her child. She wanted the boy punished. But Ann Hoffmann encouraged her to accept the fact that the little girl had also been a curious player and that the sort of interest the children had demonstrated was not unexpected. She apologized as well for the bathroom attendant having wandered off, allowing such unsupervised play to transpire. Softened, the mother of the girl agreed with this more tolerant approach and considered, "Maybe the trouble is that I had such a puritanical upbringing." My Italian Catholic mother who had never been on a date without a chaperone said simply, "So did I, but let's see if we can do a better job with our own children."

Almost a decade later and surely after many such anatomical investigations, my mother was telling us that neighbors had seen us and we should be careful not to embarrass the school. Had she taken this tact before? Was it a way to deal with the situation effectively without risking misrepresentation of the various views of the parents of the other children involved? Was she personally resisting judgment of our actions even as she warned us that others disapproved? What sort of jazzlike improvisation governed these educational decisions? It was as if the child's behavior was one musician's melody (was it always familiar to the experienced educator?) to which the educator responded with a new variation in phrasing, offering back to the child an artistic interpretation that implicitly invited revised action. But what elements of time, particular circumstance, and qualities of the individual child affected the educator's improvisational response? Had it been harder for Ann Hoffmann to decide in this instance what to do because her own daughter was one of the players in the scene? Or did she not discriminate? Were they all for the time they were there

Graduation, 1954.

The Mikado, *1955.*

Ann Hoffmann's children—all really at home in the school that was my home?

It may be that every teacher needs reminding that "her children" (those in her class) are really the children of other people, people whose behavior, attitudes, and understandings may support or thwart the most promising classroom efforts. There is a delicate balance in stage setting for and negotiating a positive teacher-student-parent dynamic. If the teacher is too parental, the real parent may fall into a counterproductive competitive role. If the teacher is too guarded and distant, the student may not relate well to her person or pedagogy. I used to wish my own children could see me for just a moment through the eyes of an admiring graduate student, just as I know they wished I could see them just for a moment through the eyes of anyone who was not their mother. But I wouldn't have chosen actually to have them as students, nor they to have me in any other role.

It can't have been easy for my mother to have had her own children in the school through which she was making her contribution to the world of education and to the broader and perhaps even global scene. Did she long for the autonomy that other parents had: the ability to triumph and make mistakes away from public scrutiny and without consideration of the principles and visibility of the school? Did the responsibilities of being a "professional" parent—someone whose profession was perceived as a kind of parenting—intrude on her relationship with her own children, imprinted—as we must have been thought to be—most intimately by her expertise? I believed as a child that my mother shared my longing for a regular home. Her scene switching at day's end, an apron embellishing a silky robe on a Sunday morning, always made me think she did. I suspect now that she was just trying to give us all of it. Changing costumes and stage sets to give to her own children as best she could a home beyond school even as she gave to the other children a school that was home.

With my mother's far-reaching parental arms embracing it all, the Hoffmann School was for every child some elaborate version of home schooling. And in her simple, complicated, instinctive, wise, thoughtful, brusque, impassioned practice, Ann Hoffmann worked hard and hopefully to make better the lives of the children at her school. In my father's loving tribute in which the school is described not only as democratic in its own right, but as an agent of political and social change, he explains: "This was the nub of bringing about a finer world—this doing a better job in bringing up one's children than our parents have done."

FAMILIAL ARTS

Arthur, now a 61-year-old therapist with shoulder-length white hair and a graying beard, looks like a film version of a shrink. It is only in the elfish bounce in his walk that I see the little boy with whom I played perfume factory on the beautiful stage set of the Hoffmann School. I told him prior to our meeting about the two-wheeled bicycle and how I didn't really know how to ride it. He says he was astonished by the news but that it explained a few things, most prominently my refusal to demonstrate. I take a certain pride in his retelling of my "develop your own style" excuse even as I feel remorse for yet another childhood deception.

Why didn't my ability to teach the thing I couldn't do give me some measure of stature in the face of my own ineptitude? Was this what they meant by "those that do, do; those that don't, teach"? When at age 11 I finally mastered two-wheeled bike riding, after considerable begging, I was allowed to go off on my own to the candy store on Riverdale Avenue. I rode with confidence and a giddy autonomy up the steep, pot-holed hill on 254th Street, past the toppling old gates of the former entrance to the school, and on to the smooth sidewalk that led to the bus stop where 254th met Riverdale Avenue. I was high on the exhilarating feeling of the wheels gaining speed beneath my feet. But as I approached the corner, the speed began to scare me. How would I slow it down? Had no one told me about backpedaling to brake?

Fortunately, when I consider the alternative, my slamming into the street pole at the corner prevented my rapid glide into a very busy street. There was blood everywhere from my nose and I was frightened and embarrassed. I looked big and strong, but in trying what other kids did so easily I had taken on too much. I really didn't know how to ride that bike. I heard a car door shut and footsteps running toward me. "Are you all right?" Ann Hoffmann asked me. Unbeknownst to me, she'd been following quietly behind in our deep blue 1949 Packard sedan, and instead of driving me—putting the bike in the back of the car—she pointed out something about brakes and suggested I ride slowly home. I did so shakily and gratefully, knowing this time she was near by.

As Arthur and I sit down together, close childhood friends but adult strangers, his well-worn East Side office disappears and animated co-constructions of days past fill the present space around and between us. We are 6, and he is promising that "next time" I can play the role of Robin Hood and not always Friar Tuck. We are 10, and Arthur comes back to school from a bout with mononucleosis to discover with horror that he has been cast as the lover Nanky Poo in the Hoffmann School production of the *Mikado*. I was more disgruntled than he that, a head taller than everyone else, I had to play the wicked Katasha—slightly less unseemly than playing the Pirate King the following summer in *Pirates of Penzance*. But a head shorter than anyone else on stage, poor Arthur had to sing solo as the romantic lead.

"You got to kiss Carrie Furst," I remind him, picturing clearly the petite little girl whom Arthur adored. Carrie had alabaster white skin that gave her an almost faded look and dull brown hair neatly pulled back in a ponytail. Her tiny clear-rimmed glasses made her already serious face look quite intellectual. She wore crisp white blouses buttoned up to her neck, circular felt poodle skirts, and a wide elastic belt with multiple notches around what must have been a 15-inch waist. Carrie was a year ahead of us in school and an excellent vocabulary and math maven. Her sixth-grade class (when we were in fifth) was comprised only of tiny, efficient Carrie and Alison, a laid-back girl twice her size who looked to be, but wasn't, in her midteens. Carrie could tumble and do cartwheels; Alison was awkward and slow. Carrie was a whiz at everything; Alison needed help from teachers and from Carrie. Carrie was breezy and aloof; Alison was plodding and kind.

It must have been a challenge and a delight to teach these two very different but equally engaged students. What did they learn from each other at such close range about the varied and viable ways into any topic of learning? What did they teach each other about collaboration and respect? They were awfully good friends, and I imagined they'd always be together. Perhaps they've been as out of touch as my classmates. Softening at the mention and memory of the admirable Carrie, Arthur considers whether the joy of that stage kiss outweighed his terror at standing up and singing before an audience of people. He was, he tells me, "psychotically shy," so it was no small task, no matter how thrilling, to reach out on stage for the object of his affection and say, "I will kiss you fondly thus."

"How is your sister?" Arthur inquires after the person who as a child I most wanted to be. Less than 4 years older, Trudy was 5 years ahead of us in school. "Now, she was a great Peter Pan." As Arthur mentions it, I see my big sister in that part, authentically attired in green tights and tunic, leaping across the makeshift spring festival stage. My sister was substantially taller than the rest of us when she was in the sixth grade, the first sixth grade that my mother would graduate from the school, a sixth grade in which my sister was the only student. Trudy had fought hard for the part—she wept at the thought of any other role—and was elated to be cast as the airborne Peter. My parents had taken us in 1950 to see Jean Arthur play the part on Broadway (Boris Karloff was a fabulous Captain Hook), and Trudy had repeatedly read and enjoyed the James Barrie play. But there must have been a dearth of candidates for Hook if tiny Arthur, a first grader, was cast in the role.

My sister, a talented young artist, did the makeup for the show. Arthur still relishes the experience of having a beard drawn with burnt cork all over his face. The thought of the large puckish Peter and the diminutive fearsome Hook sends us into gales of laughter, even though we know that none of that occurred in the audience at Hoffmann School. Suspension of disbelief was de rigueur in that setting, and the respect for children playing parts and speaking words transcended any calamity of proportion in portrayal. "How many plays did we do a year?" I ask Arthur. We both think at least two or maybe, including the summer day camp, four major productions. We are especially grateful for all the Gilbert and Sullivan and the witty lyrics and lively music that still play in our heads. I loved my Pirate King costume: jeans, a red and white striped tee shirt topped by a leather vest, a bandanna for my head, one hoop earring, a smoky charcoal beard, and tall black boots. I can almost re-create the moves, the words, the feeling of transforming my countenance (furrowing my brow and raising my shoulders slightly) into that of a mighty pirate.

Stamping my foot on the wooden stage, I lift a stalwart aluminum–foil coated paper sword to the skies: "Oh, better far to live and die, under the brave black flag I fly, than play a sanctimonious (punctuating that word, whatever it meant) part with a pirate head and a pirate heart" (trying not to crack the note on "heart"). Next, I stealthily sneak to center stage and scowl as I sing (perhaps too softly, but I'm trying), "Away to the cheating world go you, where pirates all are well-to-do, but I'll be true to the song I sing, and live and die a Pirate King." And then the wild chorus joins in thunderously, "Hooray!" "It is a glorious thing to be a Pirate King. It is!" Amidst the relief of having my solo over, I am grateful for the voices of the other children helping to carry things along.

Accompanying our variously tuned voices, the well-tuned upright piano was dramatically pounded by our beautiful, broad-shouldered, brown-skinned music teacher, Ruth Lipscomb. Her eyes fully on us, her head would nod both as a gesture of sustaining approval and to help us keep the beat. A student who attributes to Ruth his lifelong participation in music remembers, "She could play the piano in such a way—she would raise the pitch of whatever she was playing so that it sounded like the voices of the kids." And that was it. We felt her accompaniment doubled our effect. Our dashing drama teacher, Marie Hawthorne, petite and expressive with saucer green eyes and a crown of flashing red hair, would carefully turn the pages of the score. As she sang along, Marie moved her lips with exaggerated detail to remind us of the correct pronunciation. The two ladies on the bench swayed synchronously and encouraged us on as the piano music swelled and filled our earnest thespian minds with the sound of a full orchestra.

While Stephen starred as the Mikado in sixth grade, Jacob was selected to play Pooh Bah, "The Lord High Everything Else." Jacob's participation in the Mikado is his most positive memory from school even though he believes that he was asked to mouth the words of the songs and not to sing. "Quite rightly," he says, but I am alarmed that this common trespass on arts learning was committed at that progressive haven for individual attention. I feel Jacob's compensatory pride as he tells me, "Nonetheless, mine was the biggest part. I had the most lines." Undaunted and surely by coincidence (the opportunity arose when the regular drama teacher didn't show and the job paid more than other counselors'), Jacob went on as a camp counselor in later years to direct his own musical productions. "Did you ever ask a child to mouth the words?" I ask him, wondering if he had rewritten the injustice he'd endured. "Never." He continued, "Besides having a terrible voice, I'm tone deaf. I wouldn't have known which of them could sing!"

Our shows at Hoffmann were always musicals even when that meant that music had to be written for a Shakespearean play or a popular children's book story, and with such a small student body, there were or seem to us to have been parts for everyone. Preparation over time for a production was filled with directed efforts (like set painting and costume design), mounting anticipation, and shared pleasure. Our teachers were overtly enthusiastic and visibly knowledgeable about the productions. School psychologist Dick Robinson believes the most loved and admired teachers at the Hoffmann School were the ones who taught the arts, and they were all working artists and/or artist-teachers. Our drama teacher Marie also taught acting at the American Academy for Dramatic Arts. Our music teacher Ruth was a concert pianist who performed at Carnegie Hall and was described by *The New York Times* as an "exceptionally talented artist whose musicality brought out the composers' feelings." Our dance teacher Sarah Bartlett was or had been a dancer in the New York City Ballet. And a string of visual arts teachers were all working professional artists.

The walls of my apartment in Boston, as did those in my family's New York home, showcase original works of art by Hoffmann School art teachers and other artists whose paintings were sold at the many fundraising gallery shows organized by the school's officially incorporated PTA. Three dark and captivating paintings, made by a Mexican artist who taught in the earliest days of the school, are placed at a distance from four of the light impressionistic images of beach and skating that preoccupied another of the school's art teachers, talented Long Island painter, Tom McArthur.

Tom converted into a studio the empty apartment in the attic of the school's barn that had no doubt once housed the keeper of the horses and carriage of the original estate. Before his renovation, my sister and I would enjoy sneaking up the stairs in the back of the open barn space (school children were not allowed to go there) to that magical haunted place. The light would stream in through the dusty windows, illuminating patches of faded, pastel-colored wallpaper. We would walk around the creaking floors, noting domestic details like the stained glass panels in the door of the nonfunctioning bathroom, imagining which empty room had served as what, occasionally discovering pieces of broken furniture, once discovering in a barrel a litter of young kittens.

Tom swept the space out, painted it white, got the plumbing working, and installed a skylight in order to convert what must have been the main room into a studio to which he would retreat in breaks and after-school hours. Turning our playhouse dreams of that space into a reality, he would sometimes spend the night or even stay the weekend, sleeping on a metal-framed bed he'd dragged up, so that he could keep going on his latest work in progress. How privileged the school children were to be able to encounter Tom, when he was not leading a class, actually at work in his own studio. Before the 1970s, when artist-in-residence programs were organized to make up for the dwindling amount of arts education in the schools, Ann Hoffmann saw artists at work as enrichment to a full arts program.

But sometimes Tom would retreat to that studio to steal a swig or more of whiskey or even in desperation rubbing alcohol from the school supply closet—all out of the surveillance of his wife, a gifted kindergarten teacher, dignified and creative, who I imagined struggled sorrowfully to keep husband sober. Their daughter Miranda was 6 years old and attended the school. Miranda had the look of an angel—as if there was a light following her, illuminating her silky straw hair, storybook appearance, and gentle presence. She worshipped her father, as did we all: the thick Irish brogue with which he praised our work, the one of his two eyes that seemed, when he painted or assessed children's work, to pop out of his head in order to accommodate his long and intense artistic vision.

On some weekends, Tom would teach my father to paint and give private oil painting lessons to my sister and to me. He was an inspiring teacher and an inspired artist, and he taught us to see beyond concrete objects and to think like expressionists about movement, light, and feeling. But I could hear the grown-ups talking in quiet tones about "what to do about Tom," who sometimes stumbled when he walked and perhaps even had been fired from other places, although as he was recognized by my mother for his own talent as an artist and for his natural rapport with kids. There was something too about falling asleep with the lit cigarette that always hung from his mouth, an experience with or just the risk of fire. Although his wife taught for many years at the school—after their daughter had graduated—Tom did not stay very long.

I wonder how many artists Ann Hoffmann took a chance on, inviting them to teach, to share their expertise with artistic media, and to mine the deep attention their work inspired in children. Artists as teachers throughout the faculty were role models at Hoffmann. In my years as an educational researcher, I've observed the magic that artists hold for children; the draw of their far-reaching vision, the tangible evidence of their skill, and their daring in living outside of conventional norms. My mother must have known the promise of artists as "natural" teachers, teachers that children would seek out on their own, admire, and emulate. Did she also feel that children could help artists? Was being among children as much an agent of healing as participation in the arts is often thought to be? Was Chester's time in his chair such an opportunity for repair? Was Tom's invitation to be at home in the school of similar promise?

I feel his gratitude for the many chances my mother gave him in the oil painting Tom did that she kept forever in her office: a sketchy study of a few children in the library. Its simple strong vertical lines and muted brown tones capture the dignity and intimacy of the school. On my fortieth birthday, I found deep in some box a beautiful watercolor that Tom had either made for me or given to me upon my request. Whatever the original circumstance, the forgotten image was received anew as a gift across time and space. It is signed in the corner—1956—the year after I graduated from Hoffmann School, the year I was 12 and fitted with braces and ashamed of the shape of my nose and the many blackheads on my face. Hidden within pen and ink scribbles that add context to the large orange daisy in a group of blue cornflowers, I find that Tom had written: "Jessica Hoffmann is a very regular gal and very kind in the bargain at that." It was comforting again or still.

At Hoffmann School we studied music and visual arts on a daily basis and did not know until we moved on to other schools that some people think it more important to spell accurately than to draw with expression. Beyond these daily disciplines, theater and dance activities were serious, frequent, and all consuming. These were times when we demonstrated what we could do, the roles we could interpret, the songs we knew, the costumes and worlds we could collectively create. We owned our various parts and got into them with verisimilitude and the sense of play that seemed to infuse our daily lives at school. Ann Hoffmann may not have thought we would grow up to be stage actors, musicians, dancers, or even camp counselors directing musicals, but she clearly believed that if we were to live fully in this world, we would need to learn to move like dancers, to pretend like actors, to see like artists, and to know the beauty of words and the joyfulness of song.

MOTHER-IN-CHARGE

On a particular autumn Saturday afternoon when I had just started the eighth grade at the Riverdale Country School, I was working with my mother downstairs at the Hoffmann School. She had a small roster of late-entry prospective interviews and I was serving my customary role (between the ages of 10 and 16) of showing the schoolhouse and grounds to the prospective students while their parents met with my mother behind her office's closed door. At the end of each visit, Ann Hoffmann would honor me by inviting me into her office and asking, "Well, what do you think? Tell me about so and so. Is she a good candidate for the school? Will she like it here? What seems special to you about this child?" A child myself, I felt, as I have continued to feel, that it is a great privilege for teachers to consider children's individual strengths and needs, and a great challenge for parents to decide what school their children should attend.

When my mother worked on Saturdays, she wore the same straight skirts or fitted suits that she dressed in daily for her role as school principal. No wonder she longed for Sundays in which pajamas and bathrobes were required garb. I too dressed neatly for my Saturday job and I was proud when my mother would tell me how I had a way with little children, how their time with me made them all want to come to the school, how destined I was to grow up to be a teacher or maybe even the principal of the Hoffmann School.

My mother was the image of virtue. She stood straight up tall, wore grown-up clothes, kept secrets, and never spoke behind the backs of her friends. I sometimes felt I was the opposite, that the pendulum had swung and hit me in the head, knocking me unconscious and unable ever to fill her thick-heeled tie-up shoes. At Riverdale, surrounded by girls my age, I had come to enjoy the delicious closeness of saving seats in class, the edgy pleasure of passing notes that others really should not see, and the playful but acidic ranking of girls in order of such important virtues as "prettiest," " best figure," "best nose," or "most popular." The rankings cruelly went for "worst" in each category as well. My mother used to say, "If you want to learn something about yourself, do something for someone else." But my friends at Riverdale and I held values that tugged in other directions. We wanted to be shorter than boys, have socks that didn't fall down (even if it meant gluing them to our calves), small feet, tiny waistlines, and at all costs great clean hair that was neither too curly nor too straight.

I had proved inadequate to most of these objectives even as I glued my socks up, stuffed my feet into loafers a half size too small, and washed my hair almost every day. But when I worked with younger children, made them laugh, captured their engagement, celebrated their vision, I felt I was experiencing a more possible and plausible reality—perhaps even sharing my mother's talent and world. That world, our father repeatedly told us, was comprised of womanly wisdom—instinct and heart—even as his orb of words and law relied on intellect and mind. I revered my mother's particular wisdom, whatever it was made of, and felt when I was entertaining or guarding or teaching little children that I had some of that mettle. I was Ann Hoffmann's daughter and mentee, and perhaps I had inherited from her and maybe even from her mentor Rebecca a certain magic that would sustain. In 1946 my father wrote that Rebecca, "always turned her head at the sound of a young child's laugh." And almost 50 years later, he would write of my mother, "Her love for children was intense. Her face would light up with the sound of a distant child, even if there was no further contact with it." It could be written of me today.

At any rate, Ann Hoffmann did not tell lies. But for me, living in that castle in the Bronx that friends at the Riverdale Country School envisioned more as my home than anyone's school, lies were still tempting agents of self-promotion and esteem. It was that autumn Saturday when there was an unexpected knock on the glass and mahogany double doors of the schoolhouse. Standing there in soft-colored Brooks Brothers shetland sweaters and straight khaki skirts were two girls from my class, two girls who had friends at the Boys' School who were there with them, wearing herringbone tweed sport coats and striped ties. Had they stopped by after some function or tea dance to which I hadn't been invited? Wherever they came from, it was one of my lies that had brought them to our door.

I stood at the front door with them for an amount of time that concerned my mother and brought her out of her office, around the corner past Chester's chair, and down the hall. Perhaps as she approached, she could see from my posture or the rapid speed of my words that I was in an awkward and stressful situation. But as I heard her strident shoes tapping authoritatively down the hall behind me, I felt the end was near. I introduced Ann Hoffmann to my friends and theirs at the door. "What's going on?" my mother asked.

I could feel the heat in my face as I turned toward her to explain. "They've come to see the lobsters in our attic." She looked at me sternly.

I continued, "The ones we raise in big barrels that we enjoy eating with melted butter in the summer." Now that story had seemed so preposterous to me that I was sure it would be received more as humor (like my made-up word *splashical*) than falsehood. I wasn't quite sure when, how, or whether my friends' literal listening had turned my spoken fiction to heard reality. Would my mother laugh it off and tell them they should have known I was kidding? Nothing seemed funny at that moment.

The space between my mother and me felt dark and frightening. I was exposed as a person who, rather than learning about herself by doing for others, lied about herself in hopes that others would like what they learned about her. Ann Hoffmann looked hard at the well-dressed "popular" quartet, and she looked back at me. Then she looked at her watch. "Well," she said. "It's two o'clock. I won't have them disturbed at this hour. Why don't you kids come back another time, and be sure to call before you drop by." Then she breezed back down the hall.

The somewhat dazzled teens apologized for intruding and took off. I don't know how long it took me to move from the door or how long I spent in Ann Hoffmann's office listening to a lecture I could have written, so well did I know her beliefs and values. But I had been saved. She was on my side and I knew it. At that moment, I might have been Chester or Bruno or any other Hoffmann School child who knew what it was to have that champion. And that champion was my mother.

"We were always outside," Arthur points out with that tone of regret that sometimes edges the voices of older people bemoaning the loss of the good old days. At school we think we had "free play" twice a day. Sometimes other activities, like our gardening or leaf collecting in science, our mapmaking in geography, or rehearsals for plays, also took us out under the trees. Indeed, at Hoffmann School, and in the tradition of many progressive schools of that and earlier times, learning seemed to be almost as much an outside as inside encounter. Pictures from catalogues of the Hoffmann School of the 1920s show the littlest children in an "open-air kindergarten" and older children seated at desks on chilly days with blankets hugging their shoulders and covering their heads.

Arthur hated fractions in fifth grade. Our teacher, Betty, noting both his ennui with the subject and his passion for building model airplanes, pointed out to Arthur that the use of balsa wood in model aircraft construction relied on fractions. She asked him to note the application of fractions both in the layout of individual sheets of balsa and in the cutting and shaping of it into his planes. Arthur spent a whole day at his desk, logging fractions, building planes. One plane was a seaplane, and with permission, Arthur went down to our duck pond to test its viability in the water. "Did an adult go with you?" I ask, thinking of all the risks involved with children on their own wandering off on all that land. He didn't think so, but I wondered if the grown-ups were hovering somewhere out of sight, as my mother seemed inclined to do, at a distance such that children felt free on their own. "There was this great sense of openness," Arthur points out, "a sense that you were not trapped or stuck wherever you were. Even if you were doing important things in the classroom, if it was needed, you could go. It was the opposite of chaos; you were always expected to be somewhere but never forbidden to wander."

This story of individual attention and independent learning was the kind that school psychologist Dick Robinson had noted as a striking feature in the makeup of the school—something optimal about classes of less than 12 children, and the robust sense of self-agency that outdoor freedom can provide. Small classes were another tradition that stemmed from the earliest days of the school, when my great-aunt Rebecca explained the school's policy: "Classes are limited to small numbers. Instruction is adapted to meet the needs of the individual child. [This] is aimed to develop alertness, initiative, open-mindedness, understanding of the world about the child and the ability to do original thinking."

Every Friday, Dick Robinson visited the school for his weekly consultation with Ann Hoffmann, teachers, parents, and/or children who needed to be tested or treated with therapeutic discourse. On a typical day, my mother spoke with urgency. "You need to speak to Sally," she said with her standard, "right away." "What's up?" Dick asked, and she explained that Sally's parents did not "get it" about responsible parenting. They thought it appropriate to take Sally with them when they went out late at night to New York's hot spots (then the Stork Club was a frequent call) and to let her fall asleep at table at restaurants or theaters. The child was exhausted and frequently "depressed." Today she was disappointed about the role she got in the first-grade play. Dick went to the classroom but didn't see Sally there. When he returned to my mother, she explained with her usual omniscience, "No, no, Sally's outside sitting in that tree."

Dick traversed the small green hill between the schoolhouse and the tree. At thirty-something, he was tall and thin with dark closely cropped hair and thick black eyebrows that arched as if in amusement as he peered out over thick horn-rimmed glasses. With a large nose, wearing tweedy clothes, his manner was both easy and refined. "Hi, Sally," he called into the tree. "What are you doing there?" Sally spat back her response: "Where else should I be? I'm a fucking bluebird in the school play." From that quick exchange grew a friendship, the kind many of us had with Dick, in which Sally spoke to him regularly about her concerns, Dick spoke to her parents about the needs of children her age, and a new set of skills and possibilities emerged. Now in his eighties, looking much the same as he always did although everything that was black is grey, he clearly enjoys reflecting on this back and forth, so typical of his exchanges with children and parents at the school. He beams as he shares Sally's grateful parting words, "Thank you, Dick Robinson. I'm enameled of you."

"How did folks regard the school?" I ask Dick candidly. "As a school for looney kids, I guess," he says fondly, mimicking the ways his colleagues would say of his consulting: "Oh, you're at the Hoffmann School." I wonder if the small cohort of multicolored, variously sized, and closely bonded children ever realized that even as internally we felt that we were unique, chosen, and well held, externally we were thought to be loonies. "One important thing," Dick continues, "was that uniformly the child psychiatrists that I used approved of the school. . . . One absolutely superb child psychiatrist thought the school was wonderful [he sent his child there] because it was a good mixture of structure and flexibility. It could meet children's individual needs and also provide a good deal of structure."

A child psychiatrist who is an alumna of Hoffmann School, told me that there was "a certain kind of child" whom psychologists referred to Hoffmann School: the child who was "vulnerable and needed more protection." Speaking of students in the 1960s and early 1970s (when Dick was ending his tenure at Hoffmann), she specifies that there were no "aggressive kids at Hoffmann School. Ann didn't tend to take them." I wonder as I hear this whether Fred, the bully remembered by my classmates, had somehow slipped under the bar. Or perhaps he was a child who needed more protection, like Jacob whose "acting out" came from a place of desperation.

"How did you happen to come to the Hoffmann School?" I finally ask Arthur, "Do you remember?" "Oh yes," he replies quickly. At 5, he had been so miserable in the public kindergarten that he attended in the Morningside Heights neighborhood in which he and his parents originally lived that his family made the move to Riverdale in hopes of better public education. In Riverdale, the threesome lived in that garden-level apartment that because of its separate entrance seemed a lot like a private home. The family lived on a very limited income primarily because the medical bills for Arthur's diabetic father sapped whatever resources the bookish engineer could accrue. It is hard to estimate Arthur's childhood pain seeing his chronically ill father "carted off to the hospital in a coma-tose state every 6 months or more." Arthur's father was darkly handsome and, like my own father at that time, painfully thin. His mother, Virginia, was like Arthur, sprightly and strikingly animated.

I never saw Arthur as the tremendously shy and worried little boy he tells me that he was. At Hoffmann, he was truly well liked and seemed as comfortable with ideas in the classroom as he was with any game we played outside. Jacob remembered Arthur as "the teacher's pet" and con-fessed that "if he had had a friend at school," he'd have liked it to be Ar-thur. I admired Arthur's ability to climb high trees, run too fast to catch, and—thanks to me—ride a two-wheeled bicycle. But again, I confront the limitations of outside perceptions, not only because Arthur now tells me how terrified he was but also because in so many photos from that time in his life at school, I see how infrequently he even tries for the cam-era to force a smile.

Arthur tells the story of his family's first visit to the school, his first encounter with the pastoral grounds—"it seemed like what heaven would look like"—and the feeling of comfort that abounded around him. He describes my very tall father taking his small hand and showing him the duck pond as his parents met privately with Ann Hoffmann. I am touched by this recollection for two reasons: first, because it reveals again how deeply involved my father was in all aspects of the school that his aunt had founded and my mother ran; and second, because I hadn't known that my father had once held my Saturday tour guide position.

When Arthur returned home, his parents sat him down to prepare him for the inevitable. "We liked the Hoffmann School as much as you did, but there's no way we can afford to send you there." Sad but resolute, tiny Arthur set off for first grade at the local Riverdale public school, PS 7. As he describes the scale, angularity, and steel edges of the school build-ing, I realize how small he was and felt. All that stands out for him from that first day was the unrelenting terrifying sound of the fire drill bell, the clanking of leather-soled shoes on the institutional metal stairways, and the humiliation of his fear. "They could have dropped me out of a win-dow," he explains, "and I'd have been happier."

Coming home that day, there was a knock on the door. It was Mrs. Palmer from next door telling Arthur's mother, who did not have a telephone, that "some woman has been calling all the neighbors and wants to speak to you." At this moment in his storytelling, Arthur's voice begins to tremble. "And it was Ann Hoffmann, and she told my mother that she wanted me to come to her school and she didn't care if we could pay." He is crying as he explains to me, "She had to work to get me. That really made the rest of my life."

Chapter 3

Destiny and Transition

*Anna Luciano (left) when she first came to work
with Rebecca Hoffmann (right), 1935.*

THIS IS AMERICA

WHEN ANNA FRANCES LUCIANO first started working at the Hoffmann School for Individual Attention in 1934, she was 22 years old. In its fifteenth year, the Hoffmann School was then a day and boarding school for boys and girls from kindergarten through high school. It was located at 215th Street bordering Isham Park near the junction of the Hudson and Harlem rivers. Almost from its inception and up until its close, the school offered year-round education because the school year was extended, in the early days, by a sleepaway camp in upstate New York and later by the day camp on the school grounds in Riverdale. The year-round continuity increased the school's homelike

67

quality. Indeed, the first iteration of the camp, the Hoffmann School Camp in Putnam County, New York, which Rebecca opened in 1927, was called A Summer Home Camp for Young Children. In its later locations in Billings, New York, and Southington, Connecticut, it was simply called Cedar Oak.

The year my mother joined the faculty, the Hoffmann School brochure voiced a set of beliefs that prevailed from the school's inception in 1921 to its closing in 1980. It began with the claim that the function of modern education was to cultivate in children both freedom of inquiry and an open mind so that they can adapt to a "society chiefly characterized by change":

> The Hoffmann School looks not to similarities but to differences.
> It believes that children vary, that they are able to make selections,
> and consequently, that they should be given the freedom to pick
> and choose among the many ideas that are presented. In the formal
> school process of the past, these ideas were implanted from without.
> Today progressive thinkers recognize that education does not begin
> with subjects, education begins with children.

Not subjects, but children; not similarities, but differences. Inspired by such rhetoric in the second official teaching experience of her career, Ann rode the subway daily from her Brooklyn home, lugging whatever materials she had collected for whatever project she was planning for the day. While others on the train sported briefcases or piles of books, Ann would often have a box filled with chunks of wood for children's carpentry or scraps of fabric from her mother's sewing for cloth collage. With bits of her long black hair straying from the neat bun at the back of her neck, smooth alabaster skin, and darkly lashed light blue eyes, she looked more like the windswept heroine of a romantic novel than an innovative young teacher on her way to school. Even in her twenties, Ann wore sensible, tie-up shoes and dressed carefully with respect for her position as an educator. Her posture was regal, her nose aquiline, and the space between her two front teeth added playful warmth to her wide smile and earnest countenance.

My mother told me that she had never felt young. The oldest of five children, she felt responsible not only for her own behavior but also for that of her sisters and brother. As the oldest daughter, it was Ann who would attend with her parents the formal gatherings of the Santa Ninfa

Malcolm on steps of Hoffmann School in Riverdale.

social club in Brooklyn, where my grandparents had met as young teen-agers when they first came to this country from the little town in Italy that bore the club's name. A first-generation American, my mother balanced her family's attachment to Italy with the responsibility of introducing her siblings to life and school in the states. What to wear, how to write it down, what to serve or say and to whom—these were questions with which her little sisters barraged her at home and in the letters they would send after my mother moved away. I could tell from the relationship that I witnessed between Ann and her baby sister, our aunt Gigi, that my mother was as much our aunt's mother as ours.

A teenager when their father died, Gigi (Geronomola) was almost always at my mother's side. She worked as an art teacher at the Hoffmann School when she lived with us in her youth and as a school receptionist in middle age. Driving daily from New Jersey, she worked at a desk in Ann Hoffmann's office, visited weekends with our family, and was never more than a daily phone call away. In private talks with my sister and me, Gigi would complain about and celebrate both our parents more like a big sister than an aunt. My mother's voice would soften when she spoke Gigi's name, oddly, even when she was less than pleased with her. And when her little sister, at age 48, died of ovarian cancer, my mother wept so deeply that I felt she might disappear. Ann spoke with grave earnest the same words that Gigi had spoken when she heard my mother had a cancer in her breast: "Why couldn't it be me?" Gigi died in February 1977. "Bad things always happen in February," my mother told me with the same sense of Sicilian superstition that lets me believe that if there is a parking space out front, you were meant to shop at that store, or give that lecture, or drop in on that friend. My mother died of ovarian cancer in February 1980.

The other sisters, Chicky (Frances) and Muggy (Maria) also looked up to and were very close to Ann. The flood of letters to Washington, D.C., when my mother married and moved there with my father in 1939, spoke of the pain of her absence ("Honest, I miss you terribly"), their forgiveness of and growing affection for my father ("Tell Mal that I think he is okay"), and the hope they shared that she would visit them or even just write more often ("You made us so very happy the other night when you called. Tears of joy appeared in everybody's eyes especially Papa's.") As I pour through this box of letters that my mother held dear, I imagine a gracious drawing room in another age in which children are centerpieces and writing letters is a major and exciting activity.

Uncle Nino, my mother's only living sibling, tells me that on Saturday afternoons the Luciano family would sit around the radio and listen to opera. I envision them all at attention, enjoying the heroic scores and actually understanding the meaning of the words of the great Italian operas. Perhaps the centrality of music in her home contributed to my mother's emphasis on music at Hoffmann School. For Uncle Nino, the impact was profound. After studies at the New York College of Music and service in the Army Air Corps, he sang leading operatic roles in the states and abroad and was described in one of many glowing reviews as the "brilliant young tenor of the New York City Opera Company." Instilled as well with a sense of educational responsibility, Nino taught an adult education course in 1958 that developed into what is now the Long Island Opera.

Before Flatbush Teachers Training, the branch of Columbia Teachers College at which she earned her degree, Ann went for secondary school to Adelphi Academy. There she worked hard, spent little time outside of school with girlfriends and no time at all dating boys. Her home life was sheltered and in a family in which all of the children were born in the United States, Italian was still everyone's first language. The Lucianos spoke Italian with a Sicilian dialect, but Uncle Nino explained that he, the only son, and Ann, the oldest daughter, were chosen to be tutored in "pure" Italian. Proving it paid off for Nino, one of his *New York Times* opera reviews commended his "clarity of diction."

Beyond enabling her to speak with "clarity of diction," the tutoring helped my mother to understand how dialects can invite separation and discrimination. She was a real communicator and could easily converse with anyone who spoke any version of French, Italian, Spanish, and of course English. Ann never made judgments about people on the basis of their diction. Indeed her linguistic empathy was so thick that she would immediately assume whatever quirk of pronunciation came out of the person to whom she was speaking. This was particularly amusing in the case of her friend who pronounced as *l* every *r*. Her name was Ruth and our laughter would begin from the moment my mother would answer her phone calls: "Hello Luth."

I try to envision my mother at her private high school, a place no doubt as hierarchical and snooty as my Riverdale Country School for Girls (RCS). I think of the students that joined and dropped out of our tight little class, a nucleus of 28 homogenous girls together from seventh grade to twelfth. Most often those who came and went were students of color and/or on scholarships, separated from the rest of us not only by their lack of history with the group, but also because of their unfamiliarity with what we saw as importantly cool—how clothes were meant to hang, loafers to turn up at the toes, double-breasted camel hair coats to be left open and ignored even on icy days.

My mother would never have gone along with the mean-spirited if subtle ostracizing we RCS insiders employed. It was because of my mother that a girl whom it was not cool to like, an awkward, brainy, unsophisticated young woman named Paula was included (my mother invited everyone) in my surprise sleepover, sweet-sixteen birthday party. As if I deserved it, I shamelessly accepted Paula's appreciation for my mother's kindness. Paula wrote lovingly in my yearbook that in our 6 years in school, I was the only girl in our class ever to invite her to a party. My father wrote of my mother's time at Adelphi:

> Ann's private high school in Brooklyn was alive with clique and in-trigue. She never fully shared its life. She was brought to school by her father in his big car, and called for at the close of school by a chauffer. And because she was of Italian descent she was not offered admission to the sundry sororities that congealed the school's social life, and she was rarely invited to the homes of her classmates. Since

her knowledge of school folkways was limited, she was only partly conscious of these discriminations, but when her modern European history instructor referred to the "Dagoes and the Frogs" in a hangover from his World War I training, the quiet Ann was astonished to find herself on her feet in shrill indignation. "This is America," was all she said, but it was a fine speech, and its meaning well understood.

In pencil beneath this paragraph, perhaps reflecting the vision of democracy that he believed inspired and motivated both my mother and the Hoffmann School, my father writes: "It was inevitable that Ann should become a school teacher." Or perhaps my father knew what I was to learn many years later when I taught writing at Wheelock College in Boston and asked my students, all of whom were planning careers in teaching, what teacher had "done it" for them—inspired them to decide to become teachers.[9] Expecting stories of admiration and respect, I was surprised that most of the students wrote of teachers who had abused their power—humiliating or physically harming a child in their class. Those students vowed to grow up to be teachers who would never let what they witnessed happen to a student of theirs. Perhaps my father imagined Ann's modern European history instructor similarly inspiring her through negative example.

Whatever her motivation, from my father's perspective, Ann's teaching even early on—indeed her every communication with a child—was something to behold:

> I saw her in action as a schoolteacher and realized that this was an extraordinary young woman. Her classroom tingled with a kind of warm excitement; and she played the piano and all participated in that great learning experience of identification of notes and chords. She sat on the floor of the classroom, painting with the children and always encouraging them; one could appreciate immediately that there was a love bond between her and each child in the room. A well-known educator, Helen Parkhurst, founder of the Dalton Plan, described it to me many years later: "It was a mother-teacher-child chain of confidence. I have seen it only twice in many decades of educational work, once with Ann Hoffmann and once with Maria Montessori."

"Did your parents expect that Ann would become a teacher?" I ask my Uncle Nino, who at 85 is writing a biography of his father. "Well," he laughs commenting on all the lessons and opportunities bestowed upon my mother throughout their youth, "That [a teacher] or to be an Italian matron in high society." But Nino felt that from the moment Ann left their family nest in Brooklyn for the eclectic world of Hoffmann School, with summers away at the school's camp and the ever-proximate wiles of Rebecca's handsome nephew Malcolm, "It was inevitable."

An expert in language could probably have told from the almost excessive precision of my mother's speech, that she was a nonnative English speaker. But to my ear, she spoke with the clarity of voice my father wanted his daughters to emulate. He would tell us, quoting Shakespeare, that "a soft, gentle, and low" voice was an excellent thing in a woman, and my sister and I were taught to speak so clearly that cab drivers and other authentic New Yorkers would often ask if we were English. There was something also about a woman's crowning virtue being her hair, and I believed that my soft-spoken mother with her crisp articulation of English and her waist-long hair met in all ways my father's ideal.

I had no idea of the amount of prejudice Malcolm had to overcome to marry a Catholic woman of Italian descent. His mother had a stereotypical image of Italians as simple people who ate pasta outside on red and white checked picnic cloths spread on the lawn. A note written to Malcolm at law school by his mother's sister encourages him to find a nice Jewish girl and experience the comfort of "being with your own kind." In August 1936 Ann wrote from her counselor position at Rebecca's Cedar Oak camp to her suitor who had spent July at the camp, but in August took a job with the New York law firm of Webster and Garside. She sympathizes that the Broad Street law firm was wearing him thin and hints at the pressures he was experiencing around their relationship:

> Past prejudices and hates hinder the present and threaten the future.
> You have such high ideals nothing can stand in your way to achieve.
> Even if it means giving me up. You are very strong and in your
> weaker moments you can think of how much I love you and become
> a little smug (although I abhor smugness).

Malcolm's brother was to write of family attitudes in May 1938 that things were still contentious: "Mal seems much in love with Anna, which might or might not be deplored." My father expressed considerable shame that his family's prejudice delayed him yet another year (they were married in 1939) in asking Ann to be his wife. His mother, he said, lived in a big house, spoke perfect English, and had little tolerance for individuals from different backgrounds. For Malcolm, overcoming his mother's and his maternal aunt's prejudice was an important part of his coming of age: "I learned democracy in a mixed-up way while rebelling against my mother." His father's side of the family was supportive: Rebecca and the other Hoffmanns adored Ann. For Malcolm then, the Hoffmann School represented democracy, and so did my mother.

In less than 3 decades, the pendulum would swing again or further when my parents met my husband Will, whose American origins are of the Mayflower variety, rooted in rugged New England naturalism and the founding of Unitarianism at Harvard College. My mother thought Will looked like Benjamin Franklin and my father said he walked with the comfort of someone who owns the earth. Given her own experience, the clear-sighted and fair vision reflected in her love letters to my father, and her lifetime work as a democratic educator, it was not surprising that Ann would take to heart this ruddy-cheeked unpretentious man and welcome him to the mélange of our family culture. Indeed, my mother loved my husband from the start.

After her mastectomy at age 63, when she heard Will was coming to visit the hospital, my mother insisted on moving from bed to chair where she brushed her hair, refreshed her lipstick, and grabbed her needlepoint, looking when he arrived more like she was in hotel than hospital. As she anticipated his arrival, she told me of a recurrent dream she'd had when she and my father lived with my sister in their Arlington Village duplex apartment outside of Washington, DC. She was standing in a stream in the backyard behind the apartments, holding a basket and trying to catch a certain one of the many boy babies that were floating downstream around her. Was this a Bible story? She'd come close but could never catch him. Perhaps forgetting that she was pregnant with me while she was trying all this boy catching, perhaps thinking I would be just as happy to know that I'd come through in the end by delivering him to her, perhaps only speaking her usual truth, my mother looked up at me with tears in her eyes, and told me the boy baby she was trying to catch was Will.

CHANGE IN LEADERSHIP

Malcolm Hoffmann first encountered Anna Luciano in January 1935 as he arrived at Inman Station in the Bronx to spend New Year's at his

Aunt Rebecca's school "away from the arduous duties of a first-year law student at the Harvard Law School." Ann, in her first year of teaching kindergarten at the Hoffmann School, was staying over the holiday to help Rebecca take care of the boarding children who were unable to go home. Rebecca was clearly match making when she invited Ann along to meet Malcolm at the station. He first glimpsed her sitting next to his aunt in Rebecca's 1932 Chevrolet. Rebecca had a "square jaw and penetrating eyes" and her mouth "curled in the pleasure of recognition as [Malcolm] came out of the subway." He wrote:

> Next to her I realized with almost a physical start were two of the largest and shiest and most limpid sky blue eyes that I have ever seen. Her face and manner expressed not only the presence of a beautiful woman confident in her beauty but also suggested a spirit shaping her thoughts and actions which had to be reckoned with on some different level from the ordinary relationships of newfound friends. . . . From the first minute I talked to her, I sensed I was already en-meshed in a Herculean struggle which might result in the loss of my bachelorhood.

The school building in which this romance would progress was a large red-brick building with white columns at the formal entrance, a garland-covered back entrance for kindergarten children, and the windows of at least 24 rooms visible from the street. In this Spuyten Duyvil manse, Rebecca had room for her day students, boarders, in-residence faculty, intermittent house guests, and more permanent extended family like my father and his older brother David, who was finishing law school in New York. As needed, Malcolm and David saw the school as home base and Rebecca as a kind of surrogate mother. Rebecca was an independent single woman dedicated to the education of children in a democratic school, but she was also an unconventional single homemaker, making home out of school for many unenrolled "children"—nephews, young adults in transition, developing educators.

The letters from the household that lived within the school to Malcolm away at Harvard Law School express collective concern for my rail-thin, never-sleeping, chain-smoking father; encouragement that he harness his anxieties and do his work; and familial wishes that he rest, eat (Rebecca suggests a "bite of food over a Camel cigarette for a pick-me-up"), get his eyes checked, and visit home more frequently. With regard to the school, in a letter dated October 1935, Rebecca tells him, "Today the sun is shining brightly and the spirit of the school is more cheerful. David and I are writing letters in a high-spirited way of promotion. Hope it will net some much-needed registration." The struggle for the school's survival was always there.

My father had been conflicted about going away to Harvard. His brother, father, and uncles had done handily in colleges and law schools in New York, and Malcolm had won a full scholarship to Columbia University. But when he was admitted to Harvard College, his family encouraged him to accept the offer and pursue whatever financial support he could secure. He was similarly encouraged to go on to Harvard Law. But it was hard to leave: His mother's depression was deepening and there was always this longing to write, to have a life—albeit at a distance from fiscal responsibility—in which he could rise daily and initiate or return to his latest precious collection of words. It was a longing that spilled over into my lifelong ambitions.

Leaving New York and his failing mother filled Malcolm with guilt. At Columbia, he could have lived at home and not incurred the expense of travel and board. But with everyone's blessing and words of encouragement, he went to Harvard and graduated magna cum laude in English literature. He was proud to have his mother attend his graduation and see him orate as valedictorian speaker for his class, but miserable to see firsthand the new depths of her illness. After pleasant exchanges with one of her son's professors, my grandmother asked if the professor knew the people who lived below her in the apartment she was then renting in a two-family house in White Plains, people she explained—her witty metaphor-filled voice dropping to barely audible terror—who were going to kill her. My father writes of a commencement speech that was filled with reflection on the interplay between the literary and the lived: "My remarks at commencement were devoted to books. I was far too young to understand the meaning of agony."

I do not know the layout of rooms in the 1935 location of the Hoffmann School where my parents fell in love; but for my father, being under the same roof as the woman to whom he was so greatly attracted made the speedometer of their relationship race wildly. And thanks to the Hoffmann School, there would be continuing propinquity. Beyond school-year vacations, Malcolm and Ann were together as camp counselors and they wrote to each other between visits throughout the year. Eight months after their first meeting, with Malcolm back at law school, Ann writes of the same concerns as his family—he is too thin, he needs to get his eyes fixed—but her tone is both playful and scolding, without much patience for self-indulgence. Her letter dated September 30, 1935, is addressed to Mr. Malcolm Hofmann, Complaint Department, Cambridge, MA. Although she is speaking with tongue in cheek, she sounds between the lines destined to be a school administrator:

> In response to the letter of the 27th, I have the following complaints to make: I resent being called "gal" and "Miss Snippy." I dislike a certain young man's impertinence. His letters are illegible. And furthermore and positively so, I don't believe he is tired and feels lousy—just plain lazy. Anyway, he worries and bothers me very much and I do miss him. This is simply between your department and myself. Sort of a confidential matter you know.
>
> Here is wishing that your better judgment will come forward and assert itself and see that such things as laziness, smoking, drinking, messy rooms, disorderliness, work, and health are taken well in hand.
>
> Here is to your misery and may you keep up the good work of being miserable through my prayers.
>
> Arrivaderci, Anna Luciano

Rebecca's mentorship was invaluable to my mother; she provided ground and context for Ann's growing dedication to a progressive approach, as well as a model of confident and compassionate leadership. Rebecca saw in Ann an extraordinary talent for teaching and a belief in and capacity for hard work. Over the decade that spanned my mother's early years at the school, her marriage to my father and their move to Washington, D.C., and their ultimate return to New York in 1944, a relationship that had begun as teacher and director grew from professional to familial connection. My mother's unmistakably perfect cursive writing marks notations on early letters, revisions to brochures, and recommendations on the very few reports of children that have lasted from the time that she first worked for Rebecca. Rebecca was undoubtedly priming Ann from the start for the role of director of the Hoffmann School just as I felt my mother had been priming me. Little did Rebecca know that her health would precipitate that change in leadership sooner than she would have chosen.

When we first arrived to help the ailing director with her school, my family lived on the second floor of the school's new Riverdale location— up the stairwell that was so beautifully illuminated by the arched-stained glass skylight, and to the right—in what would later become the music room. Rebecca lived in what was to become the art room. It makes sense that she would choose that well located room with its tall French door windows overlooking the river and opening onto a balcony that later was replaced with a regulation fire escape. The rest of the building housed the 28 boarders, all boys, who were part of the population of the then approximately 80 children at the Hoffmann School.

I have a memory of Rebecca. One can never tell where memories come from. Sometimes I think that our pasts are really framed in and by photographs. Oh, how was I at 6? At 6, I had a cowboy hat and a rabbit and a bandanna around my neck and a smile that makes me think I was sort of shy—I think I was shy. And then there was that party that a friend had at a nightclub and I know I went because there I am in my crisp yellow dress tied tightly in a big bow behind my back (I always liked mine tied really tight). I loved to dress up. Or did I? Wherefore the Davy Crockett hat and red and white striped tee shirt and that sailor hat for summer days? It's hard to keep up with the clues provided by photographic images, but for certain they are breadcrumbs on the path to childhood reconstruction.

My memory of Rebecca is captured in no photograph. Nor do I believe it was just told to me. It is embodied in an action—in my ability since I was a very little girl to make a snapping sound by rubbing together my thumb and third finger (thumb up, third finger down), right hand only. I sense a presence, shadowy and tall. Is she standing over my basket? Are we in the music room? She has an arch to her silhouette, as if she were a tall, stretched-out letter C, a stance that I recognize in photos of Rebecca. Did the curve in her posture come from her endless bending down to childrens' eye level? I envision a faint smile; she is clicking her fingers close to my face and I am drawn to the presence, deeply impressed by the repeated activity, taking it in, and wanting to do it. Now even as I replay that interaction, a memory if possible from before I was a year old, I hear in my mind's ear (surely there must be one) a haunting faraway voice. "You can do it. Remember me."

Rebecca died a month after we arrived, the fourth month of my life. I don't know much more of that event than that my mother was at Rebecca's side when Rebecca's body unwillingly let go of the life within it. My mother told me it was a terrible moment, both in being that close to unwelcome death and losing Rebecca, only 59, all at once. But later my mother perhaps purposefully told me that being with her mother, Nanny,

Ann's staff meeting.

who died at 74, a quarter of a century later, was the most important thing she had done in her life as a daughter. I thought it no coincidence that the two women whom my mother helped leave this world were her real mother and Rebecca, who had been mother to so many, including Malcolm and Ann. In the end, I hoped my being with Malcolm when he left this world would compensate for my absence from the life leaving of anyone I could remotely consider my mother.

There it was. Through the unpredictable confluence of life and death and trauma and loss, in March 1944 Ann Hoffmann became the new director of the Hoffmann School, operated at first under the rubric of the Estate of Rebecca Hoffmann. Ann Hoffmann had not expected that she would be the permanent director of the school. My father's older brother, David, who had lived and occasionally taught at the school and who had been so close to Rebecca, might have taken it over. But he was in the service at that time and stationed abroad. Ann kept him abreast of her oversight, indicating in her letters that she was doing her best to keep the books and all the rest for whatever time she would. Her detailed accounts, written in a script as carefully articulated as her speech, gave the lie to her self-reference as a flighty female for whom such rigorous demands were not easily met.

Festival of Lights.

My uncle wrote to my mother in September 1944 to say that his wife Mercedes, who was now a lawyer, might alternatively do the job. Curious it seems to me, but not unexpected, that there was really a view that any willing soul could run a school. Was the act of being educated all that was needed to educate others, even or especially young children? The notion persists. After years studying and teaching in a graduate school of education, I am aware that teaching is somehow separated out from scholarship and professionalism. It is often regarded as a set of generalized skills acquired from any number of sources that serve in activities that may fall within but surely reach beyond the classroom or academy. A set of skills available to all. But teaching is as often thought of as a gift that some folks receive and others do not—an artful inborn skill that you can't really fully describe or realistically pass on. Ordinary and extraordinary.

Universities expect that good researchers will be good-enough teachers; preschools expect that good mothers or good babysitters will be good-enough teachers. These expectations beg the question: Is there no benefit or level of expertise gained from professional training in education? When it comes to early childhood, the lines between caregiver, parent, grandparent, and teacher are especially blurred. This must have been particularly true for the Hoffmann School, a homelike school populated by occasional residents who felt relative (pun intended) ownership. My mother was the only one with directed training as an educator, the only one Rebecca had specifically mentored as a teacher and administrator, yet others felt they could as easily have done it if the young Ann, who would all her life rise to her own high expectations for the behavior and responsibilities of a school principal, had not. David wrote to this effect from his army post:

> Don't worry. Something will turn up. You have done a grand thing for all of us and for me, especially, I like to think. Were circumstances a bit easier, you, or we, could carry on the Hoffmann School in a proud tradition, I believe, without the historical insecurity. But, if it proves that Mercedes wants to take over, I feel, recognizing my own bias, that she will not fail. Disparate temperaments often reach the same results at the same task. So perhaps did Joan and Esther.

My uncle likens Ann and Mercedes to two historic heroines, respectively Joan of Arc who saved the French from tyranny and Esther who saved the Jews from annihilation. I know he is making the point (we all saw the difference between our mother and our aunt) that my soft, intuitive, child-oriented mother might do a job that could be equaled, albeit through different means, by his angular, intellectual, adult-oriented wife. Ann was carefully dressed, persistently dignified, quietly well-spoken, and attentive to details. Mercedes wore no makeup, dressed mostly in black, and smoked constantly. She was conspicuously brilliant, wildly articulate, and at least apparently nonchalant. While Ann would cover her mouth to mask too loud a laugh, Mercedes had a booming laugh that was always accompanied by an almost feverish rise and fall of her liquid shoulders. In my uncle's pointed metaphor, the difference in religious orientation between the two heroines (Mercedes was Jewish) does not escape my attention, and without being facetious, I wonder protectively whether my uncle would have thought that my mother might fill in as a lawyer for Mercedes had she decided not to do her job.

This brief mention of a casting call for the hero or heroine who would rescue Rebecca's school informs my lifelong uncertainty as to whether other family members rejoiced over, were relieved by, or resented our residence at the school and my mother's position at the helm. There was clearly some consternation, but ultimately it would be family members, most definitely including my Uncle David, who offered unequivocal support to Ann's nurturing continuance of the school. It would have all been more easily resolved in a world in which the professionalism of early childhood educators was respected. Ann would have been seen as the only one qualified. She had both the training and the experience. In terms of other perspectives—the view of the gifted educator or of the intermingled parent-caregiver-teacher—she was also most qualified. But above and beyond these obvious qualifications, my mother had always at the ready that which few adults can muster: a dauntless faith in children.

However sorely or joyfully it played out and by whatever means the roles were finally assigned, in 1944 my mother assumed leadership of the Hoffmann School. And regardless of the imagined length of her initial commitment, she would direct the school from Rebecca's death that year until her own passing in 1980. Rebecca was in charge for 23 years, Ann for 36. My mother's long career would be marked in ever-changing proportion by dedication, uncertainty, inspiration, frustration, excitement, disappointment, and endless fatigue. Nonetheless, as must have also been true for Rebecca, my mother was compensated beyond measure by the personal development of children who struggled to advance, achieve, survive—children for whom that school and that educator were precisely what was needed.

REFRAMING THE SCHOOL

In the 1960s when the school population was over 100 and the day camp's was around 200, my mother wrote to me at college, "I am working too hard. I wish I could have a real assistant who could help lessen the load." Still, in a January snowstorm in 1964 she seemed bored with a couple of days off from school ("soup on the stove, pie in the oven, you in my thoughts") even though the children that year were, as she put it, "a very quiet group." In what was then 20 years of Ann's leadership, the Hoffmann School had grown in size and stability even as it maintained its tenets of individual attention and apparent risk taking in school admittance. A reporter doing a journalistic sketch at that time, writes of Ann Hoffmann, "Despising elitism, she admits a wide economic and ethnic mix of students and encourages them to cooperate on a 'real emotional-interpersonal basis and not on the false basis of intelligence or achievement.'"

In my father's manuscript in which Ann is posed at Rebecca's side selecting for admission and support children with physical and emotional challenges, the inclusion of children of war is mentioned frequently. In one such vignette two little boys, Romeo and Nick Martino, arrive at the

Hoffmann School with their father in a taxi: "Their story was one of the many vignettes of pain that were so widely known in the late 1930s to Americans by their reading but rarely by experience on a more realistic level." The Martinos, whose family had lived in Florence for 400 years, had fled Italy on account of Mussolini's installation for Italian use Hitler's Nuremberg decrees that denied Jews their citizenship. The family originally fled to Lisbon where the boys' mother had died, and en route to America, the Refugee Committee (which compensated the school) had wired the boat and instructed Mr. Martino to bring his children directly to the Hoffmann School.

Along with their school subjects at Hoffmann, Romeo and Nick learned to feel safe, even as they frequently required comforting when the occasional sound of planes flying overhead would make them shudder and weep. In the 5 years they spent at Hoffmann School, the boys grew strong, confident, and determined, my father says, "to fight fascism and to embrace democracy." Most of the boarding children had similar tales of pain and loss, rescue and revitalization. They were not an affluent group of kids sent off for refinement and supervision. Hoffmann School was never a prestige environment for the wealthy. Rebecca and Ann disallowed such associations for the school.

I somehow remember the sounds or bustling presence of the boarding children—all boys—who lived with us in the various rooms that made our Riverdale home a school. Although I can't be sure whether we ate dinner with them, or whether Emma and Estelle or others oversaw their life at night, I have a filmy recollection of children in pajamas and robes compounding my confusion of what the space we occupied might be called or who the members of my family might actually be. This situation had worked for Rebecca for whom the children and the school were seamlessly both family and home, but when Ann became director, she wanted to establish boundaries that would allow her husband and daughters their share of her individual attention. Toward that end, in June 1945 she terminated the school's boarding department, a move that was easier said than done.

"When I took over the school at the close of World War II," Ann explains, "we had 24 war orphans boarding here who had no place to go." Her efforts to find homes for these children took 2 years, about the same amount of time as it took her to redesign curriculum to fit her new vision of a progressive day school: a school with 90 children and 16 teachers. The challenge of learning the job, making change, and keeping things afloat all at once was daunting. There were no summer vacation reprieves for reflection and development. From her very first year as school director, Ann Hoffmann was also called upon to run the summer day camp.

In August of that summer of 1945 on a rainy day (always a challenge for an outdoor program), the Hoffmann School Summer Day Camp was visited by a child care consultant from the New York Metropolitan Section of the National Jewish Welfare Board (having to do with YMHAs and YWHAs). I'm not sure of the reason for the assessment, but it was scathing. The consultant's criticisms included a poor use of indoor space, the developmental inappropriateness of reading *Jack and the Beanstalk* to three different age groups, the lack of appeal of lunch served on paper plates, "benevolent but entirely uninterested" discipline, and worst, a lack of vitality, joy, and humor in the children and the school. The consultant found Ann Hoffmann inadequate to the task of school direction and her complaints about intrusive neighbors unnecessary and distracting.

My heart aches for the young director, trying (probably without preparation) on a rainy day to entertain and keep track of a camp full of children while at the same time hosting an idealistic progressive evaluator who would critique harshly details such as the technique of the assistant counselors reading aloud: "Storytelling was in the old-fashioned mode, that is the children were expected to be receptive, quiet, to listen, but not to participate. The story as an instrument for vitalizing the relationship between child and teacher was not understood, nor that the thoughts and feelings of the children might be expressed during storytelling, so that it could become a medium for a significant and releasing social experience."

Assessments like these were surely disheartening, especially compounded as they were by a community that wished the school would go away and doubters who wondered why and how the plain-speaking wife of Rebecca's nephew might take over the school and the camp. Ann's response would have been proud at the confrontation, her despair most private. But Ann Hoffmann was never threatened by assistance. She sought it out eagerly and even if she disagreed with or ultimately disregarded expert input, she preferred to have it to help light the way. With this in mind, it made great sense that she should seek the expert counsel of Helen Parkhurst, a friend of Rebecca's, whose founding of the Dalton Plan and School had made her a prominent figure in the progressive movement. She would look to Helen for help framing perspective, crafting curriculum, and training teachers. It was surely no coincidence that she first sought Helen's council that damp August. Helen represented many of Rebecca's and Ann's ideals. Parkhurst's vision of a child-centered school in which children progressed through their studies at their own pace, resonating heartily with Ann's belief in children's knowledge of their own needs, would prevail throughout the lifetime of the new Hoffmann School.

Helen Pakhurst is to this day regarded as an important force in the progressive era. It interests me that Helen's reputation seems hardly diminished by the circumstance that her resignation from Dalton in 1942 was called for by her board of advisors and concerned mismanagement of school funds. Nonetheless, the various written communications between Helen, my parents, and my Uncle David, who was the attorney for Rebecca's estate, suggest that financial challenges followed Helen from Dalton into her subsequent consulting career. Her pages and pages of record keeping of hours and responsibilities is written and rewritten and refined by details of funds she needs for other aspects of her life and funds she wants to forgive as gifts to the school. She has so much in process: a full-length novel, radio show, another book, and a meeting in Hollywood to make a movie out of something she has written. She shares all this and writes that while she is sensitive to the financial struggles of the school, she must demand payment for her services, the cost of which ranges over a 2-year period from $1,000 to $5,000. She reminds my parents that she is continually turning down "other consulting jobs for more money," but "I love working with both of you and we will go places!" Her financially based letters speak of loans from her brother, the need to pay her "large mortgage" on her farm in New Milford, Connecticut, her desire to contribute to scholarships at the school (she will turn back half of a $1,000 payment as soon as it is received), and even at one juncture to forgive $1,000 that she hopes will go to Ann as a kind of salary. The admixture of desperation, affection, and revelation bring particular moment to her mentor advice to Ann Hoffmann regarding budget: "Personal accounts and school accounts do not mix."

A "memorandum of agreement" between the Hoffmann School and the Estate of Rebecca Hoffmann with Miss Helen Parkhurst of "Your Child, Inc." is dated August 25, 1945. The agreement cites as Ms. Parkhurst's chief responsibilities:

1. Advising in educational matters and advertising her role therein;
2. Devising plans, budget, program, and curriculum for the school;
3. Effecting changes in environment that would benefit the school;

4. Helping supply and select teachers;
5. Participating in monthly teachers' meetings and selected parent meetings through the school year;
6. Helping the director and staff in whatever way educational advisors are expected to do, "subject to such reasonable restrictions as are imposed by Miss Parkhurst as to use of her time for these purposes."

This last clause may have been the source of difficulty in working out compensation for a colleague whose responsibilities ranged from attracting new parents to training teachers to actually teaching first graders how to read. In her year as advisor, Helen also conducted a course for Hoffmann School teachers, "Modern Psychological Theory as Related to Young Children," for which the College of the City of New York gave academic credit. Overall, however, it seems that Helen functioned as a sort of temporary co-director of the school. She writes without specific example of some of the trouble that may have been caused by this apparent job sharing: "There have been times when some of the teachers have tried to play Ann and me against each other. This has been rather humorous and infantile."

With these issues unpacked and resolved, the bills all paid and their friendship intact, Helen writes to my father in April 1946 that she believes she is no longer needed and that it is time for "Ann to be in charge with me only on call":

> Ann has done a wonderful job; she has grown by leaps and bounds.
> Because she is a growing person, much has been accomplished
> whereas little could have been accomplished without her understand-
> ing and help. . . . It looks like a really wonderful school. It is usually
> considered that 4 to 5 years are necessary for a school to get under-
> way, even with a well-trained staff—so in these terms surprising prog-
> ress has been achieved. Ann has at each step of the way taken upon
> herself the responsibility of making up for the deficiencies of others. I
> fear this may have taken its toll at times and I do hope she may get a
> little real vacation somewhere with you before the summer session. It
> is so important as she forgets herself.

In a letter dated September 28, 1946, the start of my mother's third year running the Hoffmann School, her first year running it without

Helen's direct involvement, Helen writes with continuing concern and informed perspective:

> I hope that you get a little well-deserved vacation sometime during the summer and that all the plans you had in mind worked out to your satisfaction. It is to be remembered that you have taken on a tremendous job and that there is need of time for you to acquire experience to carry out the program that you keep dreaming about. Even a child may have mature ideas that take still years and years to mature before getting into operation. However, the will to do a good job will get you there. One of these days as you look back, you will muse and laugh and revise just as the rest of us have, and then suddenly you will know with a certainty that you have found the way.

Parky ends that letter, "My love to the children. I heard from Wendy that Jessica was wonderful this summer but that did not surprise me." I was 3 months shy of my third birthday, 7 years shy of the encounter with Parky that would give rise to this book which I write 50 years later. A page from my father's manuscript describes a no doubt entirely fictive scene in which Rebecca and Ann are overnight guests at what must be Parky's Connecticut retreat. Parky, who is given the pseudonym "Jesse," has resigned from her job as a school director and is enjoying life on her real or metaphoric farm. The dialogue between the two women, Leona (Rebecca) and Jane (Ann) goes like this:

> "In Jesse's school," Leona says, "there were more than 120 children. One of the first progressive schools in New York. One of the best. We all thought Jesse was a wonder."
>
> "She still is," Jane said. "You have to be of solid stuff to manage a 15-acre farm."
>
> [Leona protested:] "But it seems a pity that all the fire in her, all that deep understanding of children, should be wasted on pigs, on cows . . . and hens."
>
> Jane said [and here it was again], "It is possible that Jesse decided that she was going to take care of her own family for a change. Maybe she grew tired of running a school and getting nothing out of it except altruistic reward."
>
> Leona could not quite understand this mode of thinking. "With Jesse's following," Leona went on, "she could always have started a small school somewhere else. She didn't have to give up teaching."

Jane exclaims, "There are occupations in the world other than running a school."

This was something that Leona could never understand. Her perspective was fixed as rigidly as if it had been chopped out of stone. Leona could no more be without a school than she could be without bread. She assumed that Jesse was cut from the same rock.

The story goes on with Jesse showing Leona and Jane around the farm and Leona making such taunting comments as that the noise from the large chicken coop sounded a lot like the preschoolers in the nursery or when Jesse shows off tomato seedlings, "I remember when you first introduced indoor gardening in the kindergarten, with those pans 10-feet-long on each side of the room." At that, Jesse admits through tears that she wants and needs to go back to education. My father ends the piece commenting on the young teacher Ann Hoffmann, alias Jane: "These school directors, Jane mused, were a curious breed—something like alcoholics. They couldn't stay away from it for long. Jane did not then understand that she also was afflicted with the same weakness."

Above and beyond their similarities in perspectives, Helen Parkhurst and Rebecca Hoffmann had a great deal in common. Both of them pursued challenging careers at a time when education was the most available profession for women with strong minds and a determined sense of social responsibility. They were born 2 years apart—Helen in Wisconsin (1887) and Rebecca in Russia (1885)—and in their thirties—Helen at 32 and Rebecca at 36—they both founded schools in New York City. Helen started the Dalton School in 1919 on W. 74th Street at about the same time that Rebecca was establishing the Hoffmann School in 1921 on W. 177th. These women so close in age, so similar in career trajectories, were just a hundred blocks and a few years apart in founding their schools.

Before founding her school, Rebecca's educational and professional background was in social work. With a history of working in orphanages and social service agencies, Rebecca was dedicated to serving children whose parents were deceased or who came from floundering or broken homes. I am sure that Rebecca's interest in children who had been placed at risk influenced her mentee Ann Hoffmann. Helen Parkhurst had been mentored by Maria Montessori, the first woman to become a medical doctor in Italy, whose world-famous Montessori method of education emerged as well from work with physically disabled and very poor children.

Parkhurst won awards for her work with the Montessori method, but went on to develop her own approach in the Dalton Plan, an approach characterized by individuality, autonomy, and social responsibility. Influenced respectively by Rebecca and Maria and their history as caregivers, Ann and Helen embraced a view of education that was directed more to the needs of children and their own desire to explore than to the requirements of a teacher's fixed syllabus. Rebecca had written, "Today progressive thinkers recognize that education does not begin with subjects, education begins with children." In its fundamental premises, the Montessori approach seemed very much aligned with the objectives of the Hoffmann School. It featured close observation, opportunities for learning across stimuli and age groups, the creation of a child-friendly learning environment, and experiences in which children could confidently acquire real-world life skills.

The Harvard reading specialist Jeanne Chall, a woman reminiscent of these reformers in her industry, determination, and astuteness, believed strongly in an individualized approach to teaching and learning. At one of her lively lectures, she cautioned that classroom teachers must keep track of the different stages of reading of the various children in the same classroom. An outraged young graduate student in the audience raised her hand: "That's easy for you to say. How am I supposed to keep track of reading levels when I have 25 students in my class?" Dr. Chall paused not at all: "If you think that's hard, try waitressing." It seemed at first a put-down, but then I caught the meaning. How can a waitress keep up with the different orders of 20 strangers and a teacher be unable to know the different abilities of a group of children she knows well?

Dr. Chall had an expression: "What's good for the rich can't hurt the poor." She believed that schools and other educational efforts designed to serve children placed at risk across a number of factors should be modeled after the great private schools, surely including places like Andover and Exeter, but no doubt as well by smaller innovative independent schools. There is much for urban public schools to emulate in the model that private schools provide: the small classes, individual attention, and abundance of learning in the arts. But many of the designers of these institutions, like Hoffmann, Montessori, and Parkhurst, demonstrated in the curricula that they designed that what worked with children who faced daunting physical and emotional challenges held promise for all children. Even as the students of Hoffmann School might now be labeled "at risk for failure" or "Special Ed," I wonder what the future would hold if all our students were given that label, all of them considered from the start as having different challenges that must be met, rather than inherent access to a norm that they are supposed to meet.

Helen Parkhurst was a familiar presence as a consultant during the day at the Hoffmann School and as a guest at evening parties upstairs in our apartment. When she was 8, my sister Trudy participated frequently, as did I and a few other children from Hoffmann School, in the conversations with children (Child's World Series) that Parky broadcasted on the radio in the late 1940s. Seated in a circle and speaking into big microphones, children talked in seminar style about such pressing issues as the existence of God or the qualities that make a person a hero. This kind of careful attention to children's thoughts on important issues was very Hoffmann School, very progressive, and reflective of an attitude in which children were respected as having a priori worthwhile ideas, conceptions from which supposedly all knowing grown-ups might learn any number of things.

My mother's belief in children's ability to show us what they need was built on the shoulders of powerful women who looked beyond the labels and institutions that separated bright children from dull, and regarded all children as more than empty slates awaiting the writing of the adult hand. On such foundations my mother created a new curriculum out of an admixture of past principles that were vibrant and worth retaining as well as promising new educational ideas that were sweeping the scene. Referenced throughout the descriptions of the new Hoffmann School is a balance between the best of the progressive era and the "current demands for academic excellence." From the progressive era came irreverence for a hierarchical system for passing on knowledge; from the current scene respect for academic standards and success, variously defined. The question of balance would invite statements from the new director as murky as that the school "insists on strong achievement" (sounds rigorous) but only as "consistent with the capabilities of the individual child" (sounds flexible). While rigor was a goal, flexibility was a mandate. There was much continuity and consistency between Rebecca's and Ann's Hoffmann Schools, but the statement that rings most loudly true from 1921 to 1980 is that "individual development is the keynote of the school."

Rebecca's Hoffmann School was founded initially to serve a parent body made up of working women in the 1920s: "The school is conducted as a day boarding school to provide for the education and care of the children of mothers engaged in professional or business occupations." Three decades later, in my graduating class of 1955, all the mothers were either single parents and/or working professionals. In the 1960s, Ann reported, "Most of our mothers now are working women."

Rebecca's Hoffmann School prioritized outdoor exploration and engagement with the arts, featuring "development through appreciative presentation of form, color, music, and literature by way of first-hand contact with nature and by training in the different forms of artistic expression." These are the very features remembered by the class of 1955 and beyond at Ann's Hoffmann School.

In reviewing the 1966 curriculum report of Ruth Lipscomb, music teacher at Ann's Hoffmann School and performing concert pianist, I am impressed that she notes as the aim of kindergarten and first-grade music class, "to help the child find his singing voice before he reaches the age when he becomes self-conscious." My doctoral thesis was on the same phenomenon of self-consciousness interfering with voice, but in the case of drawing: the disappearance in middle childhood of the freewheeling expressive images that children create at age 5 and earlier. I explored this phenomenon by placing alongside the work of children of various ages the work of professional artists, and considering them both with the same respect and in terms of the same criteria. My methodological approach sounds a lot like what happened without self-consciousness at the Hoffmann School—research in real time, as artful learning rather than social science.

The teaching professional artists and musicians at Hoffmann School created their own works of art within the daily operations of the school. The painter Tom McArthur in the 1950s created images alongside the children and introduced students to the importance of a place and purpose for making art. Ruth Lipscomb notes in her report the songs she has written for the 1966 Hoffmann School spring production of *The Tempest*: "Caliban's Song," "The Vendor," and the most beautiful score she wrote setting to music the classic Ludwig Bemelmans book *Madeline*. With all of them, unforgettable is the sweet sound of little children's voices singing the text, enhanced by the pitch of Ruth's piano accompaniment. The words and song lyrics of many original festival scripts were authored by the school's teaching actress, Marie de Wolfe Hawthorne. Written for various age groups, they included *A Godspenny for Meneither Plumcake*, in which an industrious girl farmer lives her dream of going off to be educated only to return home (her "place in the world") to make it the "best dairy farm in the world," and *Timothy Terrible Tenderly*, in which a disobedient young fish learns (at school) not to play "mean tricks" (1975).

The great outdoors and the daily teaching and learning in the arts stand out for all of us in the class of 1955. Psychologist Dick Robinson explained my mother's educational philosophy as a belief in all children being able to learn and being able to learn to love learning. I find that rhetoric in the early Hoffmann's School's belief in "the importance of the fact that children begin knowing by wanting to know, by being curious. It is with this underlying idea that stimulus is given to speak in classrooms and assemblies, to discuss problems freely, to participate in school newspapers, plays, and projects." And as I hear my mother's simple question to the child: "What would you like to do?", I note from the past, "The school attempts to make its curriculum the answer to a child's curiosity by including the things that interest children, the things that will enable them to find meaning in what they hear and see, what they think and do."

Throughout it all, as my father noted, there is a focus on democracy and the preparation for the child's place therein, along with the awareness that democracy is a fluid process in which children will participate, not a static entity they must learn to define: "It is the belief of the Hoffmann School for Individual Development that modern education has as its function the adaptation of the individual to a society chiefly characterized by change. Children preparing to take their places in such a society can best do so in an atmosphere where freedom of inquiry prevails, where there is cultivation of the open mind."

PARENTS AND PROPERTY

A mimeographed letter to parents from my mother the summer of 1946 is carefully marked "unsent." Reflecting her faith in parental support as well as a lack of careful planning, Ann Hoffmann asks parents, if they can, to send the school another $15 since the calculation of camp tuition turns out to be quite far from program needs. While her administrative skill would progress greatly from such desperate measures, Ann Hoffmann's relationship with and reliance on school parents, like her struggle to meet operating costs, would persist throughout her decades of leadership. Scholarships would always abound at Hoffmann School and, as Rebecca had in the 1930s (before that scholarships were "unofficial"), Ann looked for scholarship support to her devoted and highly organized PTA. She also asked parents to enrich her new curriculum with something called "parent education." Through field trips to work sites and classroom visits from parents, Hoffmann School children would gain a sense of professional options in the adult world as well as a better understanding of where it was that parents went when they took off for that amorphous location, "work."

When asking parents to raise funds for scholarships, Ann pointed beyond student financial need to the educational enrichment that scholarships provide: their ability to broaden the base of the school's "intercultural" program. *Intercultural* is a word that I thought was created in the 1980s when educators were becoming disenchanted with "multicultural" programs largely devoted to the food and costumes of various nations. Arguably, food fairs with adults and children in colorful costume say little about meaningful similarity and difference. Intercultural seemed not only more politically correct (less "us" and "other"), but also more intrinsically active (as in cultures interrelating) than the implications of multicultural (as in cultures displayed side by side). But "intercultural" appears in school brochures as early as the 1920s and through the 1970s as an apt reference to the Hoffmann School. It is a word that describes well the school's appreciation for the uniquely defined cultures and informed worldviews of the individual children in its small community.

For Dick Robinson, parent education went the other way round, with parents as recipients of new understanding. He found the parent body at the Hoffmann School not particularly "hip" on issues relating to children and child development. "Half of them were 'achievers,'" he told me, "the other half stage, screen, radio types—largely middle-class, professional, artistic families." Dick and my mother met frequently with these parents to catch them up on what would seem obvious requirements for raising happy children. Sally in the tree needed sleep and time for play, not late nights out with her parents. Children needed praise for their successes, support for their dreams, and the knowledge that their parents were not only responsible for their care and safety, but also engaged in their growth as human beings.

Ann Hoffmann clearly maintained a friendly antagonism toward parents. It was the view she expressed early on in her youthful notes, "A Teacher Becomes a Parent," where she describes as misguided the beliefs of untrained parents. As school director, she thought in most cases that if not for the parents (if Jacob's stepfather could only be on time for important events; if Arthur's mother would not treat Arthur like another adult responsible for his ailing father's care), she could really work wonders with the children. This may have been the downside of every child's status as "Ann Hoffmann's child"—sort of a (hopefully) loving competition between caretakers. But it could as easily reflect the broad and persistent challenge that all parents and teachers face, struggling to work together toward the good of their children and students.

I felt with real discomfort that my mother was harsh in her critique of Hoffmann School parents, direct about her expectations, and unmistakably open in what appeared to be irritation or frustration. Dick Robinson told me that while Ann Hoffmann never gave up on a child, the longer it took to positively rearrange a child's situation, the less patient and more angry she would grow. It astonished me that parents forgave or responded positively to her chastisement and that they loved her as clearly as they did even as or because she always told them what she thought. In her exposition on the significance of enjoying—not just feeding, clothing, and schooling—children, her chain of thought took an illustrative turn to the support of older siblings when new babies join the family:

> We have had recently a run of new baby brothers and sisters coming to our school children. And, of course, we have been told that every child has been well prepared for his new sibling, and each parent deposes that big brother loves that new baby. I walked into the 4-plus group the other day while they were playing house. One was the baby. There were about three or four big brothers and sisters walking around the room going to school and the store; mother was home with the baby. She would shake her finger at the baby and in a loud voice say, "Now be quiet—you give me a headache." No nice quiet words were used. Suddenly the brothers and husbands came home and all jumped on the baby and started pummeling him. The child who acted the baby howled and cried lustily. At this point the teacher quietly walked over to the group and asked, "Is that the way a baby is treated?" and they answered, "We are the daddies!"
> "Well, would your daddy jump on you?"—"Oh no!'
> "Why not?"—"Because he would crush us."
> "Then why do you do it to the baby?"— No answer.

I was always shocked—embarrassed—by the many surprise turns Ann took in her free-form lectures. Did she notice in the audience someone who needed a reminder to get her child ready in time for the morning school car? Is that why her thank you to parents for their contributions to an art show would suddenly turn to a lecture on punctuality? In this case, did she notice in the audience the parents of the children she describes

—parents who may have thought they had the new baby adjustment covered? Or was the mind of the juggler always balancing more challenges than could be addressed in a single topic? The enthusiastic applause after such pointed parables—and this one led with new surprise into a scathing critique of parents who ever use the expression "I gave up . . . [whatever experience] to spend time with my child"—was baffling to me. Where I might have put my mother on the top of that list of great teachers whose rapport is more with children than with adults, the parents at the school seemed to admire her deeply and, I sometimes thought, to think reverentially by association of my sister and me—the lucky recipients of parenting from the doyenne's hand. Hoffmann School parents filled the first floor of the school to overflowing when there were meetings or benefits, and they gave generously whenever they were asked to help. It was as if they had discovered this jewel in the rugged hills of the West Bronx and it was their responsibility to polish and preserve it.

It was Hoffmann School parents who helped secure the school's new home in 1946 by contracting for small shares in a group purchase arrangement that would not be untangled, allowing my parents to actually own the school, until 1967. Almost half the funds for the initial down payment on the property were raised by Hoffmann family members, friends, and parents of children in the school, with ownership in the name of Therese Hoffmann, Rebecca's older sister, and a bit more than half of the first deposit and subsequent mortgage payments put up by a group of investors to whom my parents for years paid their monthly share. In a letter to parents in May 1946, inviting them to "subscribe to an investment in the school property to any amount you see fit," Ann Hoffmann explains that the "school has spent considerable sums to make the premises a better place for children—about $10,000." She goes on to say, "To spend this money as tenants without any guarantee of permanence seems unbusinesslike."

Unbusinesslike? Reviewing documents from that period and throughout the history of the school, I see how "businesslike" my warm, empathetic, unpredictable mother had to be. There were water bills and real estate taxes to pay; teachers' union negotiations to settle; textbooks and playground equipment to select and purchase; garbage collection, transportation, and grounds and building maintenance to oversee; applications to fill yearly with the Board of Education and the Board of Health; building permits for running a school; applications to review, recommendations to write, correspondence to keep up with; and the huge efforts in the 1960s to petition for a permanent charter for the Hoffmann School, including overviews of curricula from each class, résumés of teachers, histories of the school, and clear statements of its mission and priorities. It took a lot to be able to say, "The Hoffmann School is chartered by the New York State Board of Regents (as of 1968) and has been officially listed by the New York City Superintendent of Schools. It has also been certified by the New York City Department of Health for children under six."

The detailed summaries prepared for charter review are not unlike the annual reports that teachers in every grade and subject prepared for Ann Hoffmann. Each report includes the range of skills and content knowledge that the teacher hoped to introduce (in response to student readiness), lists of books and materials that students explored, and examples of particular classroom practices carefully keyed to the targeted educational objectives. A broad objective of the French teacher, along with learning French culture through stories, art, and song was: "To furnish children with a new mode for exploring and expressing some of their fundamental experiences." "To increase tactile and kinesthetic perception," a kindergarten teacher played that wonderful game "Find out by touching," in which objects with different textures are placed in a box for students to feel and identify. The first-grade teacher created an elaborate school store to introduce monetary concepts, examples of the use of mathematics in daily life.

The science teacher was responsible for Grades 2 through 7 (seventh grade was added in 1963, when some parents felt their children were not ready to move on). In a unit on seasons for second graders, the teacher led an early autumn home-based field trip around the school grounds pointing out late summer growth plants, identifying seasonal insects, and searching for signs of small animals. He asked children to draw summer scenes that told the viewer about their summers and contained examples of summer-only activities. There were other science field trips, one to an abandoned quarry and another to the Junior Museum of the Metropolitan Museum of Art. This teacher presented different units for each grade with careful evaluation of the relative success of his program designs and each student's progress. In the then-combined sixth and seventh grade, Hoffmann School style, there was only one seventh grader, and that created difficulties. "For the only seventh-grade student, a problem of status emerged. This youngster insisted on operating alone. He wanted his own textbook, his own assignments, and his own classroom experiment work."

The many and lengthy detailed reports, exemplars as far as I could see, demonstrated that teachers actively strove to play out in their different settings the objectives of individualism and inquiry that distinguished teaching and learning at Hoffmann School. They wrote contextual introductions citing current literature in their respective areas, attended to candid self-critique, and demonstrated their knowledge of each child. A lot of work. But I think of my mother having to read and comment on it all—the singing in French class, the senses in kindergarten, the plight of the lone seventh grader—making decisions as to which teachers got it right, which needed help and direction. When and on what basis did she decide on ungraded math and reading instruction, regularly scheduled intelligence and emotional testing, and the personal goal for each older child of writing an original song? How could she make sweeping changes like adding another grade to the school as the immediate response to individual need? In a letter to me at college in 1964, a year after she has tried out the addition of a seventh grade, she writes simply, "Having a rough time getting our children into good schools for next year. We are going on to eighth grade."

What was involved in a structural change like that? An alumna of that first eighth-grade class (then combined with seventh) described the diversity of students as ranging from precocious to autistic, and the atmosphere as one of extreme comfort with difference and with ambiguity—less, she told me, about being "weird," and more about "being in our class." It was expected that "your mind would be open to a lot of things." And even as she was uncertain that the math she was getting was really at the eighth-grade level (she was not very tall and the teacher seems to have mistaken her for a seventh grader), she found her teachers "inspiring." "It wasn't primary on the agenda getting you up to snuff; it was more to get you excited about stuff."

Ann Hoffmann, the artist—responding to need, improvising, and helping children experience the fun of learning. The juggler with so many balls in the air; the acrobat leaping high, twisting, and changing direction. So much always going on behind the scenes of individual attention that was the hallmark of the school and the benchmark of my mother's educational approach. "How could she manage it all?" I asked Dick Robinson on a cold February day, 25 years and one day after her death and just a few weeks before his own. "She really believed in what she was doing," he explained to me, "and she put in tremendous energy and effort." Tremendous energy and effort? I'll say.

In the 1960s the untangling of real estate matters was not without rancor. My parents were determined to fully own the property they had nurtured and developed—the home-as-school that had connected our family—for so many years. The group that at that time held an equal share of the property (a business partner—parents and friends had cashed out of the venture) was eager to make money on its investment by asking more than my parents could pay for its portion of ownership. When the property was first purchased in 1946, it was in an area zoned for the sort of garden apartments that were being built throughout Riverdale and up to the back property line behind the sheds attached to the barn and over the brick wall where Mr. Raduli had once been a squatter. The zoning added tremendous value to any included properties. But unbeknownst to my parents—in fact without permission of any of the property owners who would be affected by the change—in 1948 the zoning was changed on the spot and when the property was finally bought, it could only be resold for private homes.

This drop in property value was devastating to my parents. In an appeal to the City Planning Commission my father explained that the extreme efforts (including heavy taxes and debt financing) that had been taken to retain the property seemed warranted because its land value was estimated in 1946 to be more than the purchase price of $46,000: "$51,700 for the land and $17,500 for the building." "In recent years it became necessary both to refinance the mortgage and to sell half our real estate equity in order to continue to maintain both the property and the school, which met its expenses with great difficulty." There were a series of appeals in the 1950s, but in the end my parents' after-the-fact protests to the rezoning of the property only resulted in further alienating them from unsympathetic neighbors. The *Riverdale Press* in May 1953 portrayed these neighbors as saving the community from a future as a "canyon of stone" and my father as having initiated "a red-hot zoning fight." The same neighbors who complained, on the one hand, about school cars and loud voices, on the other, wanted to be sure that their Riverdale homes would be bordered in perpetuity by single family homes and grounds as beautifully maintained as those of the Hoffmann School.

Days after my father's memorial service in 1997, when my sister and I fulfilled my parents' wishes that their ashes be spread on the grounds of the Hoffmann School, we were unable to enter the property. Barbed wire surrounded the borders where once blooming bushes framed the scene. The investors who had in the end bought the property to develop into several separate homes, had run out of money and left it all to ruin at the hands of vandals and wanton fire. From the top of the stone gate that we scaled to fulfill our duty, we could see the once glorious spring-fed pond caved in with mud. The windows of the school were burned out on all levels including the bay windows on the second floor through which Rebecca had once viewed the beautiful Hudson River. Smashed were the office windows through which Ann Hoffmann kept eyes on her children. The art barn had collapsed; large threatening dogs patrolled the grounds; and where Tony the gardener had once tended to fruit trees, only weeds and rubble reigned.

As I watched my parents tend it all—my mother's distress over an unpainted fence or a dangerous pot hole, the urgency with which any fault in the landscape was addressed—it seemed disproportionately crucial work. But the care of the grounds had been as important a part as any of the administrative duties of the Hoffmann School. It contributed to the beautification of a world that went beyond the school's literal parameters, permanently preserved in the imagination and recollection of every Hoffmann School child. The spectacle and safety of the grounds infused the educational experience that both Rebecca and Ann provided. The tangible stage for learning, where damage could literally be repaired, seeds planted in wax cups could grow to be flowers, and children's pretend games could find real shape and place.

Chapter 4

Ordinary Gifted Educator

Cashing out at Play Store.

A KNOWLEDGEABLE FRIEND

L IKE REBECCA, my mother knew that in the artful creation of a school the canvas or stage set must be primed, tended to, and acknowledged as opportunity and inspiration for the children who will bring the work to life. Ann expressed it as she would, "For everyone, but for young boys and girls especially, a healthful, congenial place to live is highly important. It adds happiness in addition to fostering progress." Against a backdrop that was deliberately bucolic, on a stage set with such aesthetic attention and care, the drama of education that was the Hoffmann School relied on the actors and actresses themselves—the advisors, teachers, and students—parts assigned first by Rebecca and then by my mother. Individually and collectively, all of the players embodied the purposes and themes that composed the work of art that was the Hoffmann School.

As founding director of the school, Rebecca Hoffmann had enlisted the counsel and input of educational experts including, as the school's "Educational Director" in the 1920s, Professor Frank E. Thompson (head of the Educational Department of the University of Colorado, 1906–1922) and, as an advisor, Professor Clara Byrnes of Hunter College, who had been active in the Big Sisters program in New York. In the late 1920s, advisors would include Dr. Nathan Peyser, principal of Brooklyn's progressive Public School No. 181, the head of the politically active Educational Alliance, and an expert on the challenge and treatment of juvenile delinquency; and Sarah Michel, the founder in New York of the internationally influential Froebel Kindergarten. These socially responsible progressive educators informed the school's heart and mind through lively discussions of process versus product, self-direction versus structure, and the spiritual and aesthetic requirements of quality education. Theirs was a generation of creative individuals who saw no better vehicle for furthering democracy than early childhood education.

Beyond enlisting Helen Parkhurst as curriculum advisor, Ann Hoffmann brought on board Richard Robinson, chief of clinical psychology at Lenox Hill Hospital, as school psychologist and Dr. Morris Herman, associate director of Bellevue Hospital and New York University professor, as consulting psychiatrist. Ann Hoffmann's tenure would extend from the progressivism of the 1940s through the back-to-basics movement of the 1960s and 1970s and the various pendulum swings around Head Start programs, open classrooms, and active learning. Her advisors would support her when Sputnik's launching in 1957 sounded a wake-up call to American educators that, in order to keep up with the Russians, schools needed to be more about "hard" subjects like science and less about "soft" expressive arts. Ann Hoffmann would allow the front-hall papier-mâché policeman to be replaced by a similarly made rocket ship, but she never gave in to the marginalization of the arts and she never let go of her progressive view of a child-centered curriculum. She believed in children and that that believing would see them through.

Perhaps unsurprisingly, it is hard to pinpoint particular or fixed criteria for student admission. I find ambiguous the statement, "Children admitted to the school are carefully screened for intelligence, achievement, and emotional stability." It doesn't say, "The school admits only children of high intelligence with records of high achievement and solid emotional stability." It doesn't really say much more than that admitted children are well known. "How did she choose the students?" I asked Dick Robinson. It proved an easy question: "She chose children she liked." I was initially taken aback by this response. What did it mean? On the one hand, it seemed demeaning of my mother who thought so hard and long about each child in her school. On the other, it seemed unjust to the children whom Ann Hoffmann might not like; but then again, I could not envision a child she didn't.

I had seen her in family court leap to comfort a surly adolescent who only let down his guard when his surlier father testified against him. "Liar!" the boy screamed from somewhere deep inside, and Ann Hoffmann was out of her seat and at his side. I had gone with her to Bellevue on more than one occasion to visit a boy who was sent there by the orphanage where he lived whenever there was trouble. I was horrified by what I saw: a poorly lit holding room, children wandering almost aimlessly among unidentified adults, a teenager lying across his mother's lap taking milk from a bottle. When Walter—a strange, unwashed, articulate 10-year-old—saw Ann Hoffmann enter the ward, he ran for an embrace. There for him again and again, as only she could be, she was never mawkish. She put her hand on his shoulder gently, looked him straight in the eye and spoke with impossible certainty: "I'll see you in school on Monday." And she always did.

"Children she liked." Did this mean everyone got in? Surely Ann Hoffmann was not discouraged by psychological challenges, learning difficulties, or unhappy home situations. Demonstrated success at other schools was of no interest to her; and IQ, though clearly worth noting, meant little in a school that valued more versions of potential than psychological testing explored. I know her approach was not foolproof. There were students the school couldn't help. These did not include students ("there were 5 or 6 at any given time") who Dick Robinson told me ended up in long-term psychiatric treatment. For them, the warmth of the school's atmosphere and Ann Hoffmann's consistency helped them to flourish. But occasionally there were children with very severe learning disabilities who needed more help than the school could provide. Dick told me of one boy: "I tested him and his test scores were unbelievable. But he couldn't read. . . . This is a learning disability in a very brilliant kid. Hoffmann School

Painting in the classroom.

couldn't do much for him. . . . He was finally sent to a boarding school, the first one developed for learning disabled kids and he did well there."

One alternative to grades is the activity of *holistic assessment:* the grasping of an overall quality that is more or other than the sum of individual parts. For example, the recognition of overriding insight or emotional power in an essay fraught with grammatical errors. I have served on admissions committees where, on a scale from 1 to 5, candidates are ranked on apparently measurable aspects derived from sources such as board scores, writing samples, and letters of recommendations. But in the end, committee members are asked to give an overall score—not the average of the individual scores—something that may override those individual measures: your gut feeling about a candidate. Remarkably, there was usually more agreement on this final gut judgment than on the other aspects. I think that that overall gut judgment was what Ann Hoffmann went for. "I like this child" was equivalent to "This is a fit."

In the 1930s, Rebecca specifies that the teachers at Hoffmann School must have "a full measure of patience and ingenuity." Dick Robinson remembers that Ann, in advising teachers, would always encourage them to be more "sympathetic and supportive." Apparently she encouraged our hard-edged well-loved teacher Betty to "soften" her approach even though Ann herself kept the bar quite high for both teachers and students. Ann Hoffmann didn't see herself as a "tough administrator," but others surely did. When I raise the possibility that my mother differentiated expectations for teaching and directing—that she felt she needed to be hard, but teachers should be soft—Dick's answer is immediate: "I think she was advising what she would do in that particular situation."

Bruno, the lifer (K–7) who grew tall too soon, tells me that in 1960 Ann Hoffmann encouraged students to conduct a full presidential campaign. But when the bickering and poster hanging (e.g., an elephant viciously trampling a donkey) got too heated, she insisted they cool it down. Finally, she allowed a pre-election debate between two student representatives. In front of a wary audience, one well-prepared young man launched the following argument: "Take a look at the picture of Nixon. He looks well rested and healthy. Now look at Kennedy. He has bags under his eyes. He looks tired. And why does he look tired? Because he works hard. Why does Nixon look so well? Because he's lazy and does nothing." At this, first Ann Hoffmann and then faculty, staff, and children broke out in roars of laughter. Kennedy won the school election.

Ann Hoffmann played the principal role with dedication and respect, but she could slip out of character for a laugh to ease the tension of a scene. I can see the laugh now and the tears that came to the corners of her beautiful blue eyes. Rebecca had framed for my mother the image of the appropriate principal. In pictures of Rebecca, a large dignified lady dressed in long skirts and tailored shirts with the neatly folded cuffs that Gracie admired, I see the same truly "grown-up" presence my mother strove to maintain—the role she played, Dick said, to assure herself "that she was a school administrator." Rebecca's letters and stories about her life in the margins of the school reveal that along with her earnest dedication to the causes of democracy and children in need, she had a playful spirit, adored her family and friends, and loved great parties. Rebecca had a theory that going to "lie down" (instead of answering the phone) when a bill collector called would somehow tweak the heavens in such a way that the next phone call would be from a prospective parent who was able to pay her child's way. I believe things like that.

My mother spoke little of Rebecca or perhaps Rebecca was too long dead to be spoken of frequently when I reached an age that I would have noticed. I do know that Rebecca and Ann Hoffmann shared a profound belief in joyfulness in education. For Ann, it was a determination to demonstrate that learning is fun. *Joyfulness* is a word that art teachers use to describe successful art rooms in safe discussions among those who already believe in the importance of the arts. Arts education advocates are afraid to use the word *joy* (*fun* doesn't even make it to the drawing table) in wider circles. They fear that joyfulness will be considered frivolous by those arbitrators of what gets left in or taken out of a child's daily educational fare. I am impressed that joy is addressed in full measure even in the context of whatever rote learning was required in the earliest iterations of Hoffmann School: "There is joy in doing and learning to do. There is added joy in becoming aware of rising standards of accomplishment, an increased mastery of the fundamental skills and the varied drills that are provided. Even greater, however, and surely much more important is the pleasure, the sense of achievement, that takes origin in understanding the why of the things one has accomplished; knowing what relationship they bear to each other; realizing how, separately and together, they fit into the experience of 'being alive today.'"

"That all children could learn to love learning": That was my mother's simple philosophy, a philosophy infused with joyfulness—delightedness with learning this and that, but more with the accomplishment of fitting it all together into some meaningful vital whole: the joyful experience of "being alive today." Such hopefulness and believing infused my mother's relationship with the deliberately diverse population of children she admitted to her school, as did her wish that school could make a difference in the happiness of a child. The rhetoric had changed under the administration of my plain-speaking mother. "She was never giving a prepared speech," Dick Robinson told me, "it was Ann out there telling it like it was." However she said things, whatever her simplicity, indirection, or surprising eloquence, it was never rhetoric that made a parent or child believe in Ann.

Out of their collaboration in the 1940s, Helen Parkhurst had written a somewhat opaque statement of "aims and purposes" for the Hoffmann School from which Ann selected and reworded objectives that she would retain. Ann's language was direct and simple; Helen's was complex and obtuse. For example, I get the gist but not the full meaning of Helen's section entitled "We believe":

> Human organisms cannot set up the progressions of their prob-
> lems—this is the work of the teacher, but each situation must offer
> opportunity for the kind of experiencing that will provide discipline
> and advancement for each individual child. The methods we use will
> depend upon our school population, as well as the needs of particular
> children. Our equipment must above all be social and designed for
> children, as worthy tools, to become the instrument of their will, at
> all times a means, never an end.

My mother sorted out Helen's statements and would write in her own words that it was important for the school "in order to meet the needs of growing, changing children who have a culture and status of their own," (each child has an individual and important worldview) "to strive to help develop emotionally well-balanced children" (feelings matter and school can make a difference) "who can focus on and enjoy problem solving" (the process of learning more than the product of right answers); "children who are learning much and have the ability and interest to learn more" (yes, learning excites learning); "children who respect the rights and ideas of others" (she believed in compassionate community); children with disci-plined minds in "self-controlled physically fit bodies" (whatever that meant at Hoffmann School where all kinds of bodies were respected).

A month after Ann Hoffmann's death in 1980, the mother of a 1964 Hoffmann School graduate wrote to my father that Ann had been plan-ning to attend her daughter's graduation from Georgetown Medical School. She hoped my father would attend in her stead. Malcolm wrote back, "Be sure that if I can, I shall attend. Ann was very fond of Mildred and loved her." Mrs. Paterson had included the brief comments Mil-dred made at her sixth-grade graduation. They were simple and must have been to my mother most dear: "Ann, teachers, students, ladies and gentlemen, I would like to take this opportunity to truly thank you all for a most wonderful childhood at this school."

It was an expression that appeared in letters to my mother from par-ents, "Thank you for giving so and so such a happy childhood." How much of our childhood is defined and not just expanded by school? The grounds, the musicals, the arts every day, the experience of other children who are different from and thereby the same as you. These were elements for shaping and nourishing childhood at Hoffmann School. They provided context as well for a curriculum guided by Ann Hoffmann's educational philosophy, cultivated like all the rest by artistry, intensity, and flexibility. Above and beyond meeting the curriculum standards of the New York State Department of Education, Ann Hoffmann had sound rationales for her selection of courses included in daily learning. But she always left room for unexpected opportunities.

For example, there was Latin (initiated in the early 1960s and continued for student learning as early as Grade 3) because of the opportunity presented by a friend of my sister's who had just graduated from Bryn Mawr. My mother thought this exciting young woman would be a good teacher (a "natural"), and what she was prepared to teach was Latin. And that was great. Similarly, logic was introduced and taught by an enthusiastic young professor from Fordham University; mythology expanded from Latin classes by another accomplished young scholar. Dick Robinson noted that Ann had a much better staff than other schools—better-trained and just plain better teachers. But he told me, as in all things, Ann's priorities were idiosyncratic. She cared about training, but didn't require that her teachers had been trained as teachers. Serious scholars passionate about their subject excited children as truly as Teachers College graduates eager to put into action the theories they'd learned; adults who had learned to deal with their own learning challenges were well positioned to help children do the same.

Teacher credentials compiled over the years present an interesting range. Sixth- and seventh-grade math and science teacher Marion Shiffer had a BS in education from the University of Maryland, 18 credits in law from the University of California, and a year at the Art Student's League. Dance teacher Madame Magda Szusz trained at the Budapest Royal Opera House and had an MA in Ballet from the Hungarian Teaching Academy. There were BAs in education from Teachers College, Bank Street, Ohio and Fordham Universities, Hunter and Wheelock Colleges; and history, sociology, and English degrees from New York, Harvard, and St. John's Universities. Speech, remedial reading, drama, art, and music degrees from Slippery Rock State Teachers College, Indiana University, Carlton College, Julliard, Pratt Institute, and Tokyo University.

The faculty was all well educated with educational trajectories as diverse as the students they taught—backgrounds that did not obviously foreshadow work in a small progressive school in the Bronx. From start to end, the Hoffmann School advocated a progressive approach in which teachers did not teach subjects, they taught children. That meant the creation of exciting learning adventures into whatever subject was at hand. In this, my youngest son must have inherited his grandmother's wisdom. He told me in the fourth grade, "You know, if you're interested in the subject, it doesn't matter who is teaching it; and if you've got an interesting teacher, it doesn't much matter what she teaches."

The arbitrariness of certain subjects did not apply to reading, math, science, the arts, and French. French was prioritized and taught at Hoffmann School (starting in first grade) almost consistently from the 1920s until the school's close in 1985. Like any and all of the arts, French provided another language, another way of saying and seeing and understanding. *Integration* is another term that was used consistently. Our Gilbert and Sullivan productions served to integrate subjects and skills as did our other project work: the school wide study of earth, neighborhood helpers, what makes day and night. "Integration assists toward interest," Rebecca or Ann had written.

Dick Robinson told me that what was unique about the Hoffmann School was its very small classes, quality arts instruction, and Ann Hoffmann's powerful belief that all children could learn to love learning. But he also uses the word *integration* in the list of special features he prepared for school materials:

1. Interracial student body, faculty, and staff;
2. All-denominational religious approach;
3. Avoidance of social and intellectual snobbishness;
4. Integration of children with physical and emotional challenges with children of superior or normal endowment;
5. The integration of the best of both progressive and conservative school programs.

The integration of heart and mind—individual goals and progress with generalized high expectations. As a classmate described it, "It was a warm, holding kind of environment; the structure was there but it was subtle and it was neatly presented." From the conservative was taken throughout the history of the school an attention to basics (Rebecca called them the three "Rs") and standards that went beyond the school. In this the school must have been successful, or so those of us in the class of 1955 surmised, because students who graduated from Hoffmann, that outlier school in which difference among students and their work was both a given and a goal, went on to do well and even thrive in more traditional standardized schools.

Another result of the Russian launching of the first satellite was a demand for American schools to produce students as fit as their international counterparts. President Eisenhower founded the President's Council on Youth Fitness. Calisthenics was replacing dance in public school physical education programs as surely as science and math were edging out the arts. Hoffmann School kids had always engaged in physical fitness activities such as creative dance and the most open-ended versions of team sports. In listing the athletic equipment for the school, in some or another of the school's many reports, there are included: "18 tricycles or bicycles of all sizes, 2 seesaws, 10 scooters, 9 swings, 7 slides, a large climbing turtle . . . jungle gym, etc." "Trees" and "rowboats" are listed alongside a "basketball court." It was true that children energetically climbed trees and also that the hoops for what was being called a basketball court were hung on two trees. Still, I would have thought the balls and bats of competitive sports would have counted more readily as "athletic equipment."

Ann Hoffmann scrupulously avoided competition (the word was spoken in hushed tones) on account of its unreasonable tenets (winners and losers) and the unwarranted stress (winning and losing) it put on children. There are several pictures of Ann pitching in Hoffmann School baseball games, wearing a wraparound, blue denim skirt, sneakers (with stockings, of course), and a playful sun hat with a tall Cyrano de Bergerac feather. She diligently encouraged the pace and excitement of the game, attending to the number of runs and outs more to see who was up than who was ahead in the game. Nonetheless, as I look at the graduation picture of the class of 1955, four kids of various heights, we do look pretty fit. We did play outside all the time and with abandon; we did play baseball and swing on climbing equipment; we often played games of tag—well the boys did. I told them I was too good to play, at least at their level, and hoped they wouldn't press me. It was my way of avoiding the humiliation of being slow and shamefully caught in an instant or desperately trying to tag some one of them whom I could never catch.

The 1960s writer of that sketch of the Hoffmann School described it all:

> The physical environment is singular, the teaching techniques are innovative, and the philosophy of matriarchal director Ann F. Hoffmann is a part of the air that students breathe. She believes that her

110 children are people with equal rights, and she prompts them to question the assumptions behind decisions, even hers. . . . A pacifist, she declares simply in her reasonable way that words can settle things [and] therefore fighting shall not exist. For the most part, it doesn't. . . . Mrs. Hoffmann asks students to consider [her] a "knowledge-able friend." . . . In many conflicts, students debate their case with Mrs. Hoffmann-and win. She will admit mistakes. She says, "We talk about how loyal friends can help each other."

In the interview, she tells the reporter that 80% of her students who have applied to Bronx Science and Music and Art have been accepted and goes on: "But we're a bread-and-butter school, not a velvet-pants place. Children can be themselves here. They don't have to satisfy some code, wear uniforms, for example. Some parents select a school for prestige, so they can brag. We try to be the school with the most compassion and heart. I want children to know we can accept one another . . . and live peacefully. It's the person who is important. The individual should not give in or give anything up . . . but he should make a peaceful world, which is not easy." I hear all of this in her welcome to new students a decade later in September 1974.

Dear Boys and Girls,
    Welcome to a new and exciting school year 1974–1975.
    For some of you it will be the last year at the Hoffmann School, and for some it will be the first, possibly a little frightening. I am sure you have all decided that this is going to be your best year. It is excellent to set very high goals academically, but do not be disap-pointed the first time you cannot do your homework or do not un-derstand your class work. Please turn to your teachers; they are very nice people, believe me. Teachers are eager to help. They are very pleased when a boy or girl has learned some subject especially well with them. If you are having difficulties with any of your teachers, come to me and I will help you.
    Most students of the Hoffmann School know I do not believe in guns, or any war toys and games. I also feel very strongly that here at the Hoffmann School on these beautiful four acres of grounds, we can learn to live in peace with one another. None of us is perfect but we can all learn to accept one another and to help each other in friendly ways. If you have ever been without a friend, you know how important friends are. If you have ever been bullied, you know how difficult it is to be happy.

Therefore, let us try to live peacefully, happily, learning and growing. Let us understand that we all have different ways of growing up and try to help each other.

HAPPY SCHOOL DAYS!!! Your friend, Ann F. Hoffmann

"If you have ever been bullied, you know how difficult it is to be happy." She knew everything. A postcard from Dick Robinson to his family at the Hoffmann school in 1959 begins, "Dear Hoffmanns, Emma, Estelle, Betty, etc." and then describes his European holiday, with his wife Phyllis, traveling from England to Amsterdam to Italy: "Have learned here that Swiss children, even if accompanied by parents, are not allowed to go the movies until they are 18 and that crime and violence are completely banned from TV. An Ann Hoffmann Heaven!" Responding to the question of whether the Hoffmann School was like a home, Dick told me, "It was familial. It was definitely not a democracy. Ann Hoffmann was it. She made all the important decisions. She dictated all the important dictates. She designed all the important designs. This is not to say that one couldn't discuss these things with her, but you didn't make the final decisions. She always did, and she certainly was deeply concerned with every child and certainly knew more about every child than the average administrator knows about the children in his or her school."

"But she turned to you for advice?" I queried, remembering how highly my mother regarded Dick, how when she almost had come to terms (it took a week) with the fact that at 20, I was leaving college, having a baby, and marrying a boy from rural Massachusetts, she held out as a final trial, "Let's see what Dick thinks of him." "Yes," Dick replied smiling. "I must say that in the 25 years we worked together, she never made an important decision with regard to any child without talking it through with me." Seeing my curiosity, he added, "I'm just saying that in 25 years, she never once with regard to any child took my advice." Laughing, he admitted with a tone of wonder, "Fortunately when it came to children, Ann was pretty much always right."

THE CHILD'S CHAMPION

"Living up to potential" was right up there in the ethos of Hoffmann School along with "accepting our children as they are" and "find out how you can help." "Not living up to potential" was a term I would often hear my mother use with regard to my performance in school. I think I first heard it when I was five. Although music at Hoffmann School was marked by a daily trip to the music room, the magic of song frequently entered our classroom time. I enjoyed singing aloud with my peers in first grade the familiar ABC song that sometimes ends with "Tell me what you think of me," but at Hoffmann always ended with, "Next time won't you sing with me?" I was intrigued in this classic learning tool, as I was by the highlighting of dates and names in other teaching songs, by the matching of a single alphabet letter to a musical beat. But I was confused by what, on account of the phrasing and rhythmic meter of the alphabet song, I perceived as one letter: *lmno*. I know that others have shared this misapprehension, but for me it went deep, even intruding on my ability to read.

Looking in our readers—the ordinary *Dick and Jane* fare—I would cringe when I saw the onset of any of these four letters, wondering how I should pronounce it or incorporate it into a word. *Lmno.* When I read aloud in class, I did so softly, always at the ready to become completely silent and skip over the irksome part of the perplexing complex letter/syllable/note. My mother, predictably convinced that I could read fluidly and that I was too shy to show my stuff in class, tried to persuade me to read louder, not to be afraid if it was easier for me than for others. Unable or not daring to share my confusion, I began to understand the concept of "not living up to potential." I'm not sure when I adopted the phrase as a cloak to wear through school, but for a long while I preferred doing a half-baked job of things relieved that folks thought I wasn't living up to my potential. It seemed to me better than exerting a real effort and revealing how much lower than what they expected my real potential was.

I was surrounded at school with children like Jacob who loved long words and real literature, Arthur who seemed to know by heart the Robin Hood tales we would reenact in pretend play, and a sister who frequently chose the reading of long adult novels over playing cut out paper dolls with me. A relative liked to describe the difference between my sister and me: "If Trudy asks a child if she wants to play house and the child says no, she goes off to read *Gone with the Wind*. If Jessie asks a child if she wants to play house and the child says no, she asks if the child will play cowboys or store or anything until the child says, 'okay.'" While I now see this trait as a version of my mother's "What would you like to do?", at that time I think the point was that I would rather play anything with someone than sit down alone with a book.

When it came to reading, which Hoffmann School ultimately taught me to do well, I maintained in the later grades my early avoidance. The very last days of summer, I would look at my school's summer reading books, skim through the shortest selections for key points and phrases, study carefully their back covers, and write book reports made up of my opinions and ideas rather than a careful reportage of content. Although I worried as always (and felt other children did) that no matter what I wrote, the teachers would approve rather than fault the principal's daughter, I mastered and held to an approach to reading that I saw as "reparative," as in reparation for not having done the required reading.

As a doctoral student in my early forties, I cautiously shared my childhood technique with the late developmental reading guru Professor Jeanne Chall, whom I mentioned earlier. "Stage 5!" Dr. Chall exclaimed decidedly, suggesting that what I was doing could be considered reading at the highest level—casting your eyes quickly across the page, searching for information you care about or can use, and being able to frame an analysis or articulate coherent understanding. Dr. Chall may have been poking fun at my lingering embarrassment or at the sanctity of her stages. But I have carefully revisited the description of what she calls the highest stage of reading and see her point: taking ideas away from reading is more advanced than recounting what was said.

This bizarre transformation of not living up to potential into performance at the highest level had a familiar ring. Was Hoffmann School not just a place but an approach to teaching and learning that could extend from tiny elementary school to major university? Had I for a lifetime misread as compensatory behavior my ability to read effectively? Perhaps my rewriting of the summer reading assignment gave it a compelling edge—made it for me a more interesting challenge. Had a gift of mine been shrouded in embarrassment when it should have been celebrated in the light? Or had the voice of a teacher determined to find gifts made the difference? The question of whether the assignment was done rightly or wrongly, well or poorly, is so much less interesting than the question of how and why a particular student has approached the assignment the way she has. In a world of right-or-wrong assessments the 8-year-old child exploring light and dark in a cloud of charcoal scribbles will receive less recognition than the children who have mastered the rote drawing of a cartoon character. But we may find that the scribbler is the passionate artist, demonstrating, in Hoffmann School language, her determination to live up to potential.

Is potential handed out in discrete proportions to each child? "You get this much potential, see if you can live up to it." "Oh, you've got a lot more, you need to work harder." Or is potential something that individuals define and redefine as they learn and mature? "Living up to" as in reaching, stretching, extending—not realizing potential. To say that a child is functioning below or beyond expectation may say more about whatever means we use to gauge expectation than it does about a child's performance. Perhaps my teachers at Hoffmann School were not, as I thought, fooled, but rather recognized what I was doing both as alternative and sufficient. Dr. Chall had seen abundance where I had seen deficiency, changing the ground rules in the game of performance versus potential.

A yellowing report from May 15, 1951, written by Dick Robinson and describing his psychological examination of me at age 7 years 5 months, states "the problem: Level of intelligence and functional level." As I read the lovely and carefully detailed account of my performance on the Wechsler Intelligence scale, Dick's writing brings back the moment of the encounter. He writes, "As Jessica and the examiner were old friends, establishing a relationship was no problem. Jessica was friendly and warm but seemed very desirous of keeping the relationship in the testing situation on a strictly business level." That's right. I knew that these assessments were formal mandates of the informal Hoffmann School. We were all familiar with the expression, if not the meaning of, "high IQ." And of course I was unafraid of any encounter with my trusted adult friend Dick Robinson.

Sitting up straight, I took interest in tasks like identifying emotions on various faces, but I asked Dick to hurry through the ones that I didn't like ("Let's not do this one") such as figuring out what was wrong with a picture of the bright sun casting no shadow over the figure of a man or worse, casting a shadow in the wrong direction—things I will never understand. Dick writes, "Jessica is a highly intelligent child who is not making maximum use of her intellectual endowment." He calls it "a habit problem," noting that I seemed somewhat undisciplined intellectually. "She expends effort only on those tasks which interest her and she tends to lose interest even on these as she works." He suggests as a remedy "a long-term project" like the care of a dog for which I would have full responsibility.

"Today they have a name for it," a former Hoffmann School teacher spoke into the air describing any of us who were students at the Hoff-

Woodworking and blocks.

mann School. What would they call my confusion with letters in first grade or my inability to stay on task? If it was a problem or disorder, it seems to me that I attended to too many things (the word, the song, living up to potential) and that slowed me down. Would that be called excess (attending too broadly) or deficit (not sufficiently focusing my attention)? Whatever the current labels, children who wear them are taught strategies that help them keep up with or excel within the unchanging constraints of school. For Ann Hoffmann, the burden was on the school to strategize and change. Accordingly, there was an a priori attachment to flexibility in approach and a belief that if all things were made right for us, whatever our individual challenges, we could find our way. Bruno, who was so large for his age, so frustrated and excitable, could not coordinate his eye and hand to guide a baseball bat into a moving ball. He "had a terrible lack of self-confidence," but Ann Hoffmann and the faculty reflected on his distress and, for him miraculously, changed the spring sport from baseball to kickball. It was much easier to kick the ball from home plate and Bruno found he was good at it. "They made it so I could be an athlete" he explained gratefully.

A clay universe.

At Hoffmann School, children were as celebrated for their sensitive consideration of others' feelings or having a positive attitude as they were for painting with abandon, mastering a math problem, or rendering a powerful song. There was no tyranny of "mattering school subjects" like math and science over the arts. Ann Hoffmann's explicit expectation was that we could do and learn anything and her implicit understanding was that if learning wasn't happening, it had more to do with the failing of the parents, teacher, and/or school than with the individual child. She maintained this perspective internally by adjusting conditions to suit individual children's needs, and she maintained it externally by never trusting the negative descriptors assigned to children by outside institutions. I would come to experience this firsthand.

By eighth grade, I had become deeply ensconced in the Riverdale Country School for Girls, a school my mother resented for its buttonholing of youth ("this one is mathematically talented; that one's creative") so alien to her educational philosophy and to that of the Hoffmann School. On the heels of my preadolescent experience as the only girl in my class at Hoffmann, I reveled in the sociability of an all-girls school and embraced with a passion that no doubt sent shivers down my mother's spine the homogeneity of the 28 upper-middle-class girls in my form. At Hoffmann we were surrounded by personal difference in our social, physical, and academic profiles; were encouraged at all times to pursue our individuality; and we revered the grown-ups in our cosmos whom we called by their first names. At Riverdale we were arranged by height, which meant we were surrounded by physical likeness; sang the same graces at lunch; wore the same kind of clothes; and made fun of the same teachers, whom of course, with formality, we called by their last names.

From a world of empathy and playful artistic expression, I had moved into a social milieu in which issues of popularity and conformity held sway. Much of it confused me. For example, why were we arranged by height within our individual classes? Did the lines look neater rising in size from low to high? Was the expectation that the smaller girls would be younger and more in need of a watchful eye from the teacher at the front of the line? Was there a subtle suggestion that you were meant to make friends with people of similar size? Whatever the reason, it worked for us in the back of the line. We were tallest, farthest from the teacher, irreverent, and deeply envious of the shorter girls who would ultimately not tower over their dancing partners in Tuesday's social dance class.

Our eighth-grade math teacher was Martha Malloy, who liked to dress in green and dance an embarrassing jig on St. Patrick's Day. She had enormous shoulders, or wore suits with padded shoulders, and did much of her cheerful if disinterested teaching with her back facing the semicircle of desks in which we girls sat. I had braces, top and bottom, that were secured by tiny round rubber bands that went from front to back of my mouth. With a flick of a finger I could sail those bands through the air and I did so frequently in math class, howling when they landed on the back of one of Mrs. Malloy's big woolen shoulders. At the moment of contact, Mrs. Malloy would twist around to catch the offender in the act. Enough of us had braces supported by those bands—and all of our mouths were closed tight around our hardware—that it was impossible for Mrs. Malloy to positively identify me, but I knew that she knew—and she did. At the end of eighth-grade math, Mrs. Malloy responded to my lackluster academic performance by flunking me and insisting that I be tutored over the summer and tested before being allowed to enter ninth-grade math. I was horrified and sorrowful at the thought of having to do math lessons over summer vacation, which I always spent working at Hoffmann School Day Camp.

It would otherwise be the second summer that my mother appointed me as the special counselor to a blind child. I had applied for the job as

Junior Assistant Counselor and been accepted by Director Ann Hoffmann who wrote: "In my opinion a well-qualified applicant." It was my job to help Lila Rosen get around camp with the other 6-year-olds in her group and be available to her as a friend and caretaker. Lila was really beautiful: big for her age with red hair and milky blue eyes that rolled upwards when she tilted her head at attention. Lila focused on her environment with an intensity that moved and inspired me. At her side, I would find myself noticing things that I usually didn't. "Listen, Lila, to the difference in the sound of our walking on the bathroom floor; reach down and feel the cool tiles." So many ways to know the change from room to room, indoors to outdoors, to sense the presence of individual children and to know if their countenance was happy or sad.

I kept a journal that I turned in to my mother at the end of the summer. It was filled with notes of what Lila had accomplished or suffered in a day, what new discoveries or missed opportunities she or we had found, what delight or frustration her participation with others might have wrought. Excerpts from the report I wrote that summer of 1957 when I was 13 years old do not sound like a girl who shoots rubber bands across the room in math class. I began by noting, "The first reactions of the children in her group varied. Many of the children were frightened. One or two of them teased. The teasers soon found that Lila was not an easy one to fool. One child tried to tell her the feet of a doll were its head and Lila immediately replied, "Can this doll walk on her head?" At another juncture, I point out, "Whenever Lila would play with clay, I would tell her to be careful not to spill the cup of water we used. At one time she spilled it on purpose so many times that I would not let her have any more water. I explained that if it had been an accident I would not have been angry. After that, she tried to explain her naughtiness as accidents, though when questioned more thoroughly, she had to laugh." I concluded, "Over this summer I sincerely believe Lila has discovered many things about getting along with others. Her charm and personality and intelligence will surely help her to succeed in all she attempts. Lila is the most wonderful child I have ever met and it has been a privilege and great pleasure to have worked with her this summer."

While she went to a school for the blind in the winters, Lila's story was similar to so many of the students' at Hoffmann School. Re-creating her physical challenges as unique ways of seeing, she shared her understandings with other children and enlarged their worlds and hers. Lila wrote to me from time to time until she went on to Barnard College and then to graduate school. With such extraordinary opportunities for learning, what need had I for a tutor repeating deadly class work? Perhaps I shouldn't have been surprised by my mother's directive as we left our year-end meeting with Mrs. Malloy, "You enjoy yourself this summer, Jessie."

"You mean I'm not getting a tutor?" I asked.

"I'm sure you'll do fine on that test in the fall."

At that moment, I felt vividly my mother and myself as coconspirators, resisting the mundane obligations of the mainstream. We together were brave outsiders, nodding to the conventional expectations of a cookie-cutter world, as we ourselves reached for higher goals. I had insisted on going to Riverdale, against my mother's protests because my sister had. My mother wanted me to go to progressive Dalton or challenging Brearley, two schools that seemed to her to be more about learning than button-down shirts and Shetland sweaters. But it was a time when my sister's path was the only one of interest to me, if not just to increase my chances of becoming exactly like her, at least to have the chance of benefiting from her experience. What was it like for the principal as parent to encounter a teacher she wouldn't have hired at a school she would have run differently?

In the end I believe my mother welcomed the opportunity that Mrs. Malloy had afforded me to realize the difference between the active personal learning I was doing as Lila's counselor, in which my mother believed, and the passive impersonal learning that my mother despised and that had failed me. Surely I was a Hoffmann School kid, aligned with difference and self-respect even as I had become a Riverdale Country School cutup, longing for acceptance and popularity. At summer's end, my mother told me I was expected at the Brearley School in the fall. I wept and begged her not to take me away from my school friends whom I loved dearly. My mother's lesson lost on me, I returned to Riverdale for ninth grade. I took Mrs. Malloy's math test and, as Ann Hoffmann had expected, I made no mistakes.

DECEPTIVE SIMPLICITY

Among the yellowing pages of my father's writing, I find this description of my mother who must then have been in her early thirties:

I think that she is beautiful, and my opinion is expert since I am her husband. I think that her beauty is not of the surface only but in the clean design of the engine that runs her. She is remarkable for the premature whiteness of her hair, for the blue cast of her gentle eyes which suggest that compassion can still reside in the human spirit, for the firmness of her ruler-edged nose, and for the deceptive simplicity of her speech which always seems to formulate universal truth in the casual expressions of the housewife. Mostly she is remarkable for the faith she has in people and in our democracy.

"The casual expressions of the housewife." I see it again and wonder to what extent my mother may have cultivated this image, deliberately softening the edges of her "hard-nosed executive" image with the ways and words of the wise, if unworldly, housewife. Or did it go the other way round? Was she sharpening the contours of her warm being in order to play the part she was given?

Ann Hoffmann was in many ways ahead of her time. Her ongoing challenge of balancing full-time career and busy home life was, in the 1940s and 1950s, outside of the norm. Upstairs in our apartment and in the presence of my father, it seemed to me that what she really longed to be was that plain-speaking housewife who enjoyed coffeeklatch mornings, luncheons with friends, shopping in town, and evenings free for dinner making, dishwashing, and family hearthside gatherings. My mother's supposed longings, as I invented or perceived them, remind me of one of my favorite stories, *Tonio Kroeger*, written by the great German author Thomas Mann,[10] about a struggling young poet whose life is his art. Above and beyond Tonio's compulsion to write, the thrust of the story is his struggle to make sense of the painful distance he feels from the subject of his extraordinary art: ordinary life. Tonio is the quintessential outsider artist, longing for the simple life of the blond-haired, blue-eyed people whom Mann situates at the center of society, luminously in the dance, while Tonio stands darkly on the edges. "How I long for the commonplace," Tonio declares.

Tonio's longings reminded me of my own perhaps real and my mother's apparent longings for a regular life in a regular home and of how she struggled every day in her work as Tonio did in his to create something new that had not been there before. Tonio's artistic medium was the tone and meter of words while hers was the strengths and foibles of children. His aesthetic objective was a unified work of art, hers the unleashing of human potential. But just as Mann's reader must doubt the self-pitying of Tonio, who seems to see his talent as a burden, it was always unclear whether Ann Hoffmann reveled in the part she played or longed for reprieve. Either way, the Mann story afforded my first realization that my mother was an artist and that in spite of or along with the many triumphs of her artistry, she suffered mightily for her art.

Surely she and her school stood on the edges of the dance, alongside and embracing the Tonios who could or would not fit in with the rest. Surely she was most interested in children who for a range of circumstances were outsiders to the celebrated norm, even as she saw all children as outsiders, looking longingly from the sidelines, aching for approval from the dancers who comprised the adult world. In the draft of an article ("Are We Enjoying Our Children?") that she hoped to publish in the *Ladies' Home Journal* in 1948, Ann Hoffmann asked parents to "live *with*" their children "not around them or near them," to put in perspective competitive measures of IQ scores (never predictors of "a fine eagerness and a wholesome attitude toward life"), and to celebrate their children, whatever their relative strengths:

> Let us accept our children as they come . . . and help bring out the best in them by always being proud of them, praising them, and giving them the warm security which this anxious world rarely provides outside of the home. Most of all, let us try to enjoy our children by sharing life with them, not in the adult world, but in the world of children which we may once more be privileged to enter if we have the fortitude to ask over and over, "Now what would I do if I were 7?"

Ann Hoffmann did not shy away from the areas in which children needed to improve; she embraced them. But she also saw children's strengths (whatever their nature) and successes (no matter how small or in what arena) as mandates for celebration. She called upon adults to pause for a moment from their dancing and praise whatever new step a child had invented—regardless of whether it went well with the music. With all of this came an emphasis on respect: on the dissolution of circles that let some but not all in; on a lack of hierarchy among activities and people; and on the mutuality of heart and mind. Outside the lines people drew, Ann Hoffmann found place and need, and she answered the call.

In her article (a piece that informed or was based on a PTA talk), she stresses the importance of parents spending quality time with their children, advocating for the sort of life we enjoyed at home on Sunday mornings, lingering in our bedclothes, eating scrumptious breakfasts all together, savoring the pastry and jelly donuts that Estelle would bring us from a Spuyten Duyvil bakery. Throughout the piece, my mother strikes that familiar but almost punitive tone with parents, instructing them to look beyond the surface of their children's lives and to value their children explicitly as she did. She speaks with clarity and purpose that reflect and belie the "casual expressions of the housewife:"

> I know parents of an 8-year-old who are so eager to see this child excel in schoolwork that they do not consider any phase of his emotional behavior important. This 8-year-old is starved for outside interests which his parents do not help create; he is constantly prodded with "Do you know your times tables?" "Why are you still using manuscript? Don't they teach you writing?" These proddings are unduly disturbing to a child. A youngster wants reassurance that he is tops. He wants to learn that what he is doing is approved of by friends, parents, and teachers. If your child reads well but is poor in arithmetic, praise him for what he can do. Don't call your child stupid or the teacher inadequate and the school lax—find out how you can help him.

"Now, what would I do if I were seven?" An invitation to cross the edges of the dance, the unnecessarily deep divide that can separate the world of adult and child. In such boundary crossing, Ann Hoffmann was motivated by her passion for helping children. She explained, "When a youngster is not succeeding in schoolwork, our school does detective work"—another face of listening. Listening for stories that make sense of behavior. Really listening when a child tells the story of last night (Another night with parents not home? A night when a new sibling sapped everyone's attention? A night when a child was sent to her room for not doing homework—or no one cared?) provides context for understanding the child's countenance and performance.

In a 1962 letter to the Ford Foundation, requesting much needed (as usual) funding for the school, my father describes my mother's dauntless detective methods: "Mrs. Hoffmann is in almost daily contact with a number of parents by phone or visit and supplements the curriculum with a genuine effort to ascertain and correct the reasons why the child does not perform at his best level. Often the reason relates to problems of home living in which Ms. Hoffmann willingly intrudes in the hope of helping the situation." Ann Hoffmann chose for admission to the school, not students with records of proven success, but children who interested her and whom she liked. And she supported those children in every way she could—looking below the surface when things were hard, "intruding" as she felt it was needed, dedicating herself and more time than could be measured to those she represented even in the "anxious world" beyond Hoffmann School walls.

While I don't think it was common knowledge—certainly not among the teachers who struggled with low pay and the suspicion of inequity in salaries—in the almost 40 years that she directed the school, Ann Hoffmann never drew anything that could fairly be called a salary. My father wrote in 1992:

> She ran a school for about 100 children for over 35 years, all four seasons of the year, nights running into days, living with her parents' and children's concerns and the most she ever took out from the school as money in a single year was $3,800, but generally she took nothing at all and often it was my duty to make up a deficit out of the proceeds of my law practice. Her work was for children and she thought that she was in the direct line of fire in the war against civilization. She said that if the children could not achieve, were not strongly motivated, then our civilization was failing more surely than through outright destruction by warfare. Though most use their memories and some intelligence, they must also develop good work habits, they must utilize their lives effectively, but mostly they must walk on this strange planet with a sense of wonder. . . . My wife thought in metaphors.

Speaking of metaphors, the representation of my mother as a defender in the "war against civilization" may seem hyperbolic. But ordinary dedicated educators are guardians of culture, fighting for children against the corruptive tides of changing values and ethics, steering clear of devaluation and burnout to make substantive difference in our children's lives. One of my former graduate students, a splendid New York City public school principal named Rebekah Marler, spoke in 2007 of the same battle: "Those who work in schools know that above all other social institutions and organizations, schools are truly on the front line of the battle to uplift or destroy humanity." She identifies as "the most pressing issue in school reform today . . . the never ending resistance to creating schools that are about the business of helping children make unquantifiable meaning in life by integrating the heart, mind, and spirit."[11]

Across the half century that divides them, Rebekah Marler and Ann Hoffmann are united by their fighting spirits and their belief in the arts as agents to humane education. Rebekah found in her graduate studies that she had two strikes against her in the field's silent hierarchy: (1) Her specialty was early childhood, an area thought to require less knowledge and skill; and (2) she focused on the arts, subjects that are marginalized in mainstream schools. In a saner world, educators would not need to rail against the kind of standardized measurement that makes a nuisance out of students' individual differences. The early years of childhood when children frame their understanding of school would be considered most crucial, to be negotiated by the most skilled educators. Similarly, in a more perfect world, the arts—representing as they do the heights of human creativity—would be valued as the most important subjects in school.

But this was not the case in the 1940s and it is not true today. Reform is the ongoing medium of education not just because changing times necessitate alteration, but also because, when it comes to honoring timeless values, we cannot seem to get it right. Nonetheless—or on this account—generations of dedicated educators (most of them women) struggle on and create a web, joining hands across time, philosophy, and shared outrage. Progressive educators of the twentieth century disavowing a view of teaching as the filling of empty vessels with quantifiable facts—with envisioning the education of thoughtful, active, engaged citizens in a world worthy of change. Twenty-first-century educators still struggling with a preoccupation with answers that can be counted right or wrong, still longing for classrooms filled with inspired teachers and immeasurable outcomes like walking the planet "with a sense of wonder."

While Ann Hoffmann was also described as "a warm being to whom it is rare that a child does not relate as a mother figure," my classmates saw beyond the maternal view. Although she was parental, they told me, it wasn't as any sort of doting parent. She had high expectations and she was fair, but when she clapped her hands and said, "Children," everyone in the room quieted down—immediately. Sometimes all that was needed was for her to clap her hands. "She was very forbidding," Arthur remembers, " . . . scared the hell out of me." But when I ask if she was ever unkind, he is protective and deliberate: "Never." Gracie elaborated, "I saw her as the ultimate authority figure—but I did see her as kind and warm (but not mushy or anything). . . . I liked her but I wouldn't take a chance and disobey her." Gracie points to a moment of discipline that still seems strange. She realizes at 62 that in fourth grade she was spending too much of her time "torturing" Stephen, whose predilection for agitation was hard to resist. But when she set him off without a paddle in a flat-bottom boat on the school's pond, Ann Hoffmann laid down the law: Gracie would not be allowed to play with Stephen for an entire day. This still seems harsh to Gracie since she really liked Stephen and wanted to have him as her friend.

I am fascinated by my mother's disciplinary decision. Rather than giving Gracie a lecture or time-out for negative behavior—for pushing around a vulnerable child—Ann Hoffmann enforced the positive lesson that making and having friends is a privilege that comes with responsibilities. As I can't imagine I ever could, my mother seems to have understood Gracie's action as misdirected affection and known that her "strange" tact of deprivation would be effective. Again and again I ask, how did she make these individually tailored on-the-spot decisions? Did she know each of these children so well or did she know all children so well, or did she just know well how to learn from and about children? "What do you want to do?" Perhaps she didn't even need to ask.

Stephen tells me, "I know that I must have been very fond of her because I remember one time sneaking a kiss in to Ann. . . . I am not sure if we were in the office or in the dining room . . . or if she ever knew it was me." Ever knew it was him? Taking my leave from his law office, I had told Jacob as if I knew (and I did) that Ann Hoffmann would be very proud of him. In response to Stephen's speculation, I again transcend my role as the school itself, assume my mother's voice, and assure him—because it must be true—that Ann Hoffmann knew exactly who had bestowed that kiss. As I presumptuously employ her wise and unpredictable voice, I feel a kind of heady hubris.

"I would never tell her I couldn't do whatever it was she asked me to do," Arthur says simply, and, "she asked me to do very hard things." From the time that he was 10 and assigned without asking the part of Nanky Poo or asked in sixth grade to write a play about Christopher Columbus, or throughout his time there required to do ballet, Arthur felt the standard being raised by this champion of children and her expectations lying somewhere just beyond his reach. While Jacob chose the path of "acting out" in school to cover up his refusal or struggle to do homework, Arthur worked as hard as he could to get the work done. He remembers crouching under his blankets with "a flashlight and blunt pencil" after his parents had sent him to bed, trying to come up with the third of the three minimally required sentences on Columbus: "My entire play was: 'Christopher Columbus had an idea. The world was round.'"

At 16, Arthur was given $200 and the keys to the Hoffmann family station wagon to buy and replace shingles on the roof of the school's art barn. The next summer he was asked to drain and paint the camp's swimming pool, a fenced-in 40' long by 20' wide inground pool installed in 1954 in the grassy field between the Arts and Crafts Barn and the spring-fed pond. The side of the barn that faced the pool was opened up into dressing rooms for boys and girls. A makeshift outside shower allowed swimmers to rinse off before and after entering the chlorine blue water, and a stone pump house at the opposite end of the pool kept the water circulating and clean.

Arthur holds back a smile as he vividly describes himself sitting in the hot sun on top of the barn, hoping he had figured out how the shingles should be affixed, somehow all by himself getting the job done in time for the new camp season. He remembers that in order to start syphoning water from the pool into the pond below, he sucked so hard on the hose that leaves and mud splattered onto his face. I assume my mother would glance out her office window from time to time, and I wonder if, seeing this challenged, capable, and industrious young man, she felt some measure of angst because she had asked so much of him. Was it on account of financial constraints that she gave Arthur summer jobs one would usually hire contractors to complete? Or was this just a continuing education opportunity for a Hoffmann School graduate to live up to his potential?

A letter from Arthur's mother dated August 17, 1951, thanks my mother for a camp experience for Arthur when he was 8, and for all of it:

> Ann, I've been searching for words to thank you for the wonderful summer you've given Arthur and for the many kindnesses you've shown us all, but somehow these are things which go beyond words, as expressions of the heart and spirit, and there doesn't seem to be anything adequate I can say to let you know what these things have meant to us. I can assure you that none of your kindnesses has gone unnoticed by us, and I know you have realized the comfort they have brought and the opportunity for renewal that they have afforded us at a time when these were sorely needed.

SHE WAS THE SCHOOL

It is fifth grade and our teacher, Betty, has charged me, on account of my living at the school, with checking in from time to time over the weekend on our white rats, one of which is pregnant. It was scary duty. I was both enamored of the rats, their beautiful white fur coats and ruby-red eyes, and distressed by their enormous tails. When I would hold them to show how brave I was, how I really thought they were cute, and to introduce them for example to a squeamish friend of my mother's visiting on a weekend, I would cringe as the tail crossed my arm and reminded me of the authentic ratlike quality of these endearing pets.

These classroom rodents were not like the big black water rats that found their way up from the Hudson River to the school grounds. Gardener Tony's biggest and most watchful cat, Midnight, who slept in the gutters of the driveway and lived 18 years, enjoyed scuffling with those terrifying beasts. I believe Midnight left his victims around because occasionally our little Welch Terrier, Folly, would find them. Folly's predecessor, the big cocker spaniel that had a nervous breakdown when he was reportedly stolen from our grounds by a caretaker on the nearby estate of Wave Hill (where the Queen Mother stayed when she visited the states) would have run from such carnage. But tiny Folly would much too often deliver to me, even lay on my lap, a stiff-bodied, dead river rat, its ugly mouth open baring its teeth as perhaps it had in its last defensive posture against the wrath of Midnight. Sometimes it was hard to distinguish these smooth white, red-eyed, pink-tailed, cage-bred creatures from those monsters of the deep.

It was also always a bit forbidding going downstairs from the warmth of our little apartment to the empty dark school building which felt, with all the children and teachers gone, more abandoned mansion than beloved schoolhouse. With so many different chambers, the downstairs seemed vast and disjointed, where our apartment was compact and contiguous. Our cozy flat on top of the Hoffmann School embraced us with familial stories, intercultural pride, physical connection, and visible color and beauty. Venturing downstairs alone in nonschool hours meant leaving all that for the echoing floors and dark lonely majesty of the building below. But I rose to that challenge as a responsible caretaker of the pregnant white rat and her mate in Betty's classroom.

I would run from the apartment door across the balcony, down two steps and up two more, quickly open the door and see no activity, and race back to the safety of home. The real responsibility here was to be at the ready if the pregnant rat was having her babies. Should that be happening—and as I think of it now, the task was enormous—I would have to remove the male rat from the cage lest he eat their young. The likelihood of this happening seemed slight and my biggest challenge that Saturday afternoon was to run from the apartment to the classroom and back without encountering an untoward creek or rattle in the empty building. But opening the door, there it was. Amid a symphony of soft squealing, the mother rat was emitting these small pink cylinders from her body, and I was terrified. I slammed the door, ran upstairs, and telephoned my teacher. I needed help and no one in my family had stomach or courage to assist me.

Betty arrived an endless while later after taking the bus to the Riverdale Avenue stop and walking down the hill with her son Leon, a boy about 3 years older than me, who wore dark horn-rimmed glasses, had a keen interest in and knowledge of science, and went to Horace Mann. Leon had come prepared with a slim cigar box. They entered the classroom and shook their heads. Babies were strewn around the floor, little corpses as testimony to my lack of bravery and excess of neglect. I cried quietly and with some measure of disgust as Leon put on a pair of rubber gloves and carefully lifted the little corpses, laying them in a line in his cigar box. Betty handily moved in and separated the parent rats as Leon brought the good news that two of the babies had survived. That meant a rat for each pair of us in the class of 1955 and we would care for them and nurse them to adulthood, each of us monitoring their growth in carefully decorated baby rat journals. Jacob had not remembered that we shared a baby rat and named it Willy, but my mother had saved that journal, as she seemed to save every drawing or paper or poem I created in my whole life at home. I had cheerfully entitled the journal "My White Rat Willy," and the story of baby-rat slaughter was neither repeated nor apparently remembered throughout the balance of the school year.

We all remembered Betty as a slim woman with excellent posture and an infrequent, if well-timed, smile. Photographs confirm that she dressed carefully in dark dresses with full skirts or tailored straight suits, conservative but well suited for her long legs and lean figure. She stands in these photos proudly and to the side of whatever child or occasion she attends: her students' graduation, theatrical offering, or dance recital. Her hands are carefully folded one on top of the other as teachers and administrators are prone to do. Only in one photo (taken with my Brownie camera), that of a field trip to the Bronx Zoo, do I see the boys in my class—Jacob with thick book in hand, Stephen wearing his own Brownie on a string round his neck, Arthur disassembling, leaning in—all cuddling around her. Her mouth, well-defined by red lipstick, curls into a slight smile with that particular twist that almost can be interpreted as a snarl.

Betty's ingenious capturing of his attention around fractions and balsa wood impressed Arthur, and I know that she enthusiastically welcomed my alternative interpretations of assignments: a short children's book or limerick about whatever person in history was supposed to occupy an essay. Indeed, her positive recognition of my reinterpretation of assignments set me up for some disappointments at my next school. For example, I knew that Betty would have found creative my response to our seventh-grade assignment (at the Riverdale Country School) to do a report on a country of our choosing. Instead of selecting some place real, I chose to invent a country, along with its form of government, religions, and legislature. I approached every detail of my project with excitement and was stunned by the teacher's reaction when I attempted to present my descriptive scrapbook, filled with such magazine cutouts as a beautiful photo of the Taj Mahal that I had designated as the home of my country's highest court. I was made to do the assignment over. Humiliated, I did a half-hearted report on the birds of New Guinea. Betty would have celebrated my insight and industry. After all, you had to learn quite a bit about what makes a country a country to invent one of your own.

In spite of all this, I think of Betty as a traditional teacher. We had spelling quizzes first thing every day, for which I studied every morning before school, keeping the correct spelling of words in mind for exactly as long as it took me to take the tests. We studied cursive writing and even on our carefully ruled tablets were never able to match the magnificence of Betty's artful chalkboard demonstrations. We daily, if not more frequently, took turns reading aloud in class, from our reading texts surely, but also from *Weekly Readers,* science textbooks, and prose and poetry that we had written ourselves, as opportunities or assignments would arise.

At Hoffmann School the floating teachers—specialists who would take out of the classroom a child who needed extra academic or social support—also worked with the especially advanced students (perhaps Jacob was one of them) to extend their experiences beyond classroom level. Challenge was as much a mandate at the Hoffmann School as competency. One child's challenge might be keeping up; another's reaching way beyond what was happening in class. I didn't have out-of-class time on either count. I read well with comprehension and aloud with expression; I excelled at spelling and math quizzes on account of my strong short-term memory; and though I sensed they resented that I was the principal's daughter, I "got along unusually well" with my peers.

In my sixth-grade report card in 1955, Betty raves about me: "A fine sense of humor. Is an independent and critical thinker; has an excellent memory; excellent work habits; avid reader; has creative talent." Recommending me for seventh grade at the Riverdale Country School, Betty summarizes my *S* grades (at Hoffmann, you could get *S* for Satisfactory, *I* for Improving, or *N* for Needs Improvement) in the areas of importance at Hoffmann School (Emotional Habits; Thinking Habits; Work Habits; Physical Aspects; Language and Literature; Music and Dancing; Arts and Crafts) with a glowing review: "Jessica is an excellent student and will do outstanding work in her next school. She has been very cooperative, and it has been a pleasure to have been her teacher. Jessica has an unusual sense of responsibility [guess she forgot about the white rats], is mature in her judgment, and very capable. She has a knack for making friends and getting along with people. I shall follow her career with interest." It all reads to me like standard fare designed to make whomever at my next school reads it happy to have accepted me, but I am caught off guard and moved, perhaps because I know what it is to love teaching and to love my students, perhaps because I loved Betty, by her last sentence: "I know I shall envy her teachers."

Betty seemed strict to us, and with eleven children in two grades in one room—all but one of them boys—she had a lot to handle even as individual attention must certainly have come more easily than in a public school classroom of 25. It had been Betty's son Leon who brought Betty to the school. Leon started Hoffmann School in first grade and was promoted from third directly to fifth only to discover that the fifth-grade teacher was leaving and there was a vacancy. Leon told his mother about the job opportunity at Hoffmann School and his enthusiasm resulted in the discomfort of being in his mother's class for the balance of the year. That didn't work out, and he left for the local public school near his house on 187th Street and Broadway, where in a rough and disorganized setting in which he dodged spitballs and felt he "couldn't learn," he witnessed the awful sight of his fellow classmates in the sixth grade beating up his teacher. He was grateful when Betty found for him and helped get him a scholarship to the brainy and more structured Horace Mann.

Betty's husband, a postal worker who was shorter than Betty (significant in my literal world in which men were supposed to be taller than women), died at 96. Betty herself had just passed away at 91 the year before I found and spoke with now 66-year-old Leon. I would have loved to talk with her and regretted my timing. Betty had died of a chest illness, Leon told me, and had left this world with all of her faculties—"no pun intended." When first asked, he reported that Betty had left Hoffmann School on "good terms" with my mother for higher wages in the public school system where she taught in two other schools for a total of 15 more years, before retiring with her husband to Florida. I was impressed that even though she had a permanent place in my memory in that second-floor classroom at Hoffmann School, Betty had gone on to two more teaching chapters in a very long life.

Leon saw my father as tall, dark, handsome, and extremely warm. My mother he found more problematic and presumed to speak for more employees than his own mother—for the music teacher and the school secretary with whom his mother was friendly and had stayed in touch—when he described Ann Hoffmann as having "rocky relationships" with several people who worked around the school. He said that his mother, a veteran teacher about the same age as my mother, enjoyed the freedom that Ann Hoffmann gave her in her classroom—she could teach anything and shared profoundly Ann Hoffmann's belief that "every child, no matter what was said, had real potential."

Dick Robinson described Ann's leadership style simply: "She was very definite and clear about what she wanted and had no hesitancy about telling you what it was." Further, "she tended to be impatient with people she supervised and the teachers had a lot of complaints about that. . . . She was a firm hand and there was a consistency to the place, and what she demanded from the teachers was always consistent." Consistent, and her way. She insisted on "doing things the way she wanted to do them which fortunately turned out to be the right way for a lot of kids." For his own part, Dick was "always aware of the two aspects of her personality; one was this tough demanding lady executive type and the other sensitive, sweet, supportive, funny. There were parts of her I couldn't stand," he confided, "and parts of her I loved to pieces. . . . Her usual thing was to refer a child at 9 in the morning and to ask at 3 p.m. in the afternoon whether I had completed treatment. Her favorite phrase was 'Get with it, Professor' and she was great to work with, and we from the very beginning had a special relationship." I asked Dick why my mother called him "Professor." "Because she felt while she was an outspoken plain speaker, I was like a professor—that is, not plain spoken. I was Harvard educated and not as direct as she was. I don't think she ever accused me of using jargon, which I always tried to avoid, but apparently not successfully. I think she thought I was professorial in that sense."

It occurred to me that it might have been the younger inexperienced teachers who came and left. Veteran teachers like Betty had seemed devoted to my mother, to have "worked things out" as Dick said he and

Ann did, and to stay on for many years. But there were exceptions to the veteran rule. Teachers like Domenick A. Capone (everyone but my mother called him "Dom") originally came as a teenager to work at the Hoffmann School Day Camp. It was the summer after he graduated from Roosevelt High School in Yonkers and was off in the fall to Boston College. I first met Domenick that summer. He was heavy-set and sixties cool with shiny curly hair and a gold chain that he wore even when he swam. He had two friends who also worked at the camp; one was the lifeguard John, and they were hilarious—always making fun of each other. What seemed the most hilarious was that they called each other by their mothers' names: "Ethel, get over here." That sort of thing.

Anyway, as I would never have predicted, Dom fell in love with children and with teaching. My mother had said from the start that he was a "natural." How did she know? Under my mother's direction, he worked every summer at the camp, and then went on to earn two master's degrees in education. In my mother's last years, as the cancer she was fighting took its toll on her strength and energy, she engaged Domenick, whose son went to Hoffmann from kindergarten through sixth grade, as her assistant director.

The summer after my mother's death in February 1980, Dom took over as director of the day camp. In a letter to parents dated February 25, he wrote: "Anna Hoffmann was dedicated to the care, comfort, and happiness of the little ones. I too shall oversee their summertime recreation and growth in this tradition. Ever mindful of the high ideas of the Hoffmann learning experience, I hope to help your children enjoy to its fullest the summer of 1980."

The following fall, a dedicated and longtime French teacher, Marianne Perotta, assumed the position of director of the Hoffmann School. By that time Domenick was a master teacher who had served as an administrator in the Bronx public schools. Along with three other dedicated teachers, Marianne and Dom struggled to keep the Hoffmann School and camp going, but with little success. It was difficult to go on without my mother's remarkable charisma, administrative acumen, ferocity of faith in the most unlikely children, and cadre of devoted parents. Like my mother, and like Rebecca, this dedicated group of passionate teachers was more interested in children than in school budgets. With a surplus of scholarships and a yearly tuition about a third of what other independent schools were charging, the closing of the Hoffmann School after the camp season in 1985 was inevitable. After its closing, Domenick (perhaps unsurprisingly) went on to be Superintendent of Special Education for the New York Public Schools. His son, reflecting what might by now seem a trend toward empathetic professions for Hoffmann School graduates, had grown up to be a child psychologist.

Leon's claim that his mother was dissatisfied with the salary at Hoffmann School had a resonant ring. Yellowing pages of correspondence from 1946, when my mother's leadership was just taking hold, show the school was working out an agreement with the Teacher's Union to assuage union faculty members who were dissatisfied with their contracted salaries. Judy, a friend of mine from Riverdale, taught kindergarten at the Hoffmann School 20 years later, after she graduated with undergraduate and master's degrees in education from Boston University. Judy was always suspicious of her low salary and when she heard from another teacher that that teacher, also just starting out, was getting more money, she decided it was because she was a "family friend" that she was paid less. I asked her if she had ever confronted my mother with this suspicion and she said it hadn't occurred to her to ask or even to question that what the other teacher told her might not be true.

Judy's first year of teaching at Hoffmann School was filled with excitement and ingenuity. She cultivated plants for her new classroom, made beautiful nametags for the children's cubbies, and had a harrowing time with a fish eating fish that keep clearing her fish tank. Like Betty, she enjoyed independence in her classroom and noted that while she felt she was "ahead of her time," utilizing Boston University's latest version of project-based learning in her classroom, the teacher across the hall had graduated from Bank Street and "strictly employed" the traditional Bank Street method. The children in Judy's classroom were diverse in terms of color and background, and she found them all bright and capable even as she suspected that the older children in the classrooms upstairs were less "normal" and had problems. She explained, "We didn't have the words *learning disabilities* or *behavioral problems* then."

By the time Judy worked at the school, Ann Hoffmann was 52 years old, a decade older than she was at graduation of the class of 1955. She was a seasoned administrator in comparison to the young director my father wrote about in the early 1940s. But as Judy spoke of her happy first year of teaching and the approval from a distance she felt from Ann Hoffmann, I remembered the story of the young director hiding behind a curtain in the kindergarten room in which a small boy was called "bad" for his unwillingness to nap. I was sure that my mother no longer hid in the shadows to assess and assist young teachers, and perhaps knew in an instant which teachers had promise. My mother had told me my friend was a "natural" and, again assuming myself as school and my voice as that of my mother, I shared these compliments with Judy 25 years after my mother's death.

Ann Hoffmann, Judy told me, "was a very large presence in the school. She *was* the school. She sat in her office or walked through the halls calling for this or that . . . and she was right on top of everything. There was a certain fear of her as a boss. You didn't mess around. She was the principal of the school and that was her job and she stepped right into the role. I think there were a couple of teachers there who had been there for a while and had a rapport with her, but with the younger ones, she was 'strictly professional.'"

Judy knew she had been right that Ann was satisfied with her work in her classroom when Ann asked her back for another year. Beyond that, she saw little of her. She thought maybe it was because the older children were a handful and because she was doing very well. She had the distinct feeling that if Ann Hoffmann hadn't been satisfied with her work, she'd have heard about it. I was surprised that my mother wasn't more "hands on" as a mentor to a young teacher like Judy whom she saw as talented. But that was her way of course. She never, as far as I could see, closely monitored my work in the summer day camp's Arts and Crafts Barn that I began to direct at age 17, after two summers of assisting and apprenticing with veteran teacher Charles Taylor, who for about a decade also taught art at the school.

Charles was a painter and when children arrived to the art room, he always seemed engaged with a work in progress of his own. He wore a gray smock that was covered with paint and would be chipping glue or dried clay from his fingers, but when a new class arrived, he would stand up to his considerable height and his broad face would break into the warmest wide grin. He was happy to see everyone, in the hall, on the playground, but especially arriving to make art with him.

Charles was a wonderful teacher and among the techniques I learned assisting him were his well-known phrases for keeping children at work: "Cover that paper with color!" and my absolute favorite, "Every mistake is on purpose. Figure it out!" Lifer Bruno told me that Charlie was a great teacher: "I loved the guy. He was so cheerful, but he had a quick temper and his blood would boil." I remembered Charlie's explosions— so outsized that the children didn't know if they should howl or laugh. They did neither, sometimes stifling the giggle that could as easily refuel as dissolve his quick-lived rage. But they were never afraid; his love for them was always certain. I am sure Ann Hoffmann asked him to try not to lose his temper. I could tell they had a close rapport, and I know she was proud of his program. She would point out to me as something to emulate the honoring way he displayed children's art. Each piece would be carefully mounted, with information about the image (a title, a brief bio about the child artist, and sometimes even an artist's comment on the work) written on a separate piece of paper, never on the child's work.

I was moved by Charlie's giving the same attention to children's artwork as to the work of professional artists. This would be an idea that engaged me throughout my work with children in the Arts and Crafts Barn. I noticed that many of their drawings had the same freedom and expressivity to which I aspired in my after-hour drawing classes at the Art Student's League. I mounted displays for their parents in which I placed the children's work beside the work of great artists—a kindergartener's painting next to a print of a Miro; a drawing from our blind drawing exercises (you couldn't look at the paper as you worked) next to elegant sketches from the *New Yorker*. The parents were amazed, and I unknowingly had identified at 17 a topic for doctoral studies some 20 years later.

In Charlie's report of the art program of 1961, I see that he is well informed on the prevailing art education literature of the time. He speaks of Viktor Lowenfeld's stages of development[12] and the degree to which he considers them in designing his curriculum. Indeed, Charlie writes quite philosophically about the various projects he oversees, emphasizing completion, fineness, and joy. And although I assume he feels the autonomy of all Hoffmann School teachers, I hear my mother's voice in his statement, "We hope that finally each child will be able to lift himself by his own bootstraps, as it were, to a greater potentiality in himself. Few will remain as artists with paint or clay, but we hope that all will become artists in whatever field into which life takes them."

Ann Hoffmann did once caution me "not to play favorites" when I made extra time in what would have been my breaks between summer camp classes for a rough-edged little boy I lovingly nicknamed "Trouble." Trouble seemed generally unhappy but truly excited at the thought of making Popsicle-stick forts. He was really engaged in collecting the sticks at home and I let him work on his fort in free times but refused to include such pedestrian crafting in what I had designed as a creative arts curriculum. Beyond that caution from Ann Hoffmann, I was like Arthur repairing the roof or Judy teaching for the first time. "Okay Jessie," she'd instruct my teenaged self, "you have 200 children coming for arts and crafts every day, please write up your curriculum for the summer and get it to me by the end of the week." But her assessments of my write-ups were as offhanded as what most teachers say about children's art work: "beautiful," with that edge of affectionate disinterest that lets children know the teacher hasn't really had or made real time to look. "Excellent," she would say, although I was never sure she read it carefully, even as I refined it on my own—and frequently—as a result of what I thought worked best each of the three summers I taught art.

My curriculum was based around themes (the circus, animals, humans, the galaxy, the city, your inner self) that the children and I discussed seminar style at the start of each session before they went off to explore their focused ideas individually or collectively in different media each day. All the children at their different ages and with their different foci and skills every day explored self-selected aspects of the same topics. It made for lively collective murals, great exhibits, and a range of opportunities for experiencing the multiple points of entry that the arts allow—or in Hoffmann School terms, the equally valued individual expressions of any one topic. Throughout it all, Ann Hoffmann stood even for me at a distance that felt like approval. But perhaps the greatest compliment came when that last summer Ann put a rush on my "typing up" my summer class plans and critique so she could show it to the incoming new art teacher at the school.

Judy's first—and last—year teaching at Hoffmann School must have coincided with Betty's last year. Leon began his recollection of his mother's leaving with a similar story—that it had been on account of low pay, and perhaps even the thought of inequity among paychecks. But as we spoke further, he reconsidered across half a century that our mothers might have had some disagreement over a child in Betty's class, a child who had a malignant tumor and was dying. Leon believed that Ann Hoffmann had told Betty not to bother to teach this child to read because reading was hard for him and his time was short, and that Betty had fought to teach the child, believing that learning would sustain and not discourage him in whatever time he had left. In that "everything worked out perfectly" way in which we recount the triumphs of our parents or have heard these stories told, Leon spoke of his mother's victory, the child's outliving anyone's expectation, and his mother's decision to leave the school on good terms rather than tussle again with my bellicose mom.

Ann Hoffmann may have seemed adversarial to adults, but children appreciated her ardent advocacy. I am moved by a letter of condolence that my father has saved for me:

February 10, 1980

Dear Mr. Hoffmann,

I heard from my mother this morning, and she told me the news of your wife's passing. I want you to know that when I heard the news I felt a great loss inside me. Mrs. Hoffmann was the only person besides my own family who ever took an interest in me as a person. She was a remarkable woman who took chances on people who at one time in their lives were not meeting their potential adequately.

It is very difficult for me to tell you the sorrow I feel for you and your family but also for myself. Mrs. Hoffmann was a woman whose caring and concern for others will never be matched ever again. When I came to the Hoffmann School 8 years ago, I was having many severe academic problems and I never believed that I would be able to make anything out of my life. Mrs. Hoffmann however did believe in me and her love and caring for me made me what I am today.

I never thanked her for what she has done for me over the years and I only wish she knew the way I felt. If there is one person in my whole life, WHOLE LIFE, who made such an impact on Jeremy Fox, it would be your wife. If there is anything I can do for you or your family during this sad period in your lives, please ask me. Mrs. Hoffmann has given me so much and I only wish I could return the warmth and caring she has felt for me.

With all my love and sympathy,

Jeremy Fox

Chapter 5

Behind the Door

The family, including Bruce the dog, around 1950.

HER WARM NEST

IN OUR SCHOOL-TOP APARTMENT a long hall connected our parents' bedroom, the bedroom I shared with my sister, the tiny shower-stalled bathroom that we four shared, and the small study that doubled as living room, tripled as dining room, quadrupled as library, office, or family room. The functional transformations of the study all occurred through the moving to the center as dining table or placing back to the edge of the room my father's mighty desk, reportedly a sixteenth-century treasure that looked quite American Arts and Crafts but was held together authentically by six wooden pegs. Ann Hoffmann's warm nest was feathered with such treasures through which both sides of the family held us in a warm embrace.

Ann and Malcolm in the 1950s.

Like Chester's antique throne downstairs, the desk had been collected by our great aunt Therese, a Russian-born decorator whose nickname, because of her luminous nature, was Sunshine. Her sister Jane, on the other hand, the only Republican in our family, was called Chiefie on account of her bossiness. Sunshine and Chiefie were older sisters to school founder Rebecca Hoffmann, nicknamed "Buddy," I assume because she was a friend to all. Among the Hoffmann siblings (seven in all), the closest relationships seemed to persist between Sunshine and Chiefie, a year apart in age, and Rebecca and Abraham (my father's father) who was 2 years younger than she. Abraham was both concerned and proud that Rebecca had forfeited the comforts of their family home to take up the causes of the poor and oppressed, and he was ever grateful to Rebecca for helping his wife and children while he was away in upstate New York in an experimental TB sanatorium similar to those described in Thomas Mann's novel of the same era, *The Magic Mountain*. Abraham's untimely death at 39, shortly after the death of his youngest child Gertrude, would devastate my father and kick-start for his mother her deep emotional decline and long-term hospitalization. It was in response to these losses, that Rebecca had offered her school as a safe haven—an alternate home—for her almost grown nephews: my father and his brother David.

As the story goes, the Hoffmanns, although they were Jewish, had lived in anti-Semitic Moscow by permission of the czar. One explanation was that the family had brought from Vienna to Moscow an important perfume factory, some iteration I believed (did they open a branch?) of the French company Houbigant. I am not sure if that belief is based on fact, fiction, or the empty bottles that we found and reused for the fragrances in our play perfumery. The Hoffmanns were in any case a creative family of heady folks with close familial ties, a love of language, literature, chess, and a fierce drive for education and professional success.

Great-grandfather Hoffmann, presumably having learned chemistry in his father's perfume factory, brought to the United States (along with his family) a secret formula for something called the unbreakable doll ("Can't Break 'Em") that he patented in 1892. He opened the American Doll and Toy Manufacturing Company on W. 13th Street that his wife and children kept running after his death from tuberculosis at 54. My grandfather Abraham, a graduate of Mercury College with command of nine languages, worked in and then oversaw the doll factory while he attended law school at City College. The Hoffmann children demonstrated the family's strong work ethic and drive—what my father called the "Judeo-Puritan tradition of the necessity to work and succeed." Sunshine and Chiefie were decorators; Abraham was an attorney; Rebecca a social worker and educator; one brother an assistant financial editor for the New York Times; the other an inventor of some kind of plastic furniture sold in his factory in Chicago.

I was always curious about anti-Semitism—what it was that industrious, inventive people like we Hoffmanns had done or looked like or fallen into that made others want to reject us. When I found out that I was named Jessica because my father was having beers at the moment of my birth with a lawyer in Washington named Jesse Clemenko, I was disappointed that I was not, as I thought, named after Shylock's daughter Jessica in Shakespeare's *Merchant of Venice*. But I learned that Shylock was the quintessential stereotype, the embodiment of the image of Jews as shrewd in business, the horrible use of the word *Jew* to suggest cheating someone out of his money. The Hoffmanns' management of money seemed absolutely antithetical to all that.

My father, one of the few Jewish boys in his freshman class at Harvard College, pieced together the $400 yearly tuition out of loans, scholarships, and assorted gifts from family members. Malcolm's mother, left alone to raise two boys after the deaths of her daughter and husband, simply couldn't afford it. The daughter of a rabbi and the graduate of a business program, this grandmother whom I never met defied stereotype.

Her misjudgment in real estate was legendary. Doubting further development, she sold for almost nothing a parcel of land in White Plains (the suburb in which she had raised her children) that would become either part of a major highway or a lucrative shopping mall. Rebecca, enmeshed in the work of settlement houses and orphanages, was imbued with the spirit of invention and love of children that had inspired her doll-making father. But she had created a school that she kept and that kept her on the edge of financial ruin. Wherefore among these Jewish women was the association with money and shrewdness?

I didn't understand discrimination but wondered how a love of perfume could obscure prejudice and hatred. I was told alternately or additionally that the Czarina would not even select a handkerchief without the aesthetic input of Sunshine, who continued her design consultation from her apartment at 729 Park Avenue where she and Chiefie, outliving all their siblings, thrived well into their seventies. These two women contributed greatly to the sustenance of the Hoffmann School, not only with gifts of heroic-looking furniture, but also with emotional and financial support. They had kept Rebecca from falling off the edge of fiscal disaster and they helped Malcolm and Ann secure the property when Rebecca passed away. There was a sense of continuing what their sister had created; a sense of gratitude to my mother for carrying the mantle; and a sense that enveloped our cosmos that children (all or any of them) were the most important, creative, and vulnerable individuals in the world.

Sunshine was definitely striking and wore old-fashioned lace-trimmed dresses that accented her stately figure, hennaed red hair, and faraway dream-filled face. Chiefie, less delicate in appearance, had long white hair, wore no makeup, and dressed mostly in tailored black suits, sometimes set off with a bowler hat and pearls. She smoked constantly and seemed to have always ready at her side a copy of today's *New York Times* and a water glass half-filled with vodka, no ice. On account of these great ladies and the lush life their family left behind in Moscow, our home and the school had a steady supply of the most wonderful costumes, velvet robes laden with beads and pearls, lace vests, ornate headdresses, and long gowns so tiny at the waist that a child my size could not fit in them without the corsets of days gone by.

Down the hall of our apartment beyond the study that housed the mighty desk, the walk-through kitchen led to a long wall-shelved pantry and opened on one side to the attic-like room in which we children would play perfumery and adults would iron clothing and store necessities. Beyond the kitchen to the right, a small hallway led to the bedroom and bath reserved for my grandmother, Nanny, who for 2 years of the two-plus decades she lived with us shared her room with her daughter— my mother's youngest sister—Gigi. Their bathroom held the footed tub in which we had our nightly baths supervised by Lucy. There was a wonderful toilet that was flushed by a chain hanging from a wooden box overhead. My aunt Gigi, then an NYU college student in her early twenties, taught art at Hoffmann School and painted the tub and that box light green with large red polka dots.

I loved that bath, loved that compact apartment in which so many of us moved about and ate together every night, loved the sound of Italian spoken softly between my mother and her mother and sister when whatever they were saying was not for our ears. My mother told us that it was my father's decision that we as babies not learn both Italian and English; something about the Italian keeping us from speaking a pure English— the kind his Ohio-born mother valued—with the English edge favored by his Harvardian or Anglophile predilections. It wasn't until he was near his death in 1997 that I told my father how disappointed I was not to have learned both languages and how hollow his pronunciation objection had seemed to me. "Was that my reason?" he asked with a wry smile that challenged his 86 years. "With so many women in my house," he explained, "I think I just couldn't have stood it if you all spoke a language I didn't understand."

Though it was home to our immediate and extended family, and occupied part of the time by Estelle, Lucy, and others who kept house, the apartment never seemed crowded. Nanny sewed amazing curtains for the pink and light blue room that I shared with my sister, and as I grew older, she made clothes for me that I designed by drawing a picture. I would give my grandmother the black-watch-plaid pleated wool skirt she'd made for me a few months before and a drawing of an A-line jumper that I wished were real. When I awoke, there it would be—the jumper I'd envisioned, black-watch-plaid and created through the night in just my size, hanging on the Dutch door of our room. Such magic in that room! Tony the gardener would surprise us Easter mornings with baby chicks or bunnies in baskets under our beds. On my sixth birthday Captain Video told me on TV that there was a gift hidden in my room and there it was. An elf named "E-O" would visit me at night in the dark after my sister was asleep and speak to me in a little voice that never really sounded exactly like hers.

My mother would tell us that growing up in the grand house her father built in Brooklyn, Nanny spent many hours in her room, sewing beautiful clothes that she wore on their regular trips to the Metropolitan Opera House or clothes for her daughters, whose various sizes, like mine, she knew by heart, and ultimately even the Pagliaci costume my Uncle Nino would wear to play that part at the City Center Opera. My maternal grandfather, Vincenzo Luciano, whom I never met, was not much taller than my grandmother although his driver's license puts his weight at well over 200 pounds. In photos of him, I see in his face my mother's rounded high brows and steady gaze, her empathetic countenance, and a half smile that I hope is like mine. He cuts a dashing rotund figure, alternately dressed in three-piece tweed suits or a boating captain's blazer and hat, neatly combed white hair, always with a cigarette in his hand. He died of a heart attack in his late fifties in 1943, the year that I was born. It must have been the stress of the depression, the loss of his great business and his wonderful homes, bad investments, overdue loans, his weight, the cigarettes. My uncle Nino, his only son said his father "died of a broken heart."

A most successful proprietor of a marble-cutting factory, Grandfather Luciano had a large plant and 400 employees before the depression brought him to financial ruin. His company, Atlantic Marble, laid the marble in all or a branch of the Museum of Natural History, and Nanny used to tell us about having lunch with Eleanor Roosevelt at the opening of the museum. We wondered how that must have been for Mrs. Roosevelt, given Nanny's indifference to English. Nanny would describe the floors and wainscoting of her Brooklyn home and the shade of marble that they were—white, like the sand in the beaches of Palermo, a stone's throw from her birthplace in Santa Ninfa. Uncle Nino (who moved from opera to construction) dreamed of buying and renovating the family home, designating it as a day care center to serve what had evolved into an economically depressed community.

Renovation had become Nino's specialty from the Tavern on the Green in Central Park to the Cooper-Hewitt Museum. In the 1950s Uncle Nino renovated that attic-like room in our apartment in which Arthur and I had played perfume factory. Breaking through walls, he transformed the awkward space into a 30' living room, with a wall on one end that was exposed fieldstone and on the other, a picture window with a staggering view of the Hudson River. My mother would take her morning coffee before any of us woke up seated in front of that great window. It was unusual to see her seated and at rest, her legs crossed in front of her with the edge of her silk dressing gown falling from her rounded knee, her soft blue eyes hypnotized by whatever she was studying with restorative intensity. My parents had glorious parties in that grand room—my mother's wonderful food lavishly presented on the beautiful china and silver that she ardently collected, the wine glasses filled by my father's persistent pouring arm, the conversation always lively if heavily interspersed with my father's passionate monologues, all of which were adoringly received. In 1964 I would be married in that room in front of the same window that provided daily vistas for my hard-working mother.

The threads in the close-knit weave of our family life came from far away places, from people who faced the perils of discrimination and the challenge of self-definition—just like the children of the Hoffmann School. I wonder how familial journeys that spanned outside and in may have predisposed Ann Hoffmann to the needs of the outlier children to whom she was drawn. Of course, she would insist that all children require the kind of open affirmation and dogged determination to which our families were dedicated, the belief that any of us can and all of us should work hard to create, succeed, and care for others. These tenets were rooted on both sides of the vast ocean that I had to name in geography tests in school. My father sometimes spoke of our good fortune in having roots both in the aesthetic and creative spirit that he associated with Italians and the intellectualism and intelligence that he associated with Judaism:

> In the Western world two of the oldest living cultures are the Italian and the Hebrew. . . . it is public record that few other strains have shown such lasting and communal concepts of family, affirming in daily life that the family is a mutual-aid society, a unit fortified against the assaults of circumstance. It is a derivative from this tradition that in both the Italian and Jewish cultures, home life is centered about the children, perhaps in painful recognition that if 60 years of happiness cannot be promised to anyone, 15 or 20 can. Life in Ann's childhood home was a warm nest for children. And so was life in ours.

SOCIAL ROOTS

In 1935, with just 60 students and more space than she needed in the school building at 215th Street, Rebecca offered housing not only to her nephews and other members of her extended family but to her friends who needed a place to stay. Three of these guest residents, Sasha and Freda and their son Dicky, had been evicted from their Greenwich Village apartment for failure to pay rent. Freda was a social worker like Rebecca and a close friend of the cofounder of the Catholic Worker's Movement, Dorothy Day. Her beloved Sasha was an artist, a poet, a player of music, and a ferocious hypochondriac. Sasha, who declared himself an unofficial grandfather to my sister when she was born in 1940, was greatly loved by my parents and remained their friend long after Rebecca's death. He and his wife would come to our school home in Riverdale and walk the grounds, accompanied by their then-grown son who was limited physically in his movement by what I think was a degenerative bone disease that seemed to challenge him intellectually as well.

I admired Sasha greatly. He was mysterious and oddly handsome— to me the quintessential poet with deep eyes, a slightly hunched-over, emaciated frame, and a permanent cigarette dangling from his bemused mouth. He was a visual artist by report only—no one had seen any of the canvases on which he was supposedly working—but he clearly preferred to read Pushkin than to paint. After his death, I was given the seven-string Russian guitar that he played along with a life-sized wooden carving of his head done by a young artist who taught at the school and was hopelessly in love with Sasha. I cherish these mementos of a character that seemed of a time and place that my children will never know. It was Sasha who taught me that suffering was essential to art and to life, and that complaints were a sign of well-being. Sasha's funeral was the first I'd ever attended, and it was there as a teenager that I heard the legendary Dorothy Day eulogize Sasha with eloquence and love. At an age at which I was certain that my own parents would never die, I watched speechlessly as Dicky, then almost middle-aged, took his leave as his father's body was removed at the crematorium. With his mother's arm around him, Dicky, a large and stony version of his expressive, vital father, raised his hand as if in farewell and said simply, "Well, Sasha, then that's it."

Sasha often and obviously wore pajamas under his dark sport coat because, he explained, he was so frequently sick and needing to go to bed that dressing completely for the day was overkill. As my father described him, "his whole personality was suffused with hypochondria." A teacup seemed attached to Sasha's right hand and its contents, depending on the day and his mood, were fortified with vodka. Dorothy Day wrote in her autobiography that Sasha and Freda's friend who ran the "Hoffmann

School of Individual Development" entrusted a dozen of the boarding children to Freda and Dorothy to care for them over a school vacation that she wished to be free.[13] The story seems as improbable as Day's understanding that Sasha and Freda were living with Rebecca because they were in fact teachers at the Hoffmann School. Some version of each of these accounts must be true, or perhaps, like the other jobs Sasha describes in this passage from my father's manuscript, they are both completely grounded in fiction.

> From time to time, parents of the school children were surprised to hear the school's phone answered by a deep foreign accent. Sasha . . . customarily conversed as follows: "This is Vladimir, the gardener speaking, nobody home. I take message." Or "This is Alexis the cook; the director she out. I take message." [My father] was delighted one day when he surprised Sasha in one of his humorous Poo-Bahish explanations. It seemed that one of the parents had heard the same voice on different occasions identify itself as cook, handyman, gardener, janitor, and a visiting professor from Equador. Sasha was deftly endeavoring to rationalize his inconsistent roles. His explanation was as follows:
>   "My full name is Vladimir Alexis Andraoff Poussiekof. When I function as a cook, I am known as Alexis. When I take care of the fire, I am known as Andraoff. In my capacity of janitor and gardener, I am simply Vladimir. And I have undertaken these tasks while visiting the United States. My real profession, as I told you before, is Professor of Social Anthropology at the University of Quito, in my mother country of Equador."

In the course of this exchange, Sasha failed to obtain either the name or telephone number of the person who had called or the caller's purpose. Apparently, he knew nothing of children or modern education and he and his family avoided appearances in the schoolhouse during the day. They were, my father tells us, "night flowers, allergic to the sun, and in time Sasha played the role of nocturnal jester and critic to Rebecca." Rebecca was lonely and needed her friends as much as they their place of rent-free abode, and probably, my father writes, "it was this core of loneliness which made Rebecca, throughout her life, surround herself with little children."

I am moved by my father's reference to a core of loneliness that may have caused Rebecca to surround herself with little children. The idea of surrounding oneself with children as one might with works of art to soothe a sorrow, fill a void, or heal a wound played mightily into my mother's educational approach. Had Rebecca inspired this insight? Rebecca was surely motivated by a vision of educational reform and social justice—a dream of making the world a better place—but it is less certain whether or the extent to which running a school filled some deep need for a family she chose or did not have time to cultivate. What is certain is that, given the full-time, year-round nature of her educational commitment, the having of friends and family beyond her school children had to happen in a physical space that was immediately adjacent to, if not overlapping with, her place of work.

On at least one occasion, on a Monday morning at the Hoffmann School when the young teacher who was my mother was preparing to take her kindergarten class out to play, a "drunk Russian" as she described him—a casualty from one of Rebecca's late-night parties in the living quarters of the school—was found asleep in the big closet where the balls and bats were kept, surprising my demure mother and the children who watched incredulously as she opened the closet door. Ann Hoffmann told me with loving exasperation of the quick step she had to do, the apology she would make to the slumbering body, the reassuring smile she would give to the children, the closing of the door, and the decision to play giant steps or whatever other game there was that did not require equipment from the sports closet.

My father described the school at this time as alive with animated children's voices in the day and with animated adult voices at night. According to secrets shared, one of these voices belonged to the dashing actor from the Moscow Art Theater with whom Rebecca was rumored to have had a child, a boy who died before he was 6 years old. No one seems to know or has been willing to tell me more. Among the hundreds of photos from the old days, I look with no success for signs of Rebecca's child. And I wonder how the loss of a biological child affected this surrogate mother to so many. Around my loss of a pregnancy, my mother told me to keep close watch for the child to whom I would now be available. The loss of a biological child positioned you to parent a child whom you might not otherwise have even known. Had this been Rebecca's comforting belief? Had it been my mother's? Where and how did my mother, who extended the tradition of Rebecca's boundless motherhood to another generation of Hoffmann School children, acquire that gain-filled interpretation of loss?

Whatever its source, the perspective no doubt sustained Ann Hoffmann through the several miscarriages she would endure. I remember the pain and sorrow around one such loss when she was 40 and I was 10, though no one fully explained it at the time. She had been resting after school on her bed, but saw from the window of our third-floor retreat, neighborhood children perched on the edges of the school pond. Out of anger for their trespassing and fear for their safety, she bolted out of her bed and down the three flights of stairs to the first floor, the additional outside stairwell off the back porch, and the pebbly driveway down the hill to the pond. I watched from the window, amazed as always at how quickly she moved even as her body, especially in its current condition, seemed anything but agile. The children ran off laughing when my mother collapsed to the ground, bleeding for reasons I did not understand, weeping for reasons beyond her physical discomfort. How much I now wonder did Ann sacrifice to live to her end Rebecca's dream?

My father was 9 years old when his father died of tuberculosis 3 years after his little sister Gertrude had died of pneumonia. His mother's steady decline and startling paranoia—what they called at that time, "menopausal melancholia"—brought her to the mental hospital in which she died in her fifties. She had had a little sister named Gertrude, who died as a young child; her daughter named Gertrude died at age 4; and she never had the pleasure of meeting her granddaughter, my sister Gertrude. I was told that antibiotics would have saved both my grandfather and my great aunt; and of course some one or another antidepressant might have allowed my grandmother to live to meet us all. My great-grandfather and two of his other sons died younger than they should, one from a disease ("Spanish Influenza") that could have been treated by modern medicine. This was how history seemed real to me—that time before medicine when everyone in the family died young—and explained, my mother would tell me, my father's over-the-top concern whenever I or my sister had the slightest cold or sore throat. Lungs were a weak link in the Hoffmann family, and true to our history, I have asthma; both my father and his brother—heavy smokers in spite of their familial predilections—died of lung disease, although they lived into their eighties. Beyond those troubled lungs, what I associated with the Rebecca Hoffmann side of things was the throaty Russian accent that embellished my elegant great-aunts' take on English and evoked the same sort of attachment to another world as the persistent Italian of my mother's mother, Nanny.

I loved the deep edges of the speech of my Russian great-aunts, the way they threw themselves entirely into the articulation of certain emotive words. The "dearies, take care you rest" and "darlings" that pervade the letters they wrote my parents when they were first married and lived in Washington, D.C. The caring content of these missives ("Dear Mal, tell me about your work, how do you like it and is it interesting?") bring back to me the sounds of their wonderful voices and images of them gliding through their dark and baroquely decorated apartment. I hear Chiefie's passionate voice, arguing a point, exasperated with government, always up-to-date on what was happening in the world, considering positions from experts in the *The New York Times* or from the strongly opinionated guests at their soirees. Sharing the family's passion for theater she writes pleasantly to my mother in 1940 of opening night at the Theater Guild, the thrill of meeting the English actor Maurice Evans, the delight of seeing Helen Hayes in *Twelfth Night*.

Of course she ends the note with political outrage—this time at the CIOs (Congress of Industrial Organization's) "interference" with our defense program. I imagine Rebecca spoke with similar outrage and passion about her many causes, advocating for the orphans for whom she provided care at the Hebrew Sheltering Guardian Society or the child labor laws and kindergarten for the poor children that she represented as educational director of the New York Section Council of Jewish Women. Malcolm's mother complained that Rebecca chastised her soundly for helping little Malcolm at age 3 (a little older than I was when I was sent to Hoffmann School) to dress and undress each day. Rebecca felt that Malcolm was being deprived of the independence that the young children at her orphanage necessarily develop.

Children were Rebecca's passion, but so was democracy, and at nights, she led classes to prepare new immigrants to take the test to become American citizens. It was astonishing, therefore, for my father to discover that Rebecca, ardently vested in local and national politics, never actually became an American citizen and therefore could not vote. Reportedly, she was such a young baby when the family immigrated to this country that her father forgot to add her name to the list of his children who would become naturalized citizens. I am taken by the thought of the founder of the Hoffmann School as an outsider by birth, of her successor, my mother—a first-generation American—as newly inside herself. Both of them familiar with outside and in feathering nests for children—those quintessential outsiders to the mysterious land of adults. In a country in which everyone was an immigrant, including my husband's family whose immigration was much earlier than ours, was there some status attached to the length of time one's feet had rested on American soil? Would we find models for behavior in veteran footsteps or would we be inspired to new direction by those just joining the parade? The question remains.

My father wrote that Ann Hoffmann, "has always operated the school on the affirmation that children need the challenge, not only of the best of our culture, but also of the kind of social and personal relations which compromise our society at large." My father's view of Ann's democratic school was as a microcosm of society at a time in which people were deciding whether differences should be cultivated and celebrated or melted down into some sort of collective American brew. This debate continues in our schools today around such issues as the nearly impossible challenge of learning to read in English when another language is your first, or the question of whether it is somehow fairer to see all children as the same, rather than to honor (not tolerate) their differences. As it would today, the Hoffmann School embraced the authenticity of difference and eschewed the falseness of sameness. The children in Ann Hoffmann's wild garden were not even all flowers and the gardener's multifaceted vision lay proudly outside the norm. Both of the remarkable women who led the charge at Hoffmann School had roots in difference and otherness that were deep, and nonnative-speaking English voices that were articulate and strong.

In a letter dated August 24, 1939, four years before I was born, Chiefie writes to my parents in Washington, D.C.: "What do you think of the startling news, about Hitler-Stalin, the two countries that pretended to be the worst enemies and now swastika flags with red sickles flying in Moscow and people greeting 'Heil Hitler, Red front.' I wonder what you hear about it in Washington?" My father's letters are filled as well with commentary informed by a close watch on what is happening politically and socially in the world. Letters from my grandfather to his sister Rebecca, written 20 years earlier, address socialism and Trotsky and the "Jewish" issue in Germany and in the states. Abraham writes from his sanatorium in Trudeau, New York, that he celebrates the political and social activism that he sees at the heart of Rebecca's plan to make a school: "It is plain you have a very hard task in hand—but a very interesting and important one. It must be a most wonderful feeling in these trying times to know you are doing your bit." He tells Rebecca that he is thoroughly grateful for her help with his own "kiddies" while he is away. He is grateful for the games she has taught them and for his own part, says, "I am being sustained very appreciably by the abiding hope that I'll be able to return to usefulness and once again do something for my family and my country."

Throughout these pages of familial lore—fabric out of which a school was woven and on which a family was imprinted—there is everywhere a deep sense of social conscience, a firm belief that individuals are able and obliged to make a difference in their time. Materials from the Hoffmann School reflect this passionate view of life and justice, explaining that in the great adventure of learning, even as children surmount the many barriers that arise as the scope and development of their interests broaden, "they become better integrated to the complex mechanism we call our social order. But that mechanism is more than complex. It is fascinating, challenging; and education must start with the axiom that it is worth being a part of, that social problems are worth the solving, life worth the living." On such deep foundations the Hoffmann School would rest.

THE QUESTION OF RELIGION

Our family celebrated Russian Easter about a week after Passover, had both a Christmas tree and a Menorah, and bought new hats and coats to wear nowhere in particular on the traditional Easter Sunday. The religious significance of these holidays was entirely lost on me; just as I was unsure which of the great aunts went with which side of the family and to which houses of worship, if they ever went, they would go. I knew that mainstream Easter had to do with spring and parades and pastel clothes; Russian Easter with big parties and finely painted porcelain eggs; the Jewish high holidays with staying home from school in honor of our relatives, and Christmas with Santa Claus, lights, presents, and music from around the world. It wasn't as if we saw the relatives of German and Russian Jewish descent for some of the holidays and the Italian Catholic side of the family for others. It was always the same crowd for all the parties, with the exception of a very few of my paternal grandmother's family whom I never saw because they had never forgiven my father for marrying out of his faith.

My mother reportedly had been excommunicated from the Catholic church for marrying my father, but none of this seemed to have troubled her or her family. My parents considered organized religion divisive, the

Anna Luciano, first communion.

rituals associated with it useful only in bringing people together, and our religious heritage, if we insisted on having one, Jewish. Too many relatives had died on account of being Jewish for us to forget them and our origins. When his father was dying in a room nearby, my father at 9 sat with his brother David, aged 12, with whom he shared a room. The two boys decided together in whispers between their tears that if their father would be allowed to recover and live, if God could show to them his goodness in this small act of mercy, they would always be grateful to and believe in God. The story of this pact and God's failure to oblige was one of the numerous ways in which my father explained his agnosticism.

A letter from David to his father when he was 350 miles away from their home in White Plains, trying to heal in Trudeau, New York, gives me a vivid sense of the absence and longing the children endured. It is written with pencil in careful, childlike cursive writing on a long piece of paper, perhaps the length of legal-size stationary that David or someone for him has cut in half vertically and folded. It is dated July 1, 1918. David is 9, Malcolm is 6, and Gertrude is 4. Both Gertrude and her father would be gone in 4 years.

> Dear Papa,
> I am sending you my report card with this letter, and I am going to send you a ring I made in school. How is everything getting along with you? I am now in Grade 4a. Malcolm and Gertrude are writing to you. It was raining this morning and I could not go out, so I wrote this letter. We are all waiting for the day you come home. It is clearing up now, and I and Mal are going down. So good-bye, Papa. I hope you will get perfectly well and come home soon.
> Your loving, David

As to Catholicism, my mother talked little about it, but the wonderful sepia photo of her first communion helped inspire me to think more seriously about religious rites of passage. There she is at about 10 or maybe 11, looking more like 15, in a beautiful white silk dress and stockings with a cloche hat and a huge bouquet of flowers cascading from her lap. She looks very serious and as if she knows all about whatever she is supposed to know to be celebrated as she is. My mother received religious perspective from the person she often described as the most important woman in her life: her convent-educated grandmother, Donna Anna (her father's mother, who lived with them in Brooklyn) after whom she was named.

The notion of "convent-educated" erroneously suggested to me that Donna Anna was a nun. For my mother, it explained her grandmother's passionate love of books and the wisdom that she had to offer in times of uncertainty or distress. We were told more than once of my mother's horrific experience of having, as a child, to kiss her deceased grandmother who was laid out for a wake (how odd is that word?) in the family living room. Donna Ann, a vital beacon in my mother's life, was dead, dressed perfectly for viewing, and my mother was required to kiss her on the lips. Was it the terror and sorrow that went with this occasion that made death a subject we didn't discuss? Was it terror and sorrow and the hope that modern medicine could cure everything that led my mother to tell me as I was falling asleep that I should not worry about dying, that when I was old enough to die, "they'd have a cure for it." Terror and sorrow and her desire to overcome her last memory of her grandmother I always felt were somehow associated with my mother's ability to excommunicate Catholicism, just as it supposedly had her.

It was terror and sorrow that I associated with this terrible thing we couldn't talk about that had happened in Germany, this awful person named Hitler who was beyond the magic powers of reform that softened the edges of my dreams. My mother baffled me by saying that she would always identify herself as Jewish so that she would never have to live if the rest of us had to die on account of our heritage. It astonished me at 5 or 6—all of it, but especially her bravery.

"Would you love me no matter what?" I would ask as I was falling asleep. "If I were a bad person and had killed someone and had to go to jail, would you still love me?"

"Absolutely," she would say, giving no mention to what I'm sure would have been some measure of disappointment.

"And if we were all in a boat and I fell over and in order to save me, you had to drown, would you drown?"

"Absolutely," she would tell me. She would give her life so that I could live whenever she had the chance. I would fall asleep wondering what that must be like, wondering if I would ever feel that way about my own children, ashamed that I was pretty sure that I would never give my life for hers or my father's or my sister's. Not until I was a parent myself did I fully realize her point of view. I was at the ready with the same quick responses for my children, but they never asked such questions. I like to think they knew what I would say.

We Hoffmanns did have Seders at Passover and my father made fun of them, or perhaps it is more true to say that he had fun at them. He used to brag that he had the "fastest Seder" in New York, and we would move quickly through the little manuals that guide the event, pausing occasionally to contemplate a question like the relationship between the discriminating angel of death passing over the houses of the Jews and the thorny notion of the chosen people. I loved the preparation for the meal, the making of the sugary chopped-apple Charoses, representing the sweet times that the Jews had had in whatever period of history this holiday represented, while the bitter Maror or horseradish represented the hard times. Why were the Jews hated? That question persisted. Chosen and rejected at the same time. Was it all about the infrequency of blonde hair and blue eyes? Were there places where lightness was the norm and my dark hair and eyes might make me the ideal?

At around age 10, in 1954, I attended Hebrew School for a while, largely because it came to me, literally. The newly formed Conservative Synagogue in Riverdale was looking for a home for its school while its building was being constructed and my mother let them use the downstairs of the Hoffmann School for after-school classes. I participated in classes for a while and enjoyed the stories and songs, the sense of community, and the little bit of Hebrew that I learned. I thought it odd that the text book, which I didn't read, was called *When the Jewish People Was Young* and not "Were Young" and liked a lot the Hebrew name that I was given, Gelah, which meant "Joy." Joy was the name my father wanted to give me in the first place until my mother found out he had had a girlfriend with that name.

When the Hebrew School moved out to its new building on W. 250th Street, I occasionally attended classes, and conscientiously explored the possibility of preparing for a bat mitzvah though I feared that it could not happen, that I could not have a ceremony that said I was a grownup really Jewish girl if my mother was not really Jewish. I begged for a meeting to be held between my mother and the synagogue's leader Rabbi Kadushin, a playful, witty, and short round man whom I adored. Rabbi Kadushin was funny and wise and impressively both confident and relaxed about being a truly religious person. I asked my mother to be honest with him about her background and to ask the question for me as to whether I could have a real bat mitzvah. When she came home after the meeting, she told me there would be no problems. "What did he say?" I pleaded.

She told me, "'Mrs. Hoffmann,' he said to me, 'what beautiful blue eyes you have.'" There it was again.

I decided not to do the bat mitzvah in the end. It was too much hard work to become a genuine believer. At one point when the quest was still alive, my mother arranged for a private Hebrew tutor for me. He was a young student from Yeshiva University, a rabbi in training, who seemed always to have Noxema on his lips, a feature I found both endearing and repulsive. In my first attempts to get out of the preparations for my rite of passage, I explained to my tutor, Mr. Zenner, that I wasn't really sure there was a God. Much to my amazement, he quickly responded that there was a branch of Judaism even for that! It was after my insistence that I also was questioning the viability of organized religion and was reluctant to hang my hat in one chapel and not another, that he backed off, as did my family, who had anyway only ever been the kind of supportive that says "if this is important to you, it's fine with us."

I even wondered at the time whether my parents were a little bit relieved that I withdrew from it all. When I was deeply involved, I begged them to take the family to synagogue for the High Holidays. No one seemed interested in celebrating the Sabbath every Friday night even though I could say all the words in Hebrew to the prayer over the candles, but the High Holidays? They agreed and we all dressed up and went to the new synagogue only to find that we had missed it, and come a day late. Without apparent disappointment or remorse, and perhaps even fighting back a smile that I detected through my tears, my father took us instead for a big pasta dinner at the Stella D'Oro restaurant that had recently opened near Van Cortland Park.

It was not until many years later that I learned that my father had similarly been disenchanted with the preparation for his bar mitzvah, even though he found a way to go through with it. His maternal grandfather, Rabbi Newmark, had settled in New York as his final destination after the trip from Leipzig, Germany, to start a reform congregation in Zanesville, Ohio. The family insisted that Malcolm take the train from his home in White Plains to his grandfather's home in Brooklyn in order to study Hebrew in preparation for the bar mitzvah. The traveling was more than my father could bear, the Hebrew too hard for him to learn, and in order to "get him" through the ceremony, his grandfather ended up writing out phonetically in English what my father would say in Hebrew and also writing for my father a speech in English about coming of age. The first sentence of that speech read aptly, "I would like to begin by thanking my grandfather without whom none of this could have happened."

From such irreverent stories and experiences grew my understanding, albeit largely intuited, that for my family, Judaism was more an act of being than doing, even though we did "do" the Seders and light the candles of the menorah that was carefully placed beside the Christmas tree. Our tree, annually selected from leftovers on December 24, worked as well as any other Christmas tree even though my father preferred to call it a Hanukkah bush. Although as an adult I have touted all this as the informed child rearing of intermarriage, I can honestly say that as a child, while I trustingly embraced my intercultural foundations, I was generally completely and quite happily confused.

The weave of my developing being was mysteriously informed by the cross threads of Italy, Germany, Russia, lapsed Catholicism, and a priori Judaism, as well as the languages, traditions, and particular shades of Americanism that each of them wrought. As a child, I was even uncertain as to the boundaries between family and nonfamily. Was I not directly related for example to the beloved individuals who worked for the school: Estelle, who like my mother cooked for us at home? Or Emma, who like an aunt or grandmother helped me do my Christmas shopping on 231st Street? Or my dearest Lucy, who was my surrogate mother while my own ran a school and cared for more children than I could count? That these women had dark skin presented no barrier to my misunderstanding that we were directly related, and when it came to being Jewish and unloved therefore, I was proud to be associated with the dark outsiders and not the recent golden oppressors of the Aryan Race or the ancient gold-leafed Egyptian oppressors of days of old. And I loved whatever celebrations went along with my complex identity.

The empty chair for the Prophet Elijah who might come to join us at any minute, the hidden money we would find—a check for a million dollars signed by Elijah himself. It was wonderful, if never taken too seriously or fully explained, and I marveled that my mother, blue eyes and all, knew every detail of the holidays. My father was so generally irreverent that it surprised me that he became genuinely furious when we suggested we might like to go out to play or to school on either of the High Holidays: Rosh Hashanah or Yom Kippur. It's not like we celebrated them or ever successfully found our way to synagogue.

But I feel guilt, perhaps inherited along with the weak lungs and strong work ethic from all sides of my family, that my own children cannot tell you what the High Holidays are and have never enjoyed a Seder of my making in our own home. Even as my husband and I sought to rewrite the boundaries of organized religion and move from the rituals that divided people to an understanding of participation in all of it as citizens of the world, we abandoned the celebration of religious holidays and focused on family at Thanksgiving (thanks to my husband's New England roots) and trees and gift giving at Christmas (my favorite parts of it all).

My mother knew all the details of the celebration of Jewish holidays, I believe, for two reasons. The first is because as a child, she had religious training in her home in Brooklyn from a local rabbi who was facing hard times in the community. Her father had seized the dual opportunity of helping out the studious young man and having his five children learn about the Old Testament from a serious scholar. Perhaps she felt some connection to her own experience when she hired for me that scholarly young tutor with the very chapped lips.

Second, early in her career, my mother had taught at the Yeshiva of the Rockaways on Long Island. The Yeshiva and Horace Mann were the only places besides Hoffmann School where Anna Luciano would teach. And I suspect that it was student teaching she did at Horace Mann, which was, when she was a student, an experimental girls school on 120th Street—a laboratory for trying out ideas for the students of Teachers College. At the Yeshiva, my mother explained, she was called "Miss Ann" to avoid the association with Luciano, an improbable Jewish name. It had not occurred to me that the experience of calling one's teachers by their surnames allowed some particular insight into their origins, and I wonder if that was yet another reason—beyond the increased degree of intimacy and the notion of real rather than enforced respect—that the teachers at Hoffmann School were called by their first names. My mother was always the exception. She would introduce herself as Ann, but the children preferred to call her Ann Hoffmann.

Sorting through the boxes of ancient letters, I hear the loving mutually concerned voices of my parents' parents, their brothers and sisters, and uncles and aunts—all speaking to me without audible sound on yellowing pages that whisper "this is you." They speak in variegated voices, all of them all together, wrapped in and around each other's lives in and around the worlds of children and education. Religion in all of this emerges as a smorgasbord of ideas from which one can choose and create for oneself a sustaining belief system, if such a system seems useful for a time or forever. But if or when religious traditions like those of Catholicism and Judaism separate people and make them fear or dismiss each other, it is time to step away. Education should be about tearing down the walls of suspicion and prejudice, not constructing them.

Someone has saved for me a letter written by Rabbi Mordecai Schuchatowitz, school supervisor at the Yeshiva of the Rockaways. He is writing to thank my mother for the report she has submitted on her work with students at the school. Rabbi Schuchatowitz tries to capture in words the essence of the educator that Ann was and that shone through whatever subject she would teach. At the Yeshiva, Ann may have incidentally increased her own understanding of Judaism and its ceremonies, but as a teacher, as always, her attention was directed toward the children.

I feel deeply indebted to you for your extremely fine report. This was written not alone with skill, sympathy, and understanding, but with a great measure of love. This feeling for the children I have noticed and admired far more that I could express in a real way. This report only confirmed my feelings and I look upon it as a poem of love written by an ideal teacher and a noble friend.

MY NOBLE FRIEND

I am sitting with my mother in the admissions office of St. John's College in Annapolis, Maryland, in the summer of 1961, the summer before I am meant to go to college, the summer after my graduation from the Riverdale Country School for Girls, the summer after I have been accepted by none of the colleges to which I applied. I am 17. My mother, Ann Hoffmann, principal of the Hoffmann School, a person who when she speaks is "giving her business . . . out there telling it like it is," is 47. She is angry at the Riverdale Country School for failing me with college applications. She was not angry at me for writing all my applications in free verse (I believe the first line was "I swing on a magic hammock through life") or for giving more attention to my first boyfriend (a senior who was not likely to go to college anytime soon) than my applications. I was a good enough (or gifted) student who, from Hoffmann School perspective, had been failed by another school.

St. John's College, the "Great Books" school was not exactly on the top of the list for an artsy-craftsy, creative type like me (that was my cookie mold at Riverdale). But I'd been interested in the catalogues that my charming and perpetually disheveled Holden Caulfieldish boyfriend had had sent to my house. He lived at the dorms at Riverdale and didn't want the other boys to know where he was applying. I never read any other college catalogues. I applied originally only to Daisy Chain schools like Bryn Mawr and Vassar and also to Oberlin—which I heard about from my friends at a 2-week ecumenical summer program that I'd attended before my senior year. Besides deliberately clay-footing myself so as not to move to the next step before my boyfriend was ready, I think the reasons I wrote my application in free verse were: (1) to demonstrate my rebellion against prosaic institutional formats like college applications; (2) to single myself out as a poetic and creative person (my latest alternative to living up to intellectual potential); and (3) to provide myself with an excuse then and now for all the schools rejecting me. At the Oberlin interview at a downtown hotel, the interviewer asked me how a New York girl like me would adjust to the remoteness of Oberlin. "Where's Oberlin?" I asked earnestly, reflecting my ignorance of the broader and specific scene.

When my dear friend Carly Simon applied to Sarah Lawrence, I helped her write the application. When we got to the question of what character in literature had affected her most deeply, we agreed that Moll Flanders from the eighteenth-century novel *The Fortunes and Misfortunes of the Famous Moll Flanders,* a book that neither of us had read, would be a perfect selection. We went on about the challenges Moll (who ironically turns out to have been less than forthright) faced and how her courage and ingenuity were truly inspiring. We would laugh not only at our brazen disrespect for the assignment and our bold and creative response, but at how well we had learned the game of high school writing: "It is wonderful to find that in a classic work of fiction one can learn so much about oneself." "I am inspired not only by the engaging character of Moll, but also by the amazing writing of Daniel Defoe; and to think that he was writing over two hundred years ago about a girl who faces the same sort of challenges as I do in my daily life." "Yes, Moll makes mistakes [don't ask me what they are], but she perseveres in a way that I hope to in my life at and beyond Sarah Lawrence College."

Carly deservedly got in, but I, unsavory ghost writing collaborator, was left with nowhere to go. In retrospect, the college ritual scene at the Riverdale Country School was a bit over the top. The day that college letters were received in the mail, all the senior girls were crowded into a classroom next to the headmistress's office. One by one we were called into that office to be told directly by the headmistress where we had been accepted and where not. After that meeting, each girl would return to the classroom, speaking softly, "Not Radcliffe," but then perking up, "Pembroke." Or sometimes, if the news was very bad, the girl would not return to the classroom at all and we would run to the window to see her taking, at the suggestion of the headmistress, a solitary walk on the lower campus below the hockey field.

When I walked into my meeting, the headmistress was in tears. "What's wrong?" I asked, assuming that Oberlin was a bust because I didn't know it was in Ohio and doubting that Vassar had been fooled by the Georg Jensen circle pin I'd worn that day. But she was really red-faced and teary. "Not Bryn Mawr?" I asked incredulously, knowing well that one of the reasons I had taken the whole process so lightly was that I knew I was "in" at my sister's school.

The headmistress offered, "But I've called the University of Wisconsin, and sight unseen they want you."

"Where is Wisconsin?" I asked.

"And what about that school you talked about in Annapolis, St. John's?" She was grasping at straws.

"Don't worry," I said, wondering how I would break this to the other girls. "I'd just as soon stay in the city and go to acting school at the American Academy of Dramatic Arts or study painting full-time at the Art Student's League."

"You may want to take a walk by yourself," the headmistress suggested to the wrong person. Before I'd made it out the door, there was my mother and Hoffmann School child psychologist Dick Robinson standing right outside. There was no way I was going to feel for a minute bad about myself or even think about going to art school. I wrote the 10 essays for St. John's College and my mother and I drove down to visit.

I had done a reasonable job, I thought, convincing the admissions officer that I cared some about the great books of the Western World, that I knew that Plato was a philosopher, and that all my life I'd wanted to study math and science more deeply than I'd been invited or selected to do at a school that pushed me in the directions in which they thought I'd do best in order for me to get into the college of my choice, which suddenly was St. John's. I liked the place, so different from the arches and fieldstone walls of Bryn Mawr. The antique colonial campus—I think it's the third oldest college in this country—was set off with brick walkways, a benched quadrangle, and a stellar view of the Severn River or maybe it was College Creek. It felt intimate and inviting. Of course there were no students there, and they—the students—were what interested my mother.

My back froze as my interview wound down and the admissions director James Tolbert said, "Why don't we have your mother come in?" My mother came in gracefully, took her chair, straightened her regal back, and looked around the room. The colonial blue trim of the small windows in the seventeenth-century building were demurely far from any decor she would call for, whether it was the bright yellow she loved in classrooms or the combination of purple and red that she introduced in our apartment. I saw my mother as a fish out of water and, perhaps for the first time, as a stylish New Yorker in provincial digs. The gold earrings she wore every day, the floral enameled pin that I would inherit and a yellow lab would chew, the watch she wore with the extraordinary woven dark gold band to which she had insisted on attaching the crummy Bulova she'd used all her life—the watch she said I should have when she died because she wanted me to measure the moments of my lifetime with the same time-piece that had measured hers. Even if her clock was wound a little faster than others. These details of tasteful adornment suddenly seemed gaudy in the spare, ascetic, low-ceilinged, historic space.

Mr. Tolbert began to twitter. This lanky bookish man with tweed jacket and meerschaum pipe, whose bookshelves would have brought my father to rapture, was visibly impressed by my tidily dressed mother. The director of the Hoffmann School looked at him closely over the green reading glasses that hung from a Lucite-linked chain around her neck. I am making this dialogue up 50 years after the fact, but it felt something like this:

She scanned the room and smiled at him. "Fine."

Then a question from him: "How was the drive down, Mrs. Hoffmann?"

Her baby blues went right to left than settled on him. "Fine."

"Any questions?" Jim Tolbert advanced and I felt myself sinking into my chair.

"Well," my mother asserted as if she'd been preparing her questions for days, as if she knew all about the school (I had read the catalogue aloud in the car as she drove the 5 hours from New York to Annapolis), "children today . . . " and she smiled a smile that let Mr. Tolbert know that she knew he knew exactly what it was that she was thinking—whatever that was. And oh my god, Mr. Tolbert started nodding wildly in the affirmative as my mouth dropped observing this mysterious back and forth. Then, as the coup de grâce, as if she had said anything at all (had I heard a soft clicking of "sick, sick, sick"?), and with some emphasis she offered, "beatniks."

And Mr. Tolbert, whom I would have assumed was now writing me off his list since I came from the womb of a woman who spoke in tongues, went into some speech he obviously had given in many places under many circumstances about the diversity of the student population, the intensity of the program, the number of students who leave because they misunderstand how rigorous things are. Leaning into him for the final question-like remark, my mother asked in two words, "Maid service?"

He replied, "Daily."

I was mortified; Mr. Tolbert was in love; and my mother seemed satisfied that the school would be an interesting and relatively safe adventure for me. I had told Mr. Tolbert that my father had so little money when he applied to Harvard Law School, that he instructed the admissions director to send him the cheapest ready-made telegram when the decision was made: telegram A if he was accepted; B if he was not. And so, as legend has it, when my father was accepted to law school, the letter read, "Malcolm A. Hoffmann, brush your teeth and comb your hair and before you know it, I'll be there. Signed, Harvard Law School." A day after we returned home, Mr. Tolbert's letter arrived, "Jessica Ann Hoffmann, brush your teeth and comb your hair and before you know it, I'll be there. Signed, St. John's College." Handwritten on the bottom, "And a special hello to your wonderful mother."

So it was with Ann Hoffmann educator extraordinaire who could worm the whimsy out of the most earnest and reluctant child, inspire devotion from the most withdrawn, and charm admissions officers with half—no, *less* than half—a sentence. My junior year at St. John's College, I was hit by a bus as I was crossing the main street that separated St. John's College from the Naval Academy on the busy weekend of the Army–Navy game. I had bowed deeply in thanks to my language (Greek) tutor who had signaled to me that it was okay to cross behind a parked bus. He misjudged and I was clipped on the forehead by another bus coming in the other direction, thrown 15 feet in the air and bounced off the hood of the poor tutor's car before I landed on the street. After a posttraumatic grand mal seizure (this happens with head injuries), I was rushed by ambulance to Johns Hopkins Hospital in Baltimore where my tortured parents, who had been redirected from Annapolis to Baltimore, found me in intensive care.

I knew my mother was there when I awakened intermittently from my semiconscious state and heard her calmly tell a nurse to "just run some water" if she wanted me to void and when I heard her maternal voice close to my ear whispering, "Jessie, these people will be asking you over and over again, what is your name and where do you come from. I want no tricks." A month later, my mother would drive me again the 5 hours from New York to Annapolis after the neurosurgeon in New York changed his opinion that I convalesce at home for a year on account of my not having the disposition to survive such an experience—one that surely would have helped my mother recover from my/our trauma. I had written my tutors for assignments, and although or because it was a life-changing experience to be 19 and in critical condition for a week, in and out of consciousness for a few days, I was eager to return to school and with gusto.

My mother didn't think it funny that the St. John's students called me "Bus Stop," and she worried that I would stay up late and not take my Dilantin (anticonvulsive medicine) or forget my cane (it had become largely decorative) when I walked to class, but she helped me move back into my dormitory room and she laughed at my jokes and soaked the sight of me into her reservoirs of blue before she bravely left without me for New York. In a letter from my mother upon her return to the city and including drawings for me from a child at the school, I hear her layered voice, filled with angst, pride, and exaggeration:

> Dearest Daughter,
> I know how happy you must be to be back at school. The house is empty. We miss you. Calls keep coming for you and everyone is surprised you are back at school. So take care of yourself "bubby" and be sure you are rested and take your pills evenly. . . . My trip home was strewn with many horrible accidents and we were slowed down. . . . Keep in touch. We love you. All my love.
>
> > Always,
> > Mother.

Her last Christmas, my mother wearily made the trip to Massachusetts, slept in her permanent discomfort on a bed we made king size by dragging together two of my little boys' single beds, and, on the day she was leaving, saw me go off with my kids to change whatever errors of selection had fallen short of their Christmas expectations. She held me still at that moment with both arms outstretched as she had that day at St. John's and I could feel her fully taking me in, from the dress I was wearing, to the impatience I was feeling, to the me that she knew better than I. It was the last time I would see my mother alive.

Chapter 6

Making Sense

Dancing in the Music Room.

PERSONAL MATTERS

H IS THOUGHTS TURNING to my mother, Dick Robinson lets me know, "She was a dreamer in all kinds of ways." One of the difficulties they had had between them was around her dream for him: "I think she had this feeling that I was interested in money and things that money could buy, which was true but she didn't like it. I was not supposed to be that way as far as her vision of me."

"Her vision for me." Was this close and respected colleague of my mother after all just like the rest of us, another child of Ann Hoffmann's? What did it mean that she had a dream for him, personal expectations for him to meet? How different was Dick from Marcus, the student a year behind me at Hoffmann School, who returned decades later to visit with my mother, and reflected on his own behavior through her eyes: "She would be so disappointed."

The accusation, "interested in things that money could buy," seemed odd coming from my mother. It was my mother who taught us at Loehmann's that good dresses were distinguished by well-finished buttonholes, who collected dishes and teacups and small silver pitchers, who dragged me (with 3 days till show time) to Bergdorf's for my wedding dress, to Jensen's for stainless, and to Tiffany's for silver, and whose friends collected for me from islands in the Caribbean more extra plates in my Royal Danish Copenhagen pattern than I would ever have reason to use. My mother loved things, and she maintained objects with the same strain of democracy that pervaded everything she did. Next to an original oil painting by an artist whom she knew, she would hang a 3-dollar Picasso print, one my father had dared to improve with a magic marker. And next to that in the nicest frame of all would be a painting that my sister or I had done in school. Side by side in her velvet-lined box were an antique diamond and sapphire ring, a gold-plated charm bracelet with a charm from each graduating class of her school, and the papier-mâché pin I'd made for her in fourth grade. They were all cherished objects, equally valued, and cared for beyond deserving. But she never spoke about cost. Quality, beauty, history—but never monetary worth—were markers of value for Ann.

She took my sister and me shopping at Best and Company and bought us as many dresses as we loved, assuring us that we would have to make final decisions when we got home. We would try them on for our father at that time when, battling his own demons, he seemed most far from us, and he would say how beautiful they were and retreat to his room. Mommy would wink over her shoulder, follow him in for a conference, and return to tell us that even though we couldn't afford them, just because his love was so great and our appearance in the new dresses so beautiful, Daddy insisted we keep them all. It instilled in us behaviors that serve us still. When things are down, Ann Hoffmann's daughters know how to have a little adventure, to walk into a store and buy for ourselves (just because we love ourselves so much) something wonderful. It can as easily be a new lipstick as a coat, but the decision making involved, the self-celebration—these are comforting activities that Ann Hoffmann taught us.

Petting sheep.

Not to think about cost. She told me, as I got older and would go out to dinner on a date, never to insult my host by looking at the price of things on the menu, always to order exactly what I want. Did she learn all this in her Luciano training to be a "fine Italian matron running a big house"? Was it all a holdover from the depression she lived through that her father did not? On its account, she would never lose or throw out a penny, never waste food or anything at all. In the way in which a child collects, combines, and confuses bits of information from the air, I imagined my mother on a long line waiting for bread and had the notion that on account of her caring for others who were suffering, her name had been placed on some list that should not be mentioned.

As a little girl Anna refused to ride to school in her father's big limousine and instead would walk on her own with the driver and car following close behind. She told us of the time that she wore to school both a beautiful new ribbon in her hair and a fine new hat. Unfortunately, it was raining, and she still insisted on walking, intermittently using her hat to protect her ribbon and slipping it under her raincoat to keep it dry. She laughed, describing how funny she looked arriving to school soaking wet with a nice dry car 3 feet behind. She had grown up with opera, marble wainscoting, and beautiful clothes—the big house in Brooklyn and another on the Long Island shore. One house next door to her father's marble factory; the other by the sea she loved. She had grown up with luxury and lost it all; she cared not for money, it was not her way. Money (the lack thereof) challenged the ownership and maintenance of her school, threatened to keep out children who couldn't afford it, and kept her from lavishing worthy salaries on the great staff she loved. Money loomed as a potential evil. Folks who had a lot were not necessarily corrupt; they could be good and generous, but folks who were poor had something going for them in my mother's eyes, a predisposition for nobility, an understanding that life was hard.

Ann Hoffmann instilled in us a taste and love for fine things, even as I knew that she expected us to marry, as she did, only for love. She loved things, not like people, but she loved them. As little children we never had jelly jars (I craved the ones with cartoon characters) or plastic; we drank from the same beautiful glasses as our parents. My mother thought it important for us to learn to manage delicate objects and for children to know they were as important as grown-ups. When we were sick in bed, she would serve us tea in a beautiful flowered Spode tea pot that held all together on top of each other the brewing tea, the cream warmed by the hot liquid below it, and the sugar on top. And when something-anything would break, my mother would seize the moment to tell us, "Don't worry for a moment. It's just a thing. Things are dispensable. People are not."

Dick's voice softens as he tells me, "She and I used to talk about dreams for education, the country—dreams for our future lives. Of course one of her real dreams I love of which I'm sure you're aware is that she is a ballet dancer and she is slim and we talked about that dream frequently." I knew my mother dreamed of being a ballet dancer. She didn't get to or plan to go to the ballet very often, though I knew she loved it and my parents spoke often of something called Sadler Wells. I know it was not just a love of ballet. It was a love of the dancer's image, the elongated, lithe body that could twirl and glide easily across the floor. Hands raised gracefully in the air, back arched, head to the sky.

Ballet shoes filled my drawings. I can still draw the exact schema I used to create them as a child, the curved upright sole, the delightful criss-crossing of ribbons around a leg, grounding the wonderful tutus with their V-shaped waistlines. Some children at Hoffmann School—not me with flat feet—wore their toe shoes to dance class and they were beautiful. It amazes me that my mother's colleague, an elegant gentleman of

84 who has made time for my visit in between chemotherapy treatments for a cancer he was determined to beat, remembers my mother's ballerina dream. Did she envision herself as a dancer, moving gracefully from one challenge to another? Did she sometimes feel the need to dance in spite of her own wants, like the heroine of the 1948 movie that we would sometimes watch on our 10-inch Admiral TV, *The Red Shoes*? Dick had said that she loved what she did and was successful, but the time it took for some children and families to find their way was deeply frustrating. She never gave up on a single child, but she suffered mightily with many.

Ann Hoffmann talked about her dance dream with Dick Robinson. Was he a comfort to her as he had been to me? Throughout my childhood, I had waves of hard feelings about my impressive father. I appreciated his lofty presence and rich deep voice, and I knew it meant a lot to him to see me at the end of the day. But I was distressed that he worked night and day, ruined my eating space at dinner by resting his omnipresent cigarette on a small ashtray in front of my plate, and refused to play baseball with me when I wished to practice on the weekends. I was angry that he wanted me to wear dresses and not blue jeans (I was the only girl in my class) and to read more books like my wonderful intellectual sister. At these times of disappointment and resentment, my mother would somehow arrange (it never felt like an appointment) for me to speak to Dick Robinson.

Dick would assure me that my face would catch up with my nose, that I would be successful on my own terms, that I had my mother's warmth and would be in demand as a friend and someday even as a wife. Dick helped me not feel too guilty about the book reports and the not-living-up-to-potential thing. He thought it was funny when my father, desperate to have me enjoy the world of literature that brought his life such pleasure, reached to my 10-year-old's pedestrian values and offered to pay me a quarter for every poem I would set to memory. My father had what is called total recall and could slip into Shakespearean soliloquies as easily as other conversationalists slip in and out of clichés. "How many lines? How many lines did I need to memorize to get 25 cents?" He may have wished he'd asked for more, but "four" was the base limit he requested. And it worked, at least to some extent.

The world was filled with four-line poems. There was so much Ogden Nash; and of course there was that one about never seeing a purple cow but rather seeing than being.[14] And then I dipped into wider sources. I believe I got a dollar for A. E. Housman's "When I was One and Twenty" (16 lines) and my father loved a lofty-sounding, romantic six liner that must have been amusing out of the mouth of my unliterary self. I would be wearing my favorite tattersall "short set"—all cotton and crisp, the shorts with an elastic waist and broad, pressed cuff, the matching shirt with red buttons over a white T-shirt to make it more or less of an outfit. My mother would have cut my bangs too short, a compulsion that sabotaged my haircuts all through school, a ritualized mistake I continue to make. I would not have smiled. Arthur attributes his infrequent smiling to sadness; mine was associated with insecurity—fearing it might show that I hadn't brushed my teeth, not knowing if what I was about to say would be enhanced or demolished by a cheerful look. I take two steps forward to recite the latest quarter's worth of poetry and my father stops me, "Who wrote this one?" I am shamed. I do not know. It was Robert Herrick:

> Whenas in silks my Julia goes,
> Then, then (methinks) how sweetly flows
> That liquefaction of her clothes.
> Next, when I cast mine eyes and see
> That brave vibration each way free;
> Oh how that glittering taketh me![15]

At the time I didn't understand the laughter that lit up his face; but I enjoyed bringing him such pleasure. I can see now how funny my presentation must have been: my earnest and lucrative demonstration of memorizing words with little if any understanding of content. "Liquefaction"— that word sounded like what it was—was the easiest to remember, and extracted the greatest smile of delight.

As my father lay dying more than 40 years later, his eyes were shut and his mind seemed to be drifting to a place that felt far away. He had told us that it would soon be his time to "tour the universe." Indeed the day before, he had closed and opened his eyes frequently, asking as they opened each time, "Am I a ghost?" It was almost funny, but awful at the same time. Was he practicing or trying to die? He would call out from wherever his thoughts were swimming for his mother, my mother. Did he feel them nearby? His well-trained nurses suggested I tell him he could— that I "give him permission"—to move on. An impossible task. They also emphasized that hearing was the last thing to go.

Responsively, I read aloud to him, nonstop, poetry that he loved, all this nineteenth-century stuff about bravery and virtue—Wordsworth's one about the field of daffodils: "I wandered lonely as a cloud."[16] I read carefully and thought he listened now and then with an occasional or perhaps involuntary smile. I leaned in close and tried to let him go: "Guess it's time to tour the universe Daddy," I said. "It's okay. If you're ready, we'll be okay." Except for his nurse sitting quietly at a distance, I was alone with my father at this time that my mother had told me to honor, realizing with disbelief that my voice reading this poetry was the last thing my father was hearing, if in fact he could still hear. I didn't need Dick Robinson any more. I had made my peace with my father after my mother's death. Supporting each other in our rearranged universe, we came to know each other well and to know better what we thought about each other.

I knew he was proud of me. Proud that, in spite of my childhood rebellion against the intellectual climate he cultivated in our home, I had studied and then taught at his beloved Harvard. As a teen, I would purposefully upset him by telling his curious friends that what I wanted to be when I grew up was a housewife with lots of kids. Sometimes to really set him off, I'd mention a big station wagon. My father's expectation was that my sister and I would get college degrees and postgraduate degrees; the rest would be incidental personal data. He was the one to write in a biographical paragraph for my mother, that her "teaching career was interrupted by her marriage to Malcolm A. Hoffmann, and from 1939 to 1944 she lived in Washington, D.C., where her two children were born." But I knew that he was most proud that I had had, and that he would know and love, my three wonderful boys. I got to hear his side of the story regarding the decision that we not learn Italian along with English; and a week before he died, he mentioned an event that I always thought had brought him much distress—I knew my mother had been angry—an event that undoubtedly marked some rite of passage for me at 16.

The family was going on vacation to California. Our family rarely went on vacations. We worked summers at the Hoffmann School camp; and our mother worked during breaks preparing for the school days ahead. My parents did not leave us—till after we'd grown and left them—for excursions to other countries or to the Caribbean. The trip to the West Coast was therefore a really big deal, a benefit of my father's increased income since he had made the move in 1955 from government to private practice, a tribute to my sister's and my adult status that we would pack our dresses and makeup and take a trip that included visits to Daddy's West Coast clients. But I refused to go.

I had signed up for something called the Shawnee Leadership Institute for World Understanding, a 2-week end of summer camp experience held at another progressive mecca, the Putney School in Vermont, in which participants (from high schools and colleges) studied religions and other belief systems and reflected across cultures on peace and mutual celebration. I had never been away from home; I had found the place myself; and I didn't realize the dates conflicted with our trip. My parents had left the decision to me, though it would not be guilt free. My mother was disappointed. She would get teary sharing photos of the three of them in California sitting under palm trees at somebody's home or enjoying a luxury hotel and that West Coast buzz—family pictures without me.

"What was the name of that pinko camp you went to when you were a teenager?" my 85-year-old father asked from the reclining chair that had become his one location; the stenosis in his spine making it too painful for him to lie down; the lung cancer spread through his body making it too hard for him to stand. "The Shawnee Leadership Institute for World Understanding." I replied. "I was never so proud of you as when you made the decision to go there," he confessed to my astonishment. I realize now that Rebecca would be proud as well and that my mother, even disappointed as she was, knew it was the sort of thing she would want me to want to do. I braved a recitation from memory and leaned in close with A. E. Housman's poem: "When I was one and twenty, I heard a wise man say."[17] My father smiled a bit, noting my dropping of the word *pounds* in line three and spoke to me across time and space, from the decline to sleep that was his peaceful death, to the girl in the tattersall shorts or the middle-aged mother of three who was his girl sitting close by. "You almost got that right." They were the last words he would speak to anyone, and thanks to my mother's unrelenting affection for us both, I was there to hear them.

My mother's wedding ring was inscribed simply: "Love lasts longer than life." My parents' relationship was like that—filled with testimonies of adoration that ranged from flowers on no occasion to scribbled love notes and sentimental poems. Although my father worked at his profession of mind—lawyering and writing—and my mother worked at her business of heart—mothering and guiding—they met in a space they cultivated in between, in which they knew each other was the love of a lifetime. This is how it always seemed to me. Twenty-one lines of my mother's free form poetry scribbled late in her life on paper that has been folded multiple times, concludes,

> . . . let the void of our passing
> Quietly fill itself with remembrance
> Of dreams lovers had,
> Hoping to glide through eternity
> Forever melting into each other's reveries.

The Hoffmann School community knew my father well from school events where he would often speak and from his morning appearances leaving for his Madison Avenue office in a car driven by a school driver who had just delivered children to the school. When he would intersect with my mother, there was a visible change in my mother's countenance. She would soften from her own invention of an administrative role into an almost coquettish admirer of the lanky man at her side. He would write that he could not find, "the verbal versatility which would be necessary faithfully to describe her career or our love." My mother ends a letter to me in January 1964 with typical instruction, "I want you cherished by the man who falls in love with you. The happiness your father and I have known through hard times and good ones is what I pray for for you. One love, one man. Human feelings are within us; but that is wealth: the moon the stars. Always, Mother."

Dick Robinson said that the school staff felt on a daily basis the intensity of "Mal's emotional involvement with Ann." He described my parents as "gutsy, emotional people who were deeply involved with one another." Although I never heard my father describe Dick Robinson, it was clear that he was jealous about the close working relationship that existed between Dick and my mother. I asked Dick about it and even at his late stage in life, he spoke of his connection with my mother as if they'd seen each other yesterday: "She was great to work with and we from the very beginning had a special relationship—'we dug each other.'" He also admitted that my father made visiting at our home less than relaxed for Dick: "It was as if he boned up . . . every time I came to the house . . . 'Well Dick, in *Civilization and its Discontents*, Freud said this . . . what do you think about that?'"

I find a small handwritten letter from Dick Robinson to my parents in 1961 when he was asked to serve on the newly formed board of trustees for the Hoffmann School. In it he said, "I think you and Ann both know of my great affection and respect for both of you. My admiration of the school, its work, and particularly Ann's efforts and singular contribution to education is boundless. I shall be ever grateful for what I have learned from her."

Outsiders may not have understood Malcolm's attachment to the school—that it was his aunt and not my mother who founded it, that he helped with business and legal matters, that he made up out of his earnings for deficits in the school's operation, that he worked hard at perilous junctures to keep the school from closing. Few of us knew the extent to which the Hoffmann School was an integral part of their romance, the site of their meeting, a confluence of familial fabrics, and a work in progress to which they were lovingly dedicated. My parents' school provided a showcase for my mother's energy and talent and a home for their children that transcended traditional boundaries, making way for an appreciation of and engagement in the arts, a sense of life as learning, and an awareness of caring for others as social and familial responsibility. "Want to learn something about yourself? Do something for somebody else." My mother would say that almost as frequently as she would say, in words that once seemed absurd to me, "Nobody said it was going to be easy" and her tireless standard, "This too shall pass."

When my father was facing emotional challenges somewhere in my early childhood, my mother picked up the oars and rowed. If he was too paranoid to go to the barber on his own, she would go with him. I don't know the shape or source of his troubles or the range of activities on which they took effect, but my father at that time had a great fear of bridges and my mother tackled that straight on. After school and on weekends, my sister and I would ride in the back seat of our 1949 cobalt blue Packard sedan back and forth across the Spuyten Duyvil Creek onto the West Side Highway and across the Hudson River on the George Washington Bridge. It seemed sort of fun. I believe my mother framed it as an adventure, but I sensed my father's deep angst, recognizing that deeply breathed "Anna" that I would hear sometimes at night through the wall that separated my parents' bedroom from my sister's and mine. "Anna, Anna, I'm paralyzed." Things like that.

Sometimes I heard my mother's response, "No, you're not, Malcolm. Please. I'm so very tired." And I would wake my sister thinking Daddy needed rescue only to be reassured by her experience and the relief of my father's anxiety quieting down into soft tones of cheerful conversation with my exhausted mother. Sometimes I would dream that I was driving the car across a bridge, a very long bridge on which no matter how long we traveled, the end stayed out of sight. Everyone in the car was at ease and so was I until all of a sudden I would freeze with fear realizing that at age 8 or 9, I really did not know how to drive. Sometimes I would wake up afraid; mostly, I just kept on driving.

My father wrote a valentine to my mother every year, and one each to my sister and to me. They were always brief and handwritten usually in red pencil on index cards, pointing to individual achievements like being 6 (if I wasn't his valentine, he'd "be in a fix") or losing a tooth (his "valentine forsooth"). "Little Jessie, as you are growing up and play in concerts at your teacher's home, I hope that happiness will fill your cup so high, you'll brush off half the foam." Mine have been saved for all these years on yellowing paper bearing his distinctive scribble script and the signature heart he would draw on each index card, a heart with an arrow crossing through it. Among my mother's, I find, "To Ann, Valentine's 1951":

We are still here, locked
Fast in one life, one love, shocked
By time's racing heels, but holding our place
As dust pursues dust in frantic race,
We shall remain as through time and space,
With triumph written on each's face
I can pen no more blessed line
Than that you are my valentine.

On the card he wrote for my mother for Valentine's Day, 1979, the year of their fortieth and last wedding anniversary, the year that she was facing major surgery for the ovarian cancer that was her demise, the heart he drew has three arrows through it:

Darling, will you as you face this trial,
Hold my hand a little while?
My valentine days with you have taught
The strength of strong, fine, loving thought,
And you and I for many years
Have conquered all our little fears.
Let us now for the fortieth time
Face this day—one day at a time—
And for the sweetest girl on all the line
Thank god you are my valentine.

A month after that major surgery, my mother returned to work. A group of Japanese parents living in the states because they were involved in the media and the United Nations had discovered the school, recommended it to friends, and seen to it that Hoffmann School was included in a movie shown on Japanese television on the subject of Japanese children at school in faraway lands. The piles of letters over the years from this group of parents, one of whom called my mother "Mother" and referred to her as grandmother to her child and "to all children," were filled with affection, admiration, and appreciation. In March 1979, a father wrote: "In the severe winter, you were out to hospital, having left untold anxiety among Hoffmann kids. Now, in the spike of spring flavour, you are back to the campus with prospect of more blooms. Here is a saying in Japan . . . after rain, the soil becomes solid."

That saying would not hold for Ann Hoffmann. Her decline continued over the next year, especially after she had undertaken an intense program of chemotherapy that weakened her ability to fight off the slightest infection. For all the time that I lived in Massachusetts, raising my three boys far from my mother's daily touch, we spoke at 4:30 in the afternoon. It was a time when my children were busy (was it *Sesame Street?*) and my mother was resting after a day at school. It was a time I could tell my mother the hilarious details of my children's day; I could seek her input into any-sized parental decision; and I could speak of whatever I had done that gave me any source of pride with the shameless sense of self-congratulation that is not only forgiven but celebrated by parents.

One afternoon in that difficult last year, my mother called in distress and told me she was no longer fit to run the school. That day, dismissal had been a disaster. It was always a strategic challenge with ten limousines or vans and drivers at the ready in the driveway when school was over and none allowed to leave until every car was safely loaded with its children and the teacher assigned to the bus seated within. On this particular afternoon, when Ann was about to ring the school bell to mark the precise moment at which the car in first place of the very specific order could leave, car number three, a Volkswagen van, hastened out of turn out of its space. My mother—and she told me this through tears of shame—was so angry that "in front of everyone," she ran into the center of the driveway and, raging, banged the metal school bell against the front of the van. I believed and told her it was understandable, but "out of control" was unacceptable to this maven player of the principal's role.

Children outside the barn.

She continued working in her school into the early days of the February in which she died, showing up every morning and fighting for what she saw as the urgent needs of her children; but things were never the same. As she succumbed to the weakness and pain associated with the final infection that was more than her chemotherapy-weakened body could fight, she chastised me for wanting her to be alive in any condition (it was true) and wanted me to know that there were in this world "worse things than death."

ANN'S IMPRINT

Arthur at 61 is telling me that it is on account of the Hoffmann School that he became a therapist. "How many of us from Hoffmann School are psychologists? Our childhoods were grounded in a therapeutic environment where we were asked to understand each other." He tells me the story of his own son who tested very high in all things but math, and how Arthur realized that he needed to "play" with numbers with his son to wake him up to math's wonders. He found out that a 16-year-old patient, who was pretty much ignored by parents dealing with a dying relative and who was getting into drugs and alcohol, really loved old records, 78 rpm records. Arthur happened to have some and knew where to get more. Like Ann Hoffmann, he suggested that the parents "enjoy" their child and go after what he cared about with him. He similarly reached an isolated adolescent girl who he discovered loved writing.

He is going on with examples from his work about how, by discovering what children care about ("What do you want to do?") he finds a way to help them help themselves. In the middle of his sharing, he yells out with a broad smile, "Hi, Ann, how are you doing?" And continues, "What does the kid need? He needs to find that there is something about him that makes some sense, that he is not nuts, that somebody can relate to who he is . . . that it doesn't matter that I'm old, I still have something to offer, and if you're smart enough to be able to use what anybody has to offer, you will get what you need!"

I am overwhelmed. Is my mother still helping Arthur realize his own worth? Is he really yelling, "Hi, Ann, how am I doing?" Even as she kept pushing the isolated child that he was ("I could get lost in a twosome") to dance, to skate, to sing, to apply to Riverdale, to take the "stupid test," he read the message beneath her actions as "You need to understand that if you are going to have a life, you need to participate!" And the question he takes from her, through which he continues their dialogue as he works with child after child is, "What do you need to do what you want to do?" Hoffmann School taught him, he says, "enough about myself to find out that there really were adults who were loving people and who meant you well and could do some things." And he was right. Ann Hoffmann meant him well. She wanted Arthur in the school she was creating; she liked him; she challenged him; and she came through for him just as he ultimately came through for her and more importantly for himself.

"I think she absolutely destroyed my conception of all school administrators, for *that* she definitely was not in personality and approach." Dick Robinson had said of her and of the school, "It was a school like one you've never seen before. The atmosphere was not school atmosphere; it did not have the appearance of a school although your mother tried to impose certain routines. Suzie up in that tree saying she was a fucking bluebird was more typical of that school than any other. It was more like living in a house with a lot of kids than a school. It was a happy place." "But you said, Dick, that it was filled with screwballs," I reminded him. He looked at me over his horn-rimmed glasses with a look that was entirely familiar and smiled as if he thought I'd of course have known, "Screwballs are happy."

I would have to agree. From where I sat within and beside and in and outside of the Hoffmann School, it was like no other school I would ever know. I would never live in any other school; yet perhaps because of Hoffmann School, I lived in all of them and they in me. And if I were asked about what things Ann Hoffmann taught me, like Arthur, I would have to say that they are things I live. Unlike Arthur, I would not be able to name them clearly. Individuation, difference, the arts—these ideas have permeated all that I have done and thought within and alongside the many settings for education to which I have always stayed close: my own education, my children's, my students'.

At the Harvard Graduate School of Education, where I first went for a year in 1984 to gain the necessary skills to write the story I promised my mother I'd tell, I ended up staying for 20 (had it become my home?). I earned a master's and a doctorate, taught graduate students, and explored the artistic development of children, especially the striking similarities that persist between the drawings of young children and artists that had been of such interest to me when I taught arts and crafts in the summers at the Hoffmann School day camp. I ended up working at a research group at Harvard with the mysterious and somewhat misleading name, Project Zero (PZ). The zero was meant to represent the state of knowledge about a cognitive approach to the arts in education, an understanding of art making and appreciating as serious activities of thought (mind) and not just the intuitive sharing of human emotion (heart).

One of my father's cousins who had taught art at Hoffmann School had recommended PZ to me, suggesting that the co-leader of the group, a psychologist named Howard Gardner, was interested in the differences that persisted among children as we always were at Hoffmann School. In his development of something he called the "Theory of Multiple Intelligences," Howard challenged the narrow limits of IQ and offered alternatively a collection of lenses through which to assess the different ways that individual learners make meaning in this world. His work resonated with Ann's not just in her mistrust of IQ scores, but also in her emphasis on difference and in her belief that all children have gifts that educators must help bring to light. Dick Robinson told me, "She did not care about intelligence. She believed all children could learn and enjoy learning, and IQ didn't make any difference." What she cared about was children and helping them learn.

After a decade of research into issues related to arts education, together with the dean, my colleagues at Project Zero, and other enthusiastic faculty members, I worked to create a program at the Harvard

Graduate School of Education based on the work of former graduate students who for decades, without formal recognition, had focused their master's and doctoral work on development and education in the arts. The program featured diversity; it was populated by students from different backgrounds and settings, from nonarts classrooms to museums and foundations that supported the arts. It featured inquiry, self-direction, and variety in perspective rather than the prescription of a set course of action. It balanced freedom with structure by including a rigorous core course that charted a shared journey through information, ideas, and literature—core knowledge out of which students crafted their own questions and direction. The program attracted a number of students who had given up on more traditional settings and were interested in forging their own paths and in "getting what they needed" to do what they wanted to do. "Hi, Ann, how am I doing?"

On a particular spring morning my sister—a full professor at the Sciences Po in Bordeaux, France—was in Boston and interested in visiting Harvard with me. Growing up in the same room, we experienced the aging felt maroon class of 1934 banner that hung on our wall reminding us always of our father's attachment to Harvard. Harvard symbolized the rational world of mind that he inhabited and that intersected but stood a respectful difference from the less rational, if not irrational, world of heart in which my mother, no matter how imposing anyone found her, nurtured the children of the Hoffmann School.

We walked together into the lobby of Longfellow Hall, a classic Harvard colonial brick building with a lecture hall on the first floor and classrooms and offices throughout, and my sister's head turned quickly at the display lining the front hall. There were mannequins hanging in fishnet from the ceiling and standing at curious junctures throughout the hall, each one hand-painted by a teen participant in an urban community arts program. I explained to Trudy that graduate students in my program had set up the exhibit and staged an opening tea for the teens at which they enjoyed talking "art speak" with the students and sharing the triumph of the exhibit with their parents. My sister said nothing.

When we got to the third floor where my students' work was on display, my sister looked with tempered interest. In glass cases and on bulletin boards around the hall were artistic creations I'd asked the students, many of whom were not artists, to make in response to readings (Thomas Mann's story, "Tonio Kroeger," was one of them) and ideas within the program's core course. Students had challenged me from time to time on account of the bulk of work in the course, the fact that along with the mountain of reading and writing that came with the core, as with any other graduate-level course, they were being asked to reach beyond their comfort level and turn their "thoughts into things." It was an expression I'd borrowed from Betty Blayton Taylor, director of the Children's Art Carnival in Harlem, a community art center in an old brownstone house that had the homeyness and child-oriented grandeur—carved wainscoting painted bright blue—of the Hoffmann School.

It was time to submit the next section's collection of artistic entries and the office was filled with students. Many of them had questions for me: "Jessica, where do we put video tapes and how will they be exhibited?" "I'm doing a paper for another course analyzing the potential, negative and positive, of displays such as this program's on schoolwide regard for the arts in education."

That stopped me. "What are you thinking?"

"Well, how many people read the signage with this work and realize the depth of the questions we are asking about the arts and learning and the complexity of putting two opposing perspectives into one work all at one time? How many folks just look at all this on display and think of it as about feelings—like children's work on display on the walls in their schools—equating what we do here at this level of education with the demeaning view of the outsider art teacher as someone who decorates the school walls."

By this time my sister had retreated to my small office off the main room. When I finally joined her and walked into my office, she was sitting quietly. "Quiet" is not an apt or frequent descriptor for my sister or me. She looked up at me and broke the silence, "This isn't Harvard, Jessie. It's the god-damned Hoffmann School." And then she smiled. "It's Mommy's revenge on Harvard."

It had really not occurred to me until that moment that perhaps by championing the arts in higher education, I was championing the outsider my mother had taught me to embrace, perhaps even championing the outsider my mother was to the broader scene of education in which her approaches might face as perilous a course as have the arts. It had not before occurred to me that Ann Hoffmann was like the arts accused of being about emotion. Similarly, the buzz of her school was as different from a hushed school building as is the art room from the traditional nonarts classroom. In the art room children noisily work on group projects and make hilarious mistakes. In the traditional nonarts classroom, they are asked to sit still and listen quietly.

Had the work I did at Project Zero attempting to explain the arts as processes of thought rather than of heart, reason rather than magic, been about something more or other than the arts? Had my campaign for the arts been my effort to bring the Hoffmann School to the broader scene of education? My students said I ran a democratic classroom, and on the last day of classes in the last year that I would teach, they generously gave me a standing ovation. As they applauded, I left the front of the room and slipped in amongst them so that we were at the same level facing together—instructor and other learners—the podium that at Harvard separates the learned from the crowd. Would Rebecca have liked that? Would Ann have been proud? Were they with me in that room, delighted that I had spent that time at the American Academy of Dramatic Arts finding my voice and freedom to move and act before and among an audience?

Had I finally taken my mother's warm fuzzy, deeply empathetic, real message and grazed the rafters of Malcolm's formal grand and chilly ivy-covered halls? At the celebration of the first chair for the arts in education at Harvard University, generous supporters, giddy with their triumph in securing a permanent place for the arts at Harvard, raised their glasses and made extravagant toasts. A major donor spoke through tears at the podium saying that with all the intellect that abounded at Harvard, the Arts in Education Program had given the School of Education its heart. I was mortified. There it was again. I should have cheered.

SITTING AMONG CHILDREN

As it turns out, the Chester who decades ago sat so long in the chair outside Ann Hoffmann's office still lives in the house from which he walked daily to the Hoffmann School. It was a house his parents had rented that he bought for his mother when he was an adult and able to do so. "You walked to school?" I gasped, remembering how early and then much earlier he would arrive. "Oh yes, up and down the steep hill at 254th Street and on the snowiest days." Then, as if I needed further explanation, "I had found a home and I was always there on time." Chester, now a 57-year-old father of three tells me, as if I didn't know, "Of course you know I spent much of my time at Hoffmann School in that chair in the front hall."

His description of the school began with the chair: its comfort even though it was hard wood without upholstery, the secret compartment in its base. An elevator had been installed in the front hall to facilitate my mother's frequent up-and-down between school and home, and that too was a source of interest: "It was an unusual elevator. Fascinating." Like others at Hoffmann after my time, Chester asked about tunnels that had been found under or near the duck pond and whether they had been part—as the students all thought—of the Underground Railway. He mentioned physical details that were startlingly unknown to me.

Chester told me that his brothers had both done well in public school and that he had felt guilty about causing his parents such trouble and the expense of a private school (actually schools, counting the ones he'd gone to and left before Hoffmann). "I was quite intelligent IQ-wise," he explained, "but I had major issues when I came to the school. I couldn't read. I was probably dyslexic. Somehow I always thought I could 'learn school' at a later time, and then I was too far behind." Reflecting on the close bond that he shared with Ann Hoffmann, Chester confided, "My mother felt threatened by my relationship with your mom." Threatened seemed a good word to me for countless reasons ranging from the attachment children quickly made to Ann Hoffmann and her suspicion of "parents" as the usual stumbling block between children and their needs. In any case, "threatened" was a good word for me. How was I supposed to feel about my mother's relationship with hundreds of children like Chester? Amazed? Yes. Proud? Yes. Threatened? Maybe. Yes, definitely.

Describing what he could see from that chair, Chester appreciated the view through the panes of glass into the office, "so you could see your mom working." His calling Ann Hoffmann my "mom" seemed odd after so many conversations in which she was Ann or most often Ann Hoffmann. He explained, "She treated me like a mom in a sense, a strong mom but a loyal one." Chester told me how he had cared for his own mother for 10 years after she had suffered a massive stroke and reflected that his sense of himself as an intuitive caretaker came from his time at Hoffmann. After he graduated from Hoffmann School and was a teenager, Ann Hoffmann suggested that he come to the camp and work with young children. Chester loved that experience and says that it was on its account that he had considered becoming a teacher. His time at camp had introduced to him the thrill of making a difference in the well-being and course of another person's life. That, he told me, "had a truly positive effect" both on his self-image and his professional direction.

Ann Hoffman understood and exploited the "truly positive effect" of working with children. Tina, who lived just on the other side of Sherwood Forest beyond the school's baseball field, was 18 when her mother called Ann to ask for help. She was distraught because Tina had suffered a "mildly psychotic depression" and taken in a "suicidal gesture" her mother's "neck pills." Tina, who had gone to Hoffmann School in kindergarten and then again in eighth grade, had completed a semester of college and had perhaps put too much into her reading of Dante's *Inferno*. Ann Hoffmann came running across the grounds and through the tall bushes that separated the school property from Tina's family's house just as Tina had once walked "through the hedges" on her way to kindergarten at Hoffmann School.

Tina's kindergarten class was called the Pixies, a term which even at age 4 Tina found insulting, but she loved the art barn: "It was encouraging and free, a joyful exciting place where you could do what you want." When Tina was in eighth grade, Ann Hoffmann commissioned her to paint a mural in the French room. Tina was thrilled and put together bags of plaster and buckets of paint to realize her idea of transforming the room into a sidewalk café. The project grew to enormous consuming proportions and Tina, overwhelmed by the task, was grateful to Ann Hoffmann for putting an end to it. She did it in such a way that Tina "never felt bad about it."

Tina's classmates were diverse. She tells me, "Here I was like a bright student—a little precocious—in the same English class with this girl with autism who would be flapping and screaming . . . and a part of her brain would work and she would speak coherently, and we felt comfortable with these differences—a certain ambiguity or openness—not needing things to be tied up in knots. It left your mind open to a lot of things." Another boy named Harold would make Tina laugh till she fell on the floor: "He could stare at you and make your eyeballs vibrate." Tina found the atmosphere creative. It was a place "where you were encouraged to be whatever you are." And she remembers Ann Hoffmann vividly: "The whole time I knew her she had white hair swept up in a bun, really clear, light blue eyes, and a round face. Her face could go from very businesslike when she was in her office and taking care of administrative things—from sharp office thinking—to whimsy and fun. Sometimes she could be like the boss and then she could be very nurturing. She was somewhat plump, wore those half glasses with a string, and didn't tend to wear makeup or jewelry. But she looked feminine. She was respected by all the children as being the director and she took that role seriously, like the-buck-stops-here person. She seemed to like what she did and seemed dedicated."

To counter the effect of the pills, Ann made Tina drink coffee and kept her walking around in circles. As they walked around she told Tina that she wanted her to come the next day to the Hoffmann School. "When you get better," she said, "you have a job with the Hoffmann School. I think you're very good with kids." Tina remembers that she could barely put one foot in front of the other, but she showed up the next day and Ann had her sit in a second-grade class and be available to the children. "I felt frozen and like a zombie," Tina remembers. But each day Ann Hoffmann would tell her what a great job she had done. It was puzzling but appreciated. Hearing that she "worked well with children" made her feel good. Tina sat among the children daily until one of them approached her with a branch that she wanted to decorate for Easter and Tina began to relax and to find that she really did enjoy working with children. "And you've been sitting among children ever since?" I ask this veteran child psychiatrist. "I guess so," she laughs, finishing her description of Ann Hoffmann as a person "who had a brain and a heart."

I begin to understand better Ann Hoffmann's insistence on letting Chester sit among children in that chair. "I learned how to relate to people at Hoffmann School," Chester explains. "I'm kind of an anomaly—not a member of the crowd." An anomaly? Weren't we all at Hoffmann School? The building permit should have read, "To serve no more than 100 anomalies." Chester described the trouble he had writing as a child (his brain moves more quickly than his hand with pen or on computer) and how as an adult, dictation had set him free to discover that he was a good writer after all. As if he might be disappointing me, and as it was for so many of the children who were struggling and found safe haven at the Hoffmann School, he reassured me: "It was me that was the problem, not your school."

Chester remembered the familial details he noted from that chair. My mother planning my sister's wedding; her joking in Italian with her sister Gigi, who worked in the office; her loving relationship with her biological children. He had seen so much from that chair and took Ann Hoffmann in so fully—his teacher who really did live in a school. He told me, " I remember your mother when she was with your father. She, who otherwise was so self-confident and powerful, would just melt and she was so much shorter." I was somehow surprised that the boy in the chair was unaware of the life in Massachusetts that I had built with my husband and children and that in the end could not be uprooted to sustain Ann Hoffmann's dream. Commenting as if he knew my mother better than I, unaware that he was breaking my heart, Chester told me, "She was proud of you, Jessie; she expected you to come and run the school."

"Were you being educated in that chair?" I asked Chester directly. "I've never thought of it that way, " he responded and then rested a moment. "It's a good question. I guess it enabled me to learn whatever I am." It was as if for the first time he realized he might not have been wasting time. Again I felt the Hoffmann School, that I was reaching its arms across time and space in an embrace. So many of the school's graduates invited to work at the camp or the school, encouraged, like Chester and Tina, to sit among the children. Ann Hoffmann clearly believed that in sitting among children, in doing something for someone else who was a child, individuals could learn about themselves: their capacity for vision, creativity, and goodness; their ability to play with possibility. "You look like you've given up," I can hear her voice, "I'm expecting you tomorrow at 9. I believe you have a gift. Come sit among my children."

Chester bemoaned the fact that kids nowadays have to be good at everything and celebrated the ways in which at Hoffmann School, kids were recognized for their idiosyncrasies, and it was understood that if you didn't learn that particular thing today, it was because you were learning something else and you'd learn whatever when you were ready. I thanked Chester for his comments and insights and told him that I had started the story I'd promised my mother I'd tell with the image of him in his chair. Now, I suggested playfully, I looked to him for a way to end it. Rising to the challenge, Chester spoke carefully, "The truth of the matter is your mom was always on our side. She was our advocate."

Among the many letters my father received on the occasion of my mother's death, I am surprised to see that he made multiple photocopies of a very short one, one he received a month after she died from a psychologist who used to work as a teacher at the Hoffmann School, someone who must for him have told the story as simply and clearly as he tried to in his manuscript over half a century ago and as I have tried to today:

> The other day a child came to me in tears. I held him and said, "Let me tie your shoelaces—*that* will make you feel better."
> It did.
> One of the many lessons I learned from Ann.

Graduation, 1970.

THE DREAM

The lecture hall at Columbia University's Teachers College is packed. The seats are filled with young teachers in training. Helen Parkhurst, founder of the Dalton School, steps forward to introduce her dear friend and the guest lecturer of the day. "Ann Hoffmann, director of the Hoffmann School," she says, "is a truly gifted educator from whom you will have much to learn. Her being here is a dream come true for me. Listen carefully, students, and you will become better teachers."

My mother approaches the podium. She is dressed in a lavender linen dress with sewn-down flowered ribbons criss-crossing across her chest. She has a deeper lavender sweater on her shoulders and dark green reading glasses hanging from a chain around her neck. She turns to face the hundreds of students, standing straight and tall, her eyes scanning the audience, her arms hanging gracefully at her side. In the third row she spots a student with dark glasses. "Can you see me?" She calls out. The young woman shakes her head. "Hardly." With wordless hand signals,

Ann Hoffmann directs another young student from first row to third, and makes sure the visually impaired woman with glasses is helped to a seat front and center.

"Hello students, future teachers," she begins with the simple, direct, tell-it-like-it-is talk for which she is known, "you are embarking on the hardest career you can imagine and the most important work that ever can be done. You will have parents and administrators asking you to go in many directions. But you must always remember, education is not about or for them. It is about children. It is about you and your students, but most importantly, your students.

"Find out who your students are and what they need. Listen and they will tell you. Look carefully and they will show you. I am not a lecturer. I have never spoken before an audience this size. I have watched young teachers in my school find their way, and I know that teachers learn more from doing than from hearing what they should do. But if I had to tell them what to do, I would tell them what I am about to say to you."

Teachers,

Be excited about life. Your excitement will inspire your students.

Make a beautiful space for learning. Your children will appreciate and enjoy it. Whatever it takes, make your classroom an honorable and inspiring place to learn.

Make sure your children go outside to play. They need fresh air and grass and, if possible, a view of water. Let them run free, but always keep your eyes on them. Know where they are at all times. Protect them.

Give your children room to ask their own questions and to find out how their questions are different from each other's. Listen to their questions. Remind them that questions are powerful, answers less so.

Do not ever think of your students as all the same. They are never the same. Equality is not equivalency. Equity assumes variety. The ways in which your students may seem the same is trivial. What is important is how your students differ. Find out and remember.

I do not believe in competition. I believe in participation. Difference is not about winners and losers. It is about who you are and what you need to do whatever it is that you want to do. Make sure your children reach for their dreams, not for beating out someone else in a race. Know each child for who he or she is, not in comparison to anyone else.

Embrace the child who is least embraceable. Stand up for the child on whom others have turned their backs. Offer your hand to the child who has lost his way. Listen to all of them. They will tell you what they need.

Give your students the arts so that they will have voices and know how to use them. All children have gifts. It is your responsibility to identify the different gifts in all your children.

If a child does not interest you, ask her another question. Watch that child carefully. You will be rewarded and so will the child.

Ask your students to do more than they think they can. They will try and in the trying they will advance. Celebrate their successes; do not judge the worth of their successes. The child who struggles in spelling may care more about drawing. Care about drawing. Celebrate your children.

Believe in your students. Your trust will give them power.

Amuse your students. Their laughter will give you power.

Be respectful, and they will respect you.

Play, and they will know you are human.

Demonstrate the values you are teaching and love your students.

Embrace difference. It is a cause for celebration, not a problem you must solve.

Do not be afraid. When you make a mistake, they will forgive you and learn from you that mistakes are opportunities for revision, not outcomes that close doors.

Let them know when their ideas make more sense than yours. Trust me, that will happen. Good friends celebrate each other's ideas and are enlarged by them. Be a good friend.

Make sure you learn to dance and sing and paint and act, because you will want to do these things with your students to show them they are important. Both the arts and the children. They are important.

Every child can learn. And every child can learn to love learning. You can make the difference. Love learning.

Do not be discouraged if your classroom cannot make things right for a child from an unhappy home. Do what you can and care. Today there is an emphasis on self-knowledge. Some people say that you cannot know or love others until you know or love yourself. I say if you want to know something about yourself, do something for someone else. I encourage you to try it. Do for another, especially a child, and learn about yourself. Encourage your children to learn about themselves by doing for each other. We are our best selves when we think of others.

Artists make the very best teachers. Realize you are an artist and practice your art with passion and with love. Realize your children are artists and encourage them.

Protect your children from humiliation. They may learn from and always remember moments of humiliation but hopefully never on your account.

Do not shame your children. Remind them that grades are for their parents. Excitement about learning is what matters in school

Improvise. You may have everything set for your class tomorrow. But when a child asks an unexpected question that promises new direction, you must throw away your notes. You must have high hopes and flexible action.

I am a pacifist. I do not believe that children need to fight. I will not accept bullying. It can ruin a child's life. I do not allow weapons in my school, and I encourage you to lead your children in peaceful ways to peaceful action. You are changing the world, child by child. Demonstrate what matters.

Keep up with what the mainstream is up to. But only do what you think is right. It is okay to be an outsider. Children are outsiders, and we must help them to stay that way even as they must learn how to behave in the inside grown-up world. Outsiders resist peer pressure and develop their own ideas. They care about others and do not form cliques.

Artists are outsiders. Remember you are an artist. Your canvas is your work. Think of color and light. Balance is overrated.

You may not make much money. You will work more hours than you think you should. You will not be able to leave your work at school. Your students will live within your thoughts even when you are away from them. Think not of how well you did today. Think creatively about what you will do tomorrow. Don't worry if you're nervous. Nervousness is a sign of talent. A sign of caring. Be nervous.

You young teachers are about to ready a generation of children for their life as adults, as active participants in society, as fair and generous, forgiving, and caring people who are excited about being alive. You are about to reshape and perpetuate democracy and to change the world. Make it a better place.

What an honor and a privilege this work is. Be fair. Be generous. Forgive. Engage. Care. Have fun. And love.

As she steps down from the podium, Ann stops at the chair of the woman with dark glasses who has been nodding vigorously throughout the talk. "Why don't you come to the Hoffmann School tomorrow morning?" she asks this visually challenged young teacher. "I believe you may have a gift with children. And there is lots of work to be done."

Notes

1. All students, even those whose comments as adults have been quoted directly, have been given pseudonyms. Some of the children described are fictional composites of actual students who attended the school.

2. Ann Hoffmann was called alternately Anna (her given name was Anna Luciano), Anne (not sure where the *e* came from), Annie (mostly by my father), and Mrs. Hoffmann. The school children most often called her Ann Hoffmann, and I follow their lead throughout the book.

3. "It Couldn't Be Done" by Edgar Albert Guest was first published by the *Detroit Free Press* in 1914 in a collection of Guest's poems entitled *Breakfast Table Chat*.

4. Gombrich offers this fine explanation of composition in his widely read text *The Story of Art*, originally published in 1950 in London and in New York by Phaidon.

5. *Auntie Mame* by Patrick Dennis was originally published in 1955 by Vanguard Press. It was a *New York Times* best seller (as were two sequels). With friends from the Riverdale Country School, I saw the award-winning 1957 Broadway version that starred the great Rosalind Russell.

6. The only one-man show in history to win the Pulitzer prize (New York: Faber and Faber, 2004).

7. Malcolm Hoffmann's publications: *Government Lawyer* (New York: Federal Legal Publications, 1956); *The Long Canoe* (New York: Portage Publications, 1994); *Back and Forth* with Morris Ernst (New York: Peter Pauper Press, 1969).

8. First published in the United States in 1948 by Little Brown.

9. I borrowed this idea from my father's dear friend, the renowned lawyer Morris Ernst, who would ask this question at cocktail parties and used it as the foundation for a book *The Teacher* (New York: Prentice-Hall, 1967), in which he collected stories about their most important teachers from successful individuals, including my father.

10. You can find this story in the collection *Death in Venice and Seven Other Stories* (New York: Viking Books, 1954).

11. Rebekah is principal of PS/IS 50, a Children's Aid Society School in East Harlem, which in 2007 received the first Colin and Alma Powell Legacy Award in

recognition of the school's commitment to and practice of its "whole student" philosophy of learning and living.

12. Viktor Lowenfeld was a leading figure in the field of progressive art education. His stage theory of artistic development was introduced in his book, *Creative and Mental Growth* (New York: Macmillan, 1947).

13. This reference is on p. 153 of Dorothy Day's autobiography, *The Long Loneliness*, (New York: Harper and Row, 1952).

14. Written in 1895 by poet Gelett Burgess, it can be found in Louis Untemeyer's *Modern American Poetry: An Introduction* (New York: Harcourt, Brace, and Howe, 1919).

15. Can be found in Francis Palgrave's *The Golden Treasure of the Best Songs and Lyrical Poems in the English Language* (London: MacMillan, 1875).

16. W. Wordsworth, "The Daffodils," in Palgrave's 1875 collection (see n. 15).

17. A.E. Housman, "When I was One and Twenty," from *A Shropshire Lad* in the *Collected Poems of A. E. Housman* (New York: Henry Holt, 1965).

About the Author

Jessica Hoffmann Davis is a writer, teacher, and researcher with an abiding interest in children and art. At Harvard's Graduate School of Education, Dr. Davis was the Bauman and Bryant Senior Lecturer, the founder and first director of the Arts in Education Program, and a principal investigator at Project Zero. Her research has been arts related, focusing on children's cognition and development as well as learning in and beyond school walls. Widely published in academic journals, Davis's recent books include *Framing Education as Art: The Octopus Has a Good Day* (2005) and *Why Our Schools Need the Arts* (2008). Her website is http://www.jessicahoffmanndavis.com.